## OTHER BOOKS BY ELAINE FANTLE SHIMBERG

*Another Chance for Love* (coauthored)

*Coping with COPD: Chronic Obstructive Pulmonary Disease*

*Coping with Chronic Heartburn: What You Need to Know About Acid Reflux and GERD*

*Blending Families: A Guide for Parents, Stepparents, and Everyone Building a Successful New Family*

*Write Where You Live*

*How to Get Out of the Hospital Alive* (coauthored)

*A Heritage of Helping: Shriners Hospitals*

*Living with Tourette Syndrome*

*Gifts of Time* (coauthored)

*Depression: What Families Should Know*

*Strokes: What Families Should Know*

*Relief from IBS: Irritable Bowel Syndrome*

*Coping with Kids and Vacation* (coauthored)

*Two for the Money: A Woman's Guide to a Double Career Marriage* (coauthored)

*How to Be a Successful Housewife/Writer*

# THE
# COMPLETE
# SINGLE FATHER

### Reassuring Answers to Your Most Challenging Situations

Elaine Fantle Shimberg and Michael Shimberg

Foreword by Joseph Grenny

**A**adamsmedia

Avon, Massachusetts

Published by Adams Media, an F+W Publications Company
57 Littlefield Street
Avon, MA 02322
*www.adamsmedia.com*

ISBN-10: 1-59869-208-9
ISBN-13: 978-1-59869-208-2

**Library of Congress Cataloging-in-Publication Data
is available from the publisher**

Printed in Canada.
J I H G F E D C B A

This publication is designed to provide accurate and authoritative information with regard
to the subject matter covered. It is sold with the understanding that the publisher is not
engaged in rendering legal, accounting, or other professional advice. If legal advice or
other expert assistance is required, the services of a competent professional person should
be sought.
 —From a *Declaration of Principles* jointly adopted by a Committee of the American
Bar Association and a Committee of Publishers and Associations

*The Complete Single Father* is intended as a reference volume only, not as a medical manual.
In light of the complex, individual, and specific nature of heath problems, this book is not
intended to replace professional medical advice. The ideas, procedures, and suggestions
in this book are intended to supplement, not replace, the advice of a trained medical
professional. Consult your physician before adopting the suggestions in this book. The
authors and publisher disclaim any liability arising directly or indirectly from the use of
this book.

Many of the designations used by manufacturers and sellers to distinguish their product are
claimed as trademarks. Where those designations appear in this book and Adams Media
was aware of a trademark claim, the designations have been printed with initial capital
letters.

*This book is available at quantity discounts for bulk purchases.
For information, please call 1-800-289-0963.*

Dedicated to my son, Michael, who agreed to coauthor this book amidst all the juggling necessary between his career and caring for his two young children. His thoughtful insights were invaluable. Michael, working with you has been a delight and has added a new dimension to our relationship. I love you.

—EFS

Dedicated to my children, Zachary and Ashley, the two best things that have ever happened in my life. I love you.

—MBS

# CONTENTS

## PART ONE

## SINGLE PARENTING 101

### CHAPTER 1: Reassuring Your Children. . . . . . . . . . . . . . . . 1

### CHAPTER 2: Communicating Effectively with Your Kids . . . 7

### CHAPTER 3: Showing Affection . . . . . . . . . . . . . . . . . . . . . 11

PART TWO

**DADDY DETAILS: NEW
DAY-TO-DAY CHALLENGES**

## PART THREE

# GETTING YOUR LIFE BACK

---

### PART FOUR

## EX-MATTERS: DIPLOMACY WITH THEIR MOTHER

# Foreword

I had a dream once. A nightmare, really. It was of the kind that many of us have—the one where you show up for school and realize to your horror that there's a test. In this dream it was a final exam. I flipped through the pages of the test in a panic, trying simply to figure out what the subject was. I not only didn't know the answers, I couldn't even understand the questions. Did I even attend this class? How did I end up here? The paper sat in front of me demanding answers. I looked up at the clock and licked my lips nervously. I now had forty-three minutes of my class period left to do something I was entirely unprepared for. And my future depended on getting it right.

As I read this book I heaved a sigh of relief for every unexpectedly single father who will read it. For those who find themselves scrambling for answers to questions on a final they had no time to study for, this amazingly comprehensive work will help them not only understand the questions but find wise and balanced answers. For those who are feeling terribly alone facing time-sensitive decisions, you'll find the Shimbergs to be welcome and comforting companions.

But let me urge you to look for more in this important book than for counsel or comfort. If you find yourself facing a life final in decision-making, negotiation, communication, coping, balancing, budgeting, teaching, peacemaking, or healing—in relationship to your children—you'll find a wealth of wisdom in these pages. But what struck me as I read the Shimbergs' book was

less what it offered for the dozens of conundrums single fathers face, but more so what the cumulative effect of allowing these pages to influence your approach to fathering will be. Each of the challenging circumstances you face combine to shape both who you are as a human being and ultimately the values you pass to your children. In fact, the added emotional complexity of single parenting serves to magnify the effect your actions have on both your character and that of your children.

The further I read into this book, the more heartened I grew in the realization that it offers as much a code for life as counsel for key moments. The Shimbergs are ultimately qualified to write this book not just because of what they know, but because of who they are. Both have a deep love for children. Both have enormous empathy for single fathers. And both are the kind of human beings we'd all do well to emulate.

I heartily recommend this book both as a ready reference for moments of crisis and as a mosaic of values that define what a fine father—single or otherwise—should be.

PROVO, UTAH
JANUARY 2007

**Joseph Grenny** is coauthor of the *New York Times*–bestselling *Crucial Confrontations: Tools for Resolving Broken Promises, Violated Expectations and Bad Behavior* and coauthor of *Influence Genius: Powerful Strategies to Change Your Self, Your Business and Your World*.

# Acknowledgments

This book could never have been written without the input of so many, especially the more than fifty single dads who offered stories of what worked for them, what didn't, and what they wished they had known earlier. Although most of them did not know us before we contacted them through friends or relatives, they nevertheless were willing to discuss intimate thoughts, disappointments, frustrations, and successes in being single fathers. They readily demonstrated that dads can be loving, caring, and nurturing parents. We owe them a tremendous debt of gratitude and wish them continued happiness.

Special thanks to Dan Totcky, who shared so much of his single-father experiences and added excellent suggestions for what needed to be included in order to make this book an important guide for newly single dads. Dan recently joined our family, adding his two lovely daughters, Jenny and Elise, to the grandchildren group, now numbering an even dozen, with six girls and six boys.

A number of physicians went over our Doctor Dad chapter with a fine-toothed comb to be sure it was medically accurate. We appreciate their efforts and list them as follows: pediatricians Gilbert Pitisci, Marcy Solomon Baker, and Antoinette Spoto-Connors; and gastroenterologist and dear friend, Worth Boyce.

Nancy Hutcheson Harris, who practices marital and family law, reviewed our legal and custody chapter to be sure it was legally accurate and was always willing to answer our questions. Thank you, Nancy.

We also appreciate psychotherapist Barbara Montague for sharing her insights and willingness to share her time with us answering questions and explaining the whys of various actions and reactions. Canadian psychologist Ganz Ferrance, Ph.D., took time away from his work in Edmonton to patiently explain ways in which single dads can enjoy their kids while at the same time giving them the structure they need in their lives to prevent chaos. Thank you, Ganz, for being available for our phone calls.

Our heartfelt appreciation to Veronica Tillis who devoted hours checking for typos and weird sentences throughout numerous drafts, to Belinda Grant and Hannah Dewer who assisted with specific research, and to Bob Gettle who worked tirelessly to the powers that be.

Thanks also, as always, to our amazing agent, Faith Hamlin, who has been supportive from the beginning. Your friendship, professionalism, and great sense of humor make working with you a pleasure.

We'd also like to acknowledge and thank our wonderful editor, Jennifer Kushnier, who never seems fazed by impromptu phone calls and who always had the answers, and Katrina Schroeder, who assisted in the editing process and asked great questions.

# Introduction

Fatherhood is filled with excitement, joy, frustration, pride, and myriad other emotions. But when you suddenly become a single dad, through a divorce or by being widowed, new feelings enter the picture—fear, confusion, loneliness, and uncertainty. Mothers, it seems, no matter if they are homemakers or are employed outside of the home, seem to know instinctively how things work with their kids and how to coordinate the day-to-day management of the children's schedule and household duties. It may not be seamless, but it often appears effortless. Mom's magic, no doubt.

Today, half of marriages in the United States end in divorce, and more than half of these families include minor children. Whereas mothers used to receive full custody of these minor children, since 2000 more divorced parents are agreeing to joint physical custody in which both parents are responsible for the physical and emotional care of their children.

For dads, however, this responsibility, though welcomed, often requires a fast learning curve. The minutia of organizing children's lives can be mind boggling. What should you do about curfews for older children? How much leeway is there in the school dress code? Do the kids like broccoli, green beans, or neither? How do you make school lunches at the same time you're trying to get the kids to eat breakfast and dressed for school? How can you get them to all their extracurricular activities and still maintain your job? Who is their pediatrician? How do you cope with night terrors? How and when should you talk about the facts of life? What is the appropriate gift for their friends' birthday parties, and where do you buy leotards and training bras?

This book is a realistic, yet positive, guide, offering everything a single dad— whether separated, divorced, or widowed— needs to know in order to provide comfort to his kids while maintaining a stable environment, reducing stress for all involved, and keeping his sense of humor.

*The Complete Single Father* is not a mom bashing book. We have also closely observed the other side of being a single parent as the daughter of one us and the sister of the other is a single mom. Instead, it is a guide for reassuring dads that their challenges of single parenthood can be met successfully and that the ex-wife can be an important ally, with civility and cooperation being the key components.

What makes this book unique? This book differs from other books for divorced dads in that it is written by a newly divorced dad and by the grandmother of his children, the latter being an award-winning author of twenty books.

*The Complete Single Father* not only contains specific researched material from family lawyers, marriage counselors, psychologists, social workers, teachers, and members of the clergy, but it also includes Tips from the Trenches, the voices of more than fifty divorced or widowed dads who share their experiences, citing both what works and what doesn't work.

In researching this book, we interviewed fifty-three single dads, men from twenty-two years of age to those who were fifty plus. They were divorced dads, dads who were separated from their spouses, dads who never married but accepted the responsibility of raising their unexpected offspring, and widowers whom fate made single dads. We've talked with gay dads and straight dads, men who were highly educated professionals and others who had only completed high school. A few of the dads had sole custody of their children, many had shared custody, and others only saw their kids every other weekend and on Wednesday, or even less seldom. Some of the dads had cordial relations with their ex and said they were better friends now than they were when they were married, while others couldn't tolerate even being in the same room with their ex. In short, every single dad had a unique story to tell and wanted to share it in the hopes that it might help anyone walking the same path. This was true whether the dad was single by decree or by death. While this information benefits all single dads regardless of situation, for simplicity we refer to the children's mom as the man's "ex" throughout the book, even if she were deceased.

We've written this book in an easy-to-read format, with bullet points, subheadings, and a detailed index, making the information easy to locate when the spaghetti pot and tempers are both boiling over. If you have questions that haven't been answered please visit our Web site at *www.TheComplete SingleFather.com* or send us an e-mail at TheCompleteSingleFather@gmail.com.

# PART ONE

# SINGLE PARENTING 101

# Chapter 1

# Reassuring Your Children

*Make a memory with your children,*
*Spend some time to show you care;*
*Toys and trinkets can't replace those*
*Precious moments that you share.*
—ELAINE HARDT

The story wasn't supposed to go this way. You got married, had kids, and then it happened. Something along the way didn't go as planned. Instead of family vacations and happy memories with a wife, dog, and two-and-a-half kids, you find yourself sharing the company of your own children part time. It's not the way Disney writes it, but that doesn't mean your story still can't have a happy ending. Welcome to the world of the single dad.

Single fathers very often have a lot to learn about parenting, whether they have their children full time, half of the time, or on every other weekend and Wednesday evening. In many traditional marriages, even in today's twenty-first-century world, the wife is the dominant homemaker (even if she works outside the home) and the dad is her support staff—a parenting assistant. Dad helps in certain aspects of parenting: giving the kids a bath, doling out the occasional punishment, taking them to school, and perhaps coaching a team or two.

But few fathers are prepared to walk into a world where they are the CEO of the house and their job entails picking the kids up from school, coordinating play dates, buying other people's children presents, and being the main person to help their child or children get through life's ups and downs, all, by the way, while still having all the other traditional father roles.

## THINK OF YOUR KIDS

The first commandment for single dads is the mantra TOYK, or "think of your kids." This is an important concept as it puts perspective and priorities on all other decisions you make. Despite being a single parent, you need to show your kids that in many ways you are all still really a family. It's a different kind of family than they used to have—everyone doesn't live in the same house—but it's a family nevertheless, one in which the members respect each other, share responsibilities, enjoy time together, and create new memories.

Don't assume that your children know that you love them. You must tell them often, regardless of their ages. Kids are as insecure as adults, especially after their parents have separated. Remind them that you (and their mother) still love them very much and that although their parents have divorced each other, parents and their children will always be together.

## YOU'RE STILL A FAMILY

Reassure your kids that you're still a family, despite not being a nuclear family where everyone lives in one house. Hasten to point out that many families are different today. There are blended families, some with grandparents raising kids, some with two moms or two dads. The actual composition of the family is not as important as the love, trust, and companionship that exist between the members of each family unit.

Michael, father of a five- and four-year-old says, "I had been divorced for about a year and my son had a friend over playing at the house. He came up to me very upset saying the other boy had told him that Mommy and I were divorced and he wanted to know when that occurred and what did it mean. I explained that divorce just meant Mommy and Daddy live in different houses like we had been for awhile and it didn't mean anything about how much his mother and I loved him and his sister. My son looked at me and said, 'Oh, okay—that makes sense' and went off to play again. I realized we had never used the word *divorce* around the kids because we were afraid the word would scare them, like it scared us."

Adults often build up divorce as a big, bad thing for the child to handle. Instead, through a child's mind it can be summed up as mommy and daddy often wanting to still be friends but live in different houses. While this obviously may not work for older kids, younger children can accept and easily understand this simple explanation and are not frightened by the thought of Mommy and Daddy not living together.

## DILUTE THEIR SENSE OF GUILT

You may not realize that children whose parents have divorced often feel that they are responsible for their parents separating. They may have heard you arguing, being sarcastic to each other, not speaking, or even throwing dishes at each other, all situations that make it obvious to you that you and your ex weren't getting along. Nevertheless, your kids still may feel that they must have done something wrong to make you both fight so much. Why? Because children tend to think the world revolves around them. Therefore, they worry that something they did caused you and their mother to split up. And if they ever do confess their "guilt" to you, it may be something as silly (to you) as their not hanging up the bath towels after their bath, arguing with a sibling, watching too much TV, or even getting a lower grade than usual on their report card or not making the swim team.

## DAD'S STILL HERE

It's important for you to assure your kids right from the start that you'll always be their father and that you love them unconditionally. Tell them and show them by your actions, which, as you know, speak much more loudly than words. Also let them know that you'll always take care of them, especially if it's a situation where you suspect their mom may be telling them that money's going to be tight for her and the kids when they're with her now that you have your own home.

If you're a single dad because your wife is deceased, be aware that children (as well as teens) whose mothers have died are not immune from these feelings of guilt either. They often feel that they somehow were the cause of her death. Take time to assure them, as often as necessary, that it wasn't their fault. Try to initiate conversation and listen if they do open up to you. If they refuse to talk to you about it, or you think they're having trouble coping with their mom's death, ask your pediatrician for the name of a children's grief counselor or therapist.

## BE WITH YOUR KIDS WHENEVER POSSIBLE

Despite the custody arrangement, do your best to be with your kids as much as possible. Tom, a divorced father of a fourteen-year-old daughter, said, "I fully enjoy the time I spend with my daughter, but I put her interests first. I think it's much healthier for her to be with her friends than hanging out with me. I should add, though, that we have common

---

✔ **Tip from the Trenches**

George admitted that the hardest part of being a single dad was "trying to be sure I could keep their lives stable. I wanted to do as much as possible for them. (They were six and seven at the time of the divorce.) I wish I had known that they were more self-sufficient than I thought."

interests so that we play tennis or ski, most of the time inviting a friend of hers."

Obviously, as Tom discovered, as your kids grow older they want to spend more time with their friends. By making their friends welcome in your home or at activities you share with your kids, you show that you're there for your children and respect their need to be with peers as well.

## EXPOSING MYTHS OF FATHERHOOD

Some of these myths are old baggage dragged up from yesteryear and reported as fact. Others may describe some dads but certainly not the majority or any of those we've interviewed.

### Myth #1: Fathers Don't Show Their Emotions

It doesn't matter if you were the high-school quarterback, math club president, or the band leader, fatherhood is a time to embrace your emotions and share them with your children. Many parents today were raised by a generation that believed a father shouldn't show his love to his children.

We attended a high-school graduation ceremony where parents who were on the board were permitted to hand the diploma to their child. One father recoiled when his son tried to hug him in front of everyone, rather than manly (and unemotionally) shaking his father's hand after receiving the diploma.

All kids, but especially kids of divorce, need to actually feel the love you have for them. That means hugging them often (even in front of people), congratulating them when you can, and telling them "I love you always." A father showing emotions may not have been mainstream back in the fifties and sixties, but in today's soci-

ety, where peer pressure reigns supreme, the closer you can be with your child, the better communication you'll have when questionable decisions arise.

### Myth #2: You Have to Be Both Father and Mother When You Have Your Kids

Wrong. Unless your wife is deceased, your kids have a mom. What your kids need is for you to be a nurturing, supportive, strong, mature, and consistent parental role model. And that knows no gender.

### Myth #3: You Have to Be Perfect

No one is perfect, and if you try to be you're setting yourself up for failure. Besides, your imperfections let your kids know that it's okay to make mistakes, as long as you learn from them. Admit that you're not perfect, relax, and just concentrate on being the best dad you can be.

### Myth #4: Fathers Aren't Nurturing

One of the definitions of *nurturing* is to "give support and encouragement." Okay, so a few dads (possibly your own) may not be particularly nurturing, but you can be by allowing yourself to let your kids see what some call your feminine side, or what we call your human side. It's letting your kids know how much you love them and that you'll always be there for them. It doesn't mean not disciplining or correcting them when necessary. Nurturing your kids is playing with them, letting them see that it's okay to express emotions, and not being afraid to hug or kiss them. Of course men can nurture their children.

### Myth #5: Fathers Can't Cook

Here's another silly myth. Many of the most famous chefs around the world are men, so even if you don't have a big white hat, you can read a cookbook and feed your kids and yourself just fine.

### Myth #6: Fathers Can't Tell Their Kids No

It's hard for dads to say no, especially when you don't have your kids around you all the time or your children's mother is absent altogether. You don't want to be the bad guy. On the other hand, you know that kids can't have everything they want (and often don't even want what they ask for). When you set limits for your kids, it tells them that you care enough to occasionally say no to them. Although they probably wouldn't tell you, it makes them feel safe and cared for. So be a fair judge, but say no when you need to.

Psychologist Ganz Ferrance agrees that consistency and structure is especially important when you don't have the kids all the time. He says, "It's your job, as a dad, to teach your kids responsibility, independence, and help them understand the consequences for misbehavior. Don't be overly permissive. Visualize the differences between playing baseball or basketball when everyone knows and follows the rules, and playing when everyone makes up their own rules, disregarding their teammates. Which game sounds like more fun?"

## YOU'RE THE PARENT

It's fun to play with your kids, but always remember that you're the adult. Never get down to their level—unless it's physically on the floor playing a board game. Even if they scream at you, don't yell back. In fact, it often works better if you lower your voice and tell them that although it's all right for them to disagree with you, they must do it in a respectful way. Keep your anger under control; they're watching, always watching.

## KIDS AREN'T CONFIDANTS

While communication between you and your kids is important to establish and maintain, remember not to go overboard in the communication department. Your kids are your children, not your therapist or adult confidant. Never tell them what you think their mom is doing wrong, don't talk about your dates, and never burden them by discussing how much you're doing without because you have to pay their mother child support. Any time you're tempted to make your kid a confidant or tell tales "out of school," take a deep breath and change the subject.

## DADS CAN DO IT

Of course dads can do this parenting thing. You love your kids and want them to grow up confident, secure, and independent. Never doubt your ability. Have the confidence to know that you can assume the responsibility to parent your children and do a great job.

Naturally, there always are bumps along the way. Kids, alas, don't come with instruction manuals like your computer or VCR. You often have to rely on your gut instinct. (It's often right.) Later chapters will show you how to improve communication between you and your ex so you both are able to co-parent effectively. Once you and your ex are comfortable talking with one another about your kids and what's best for them, you can discuss potential pinch points without arguing, sighing, or rolling your eyes. But if you feel you need outside advice, call on friends and family or contact a qualified mental health counselor for an impartial opinion.

# Chapter 2

# Communicating Effectively with Your Kids

*God gave us two ears and one tongue so that*
*We could listen twice as much as we talk.*

—FOLK SAYING

It seems simple enough: Just talk to your kids. But communication is so much more than talking. It involves a great deal of listening and being able to keep your mouth shut and not interrupting. As your kids become teens, it also requires understanding this strange language they use, if, indeed, they talk to you at all.

## COMMUNICATE WITH YOUR KIDS

The first step in communicating effectively with your kids is to improve your listening skills with them, beginning with creating a safe listening environment so they know they have your undivided attention. One good opportunity is at bedtime when you tuck them in. Even older kids respond to these special one-on-one moments, when they're sleepy, the room's dark, and dad is there sitting on or by the bed, asking "How are things going?"

Another wonderful listening spot is when your kid is "trapped" in the car with you. Turn the radio off and ask your son or daughter to stow the hand-held computer game. Be sure your cell phone is on mute. In his book *Family First*, Dr. Phil McGraw advises, "Rather than just listen to the words being spoken, you have to 'listen' for the need driving the communication. Your child will only communicate with you if that behavior is rewarded by your reacting in a way that the child perceives as meeting her need." And, he stresses, "You don't necessarily have to agree with what's being expressed." That's an extremely important statement to remember because chances are, being male, you'll often want to solve the problem quickly or make a judgment. But that's not necessarily what kids want. They often just want to be heard, really listened to.

One parent listened to her young son saying he didn't know how to avoid going to someone's house without angering or hurting that person's feelings. She asked how he could best handle it. "Maybe," he said, after thinking about it, "If I really don't want to go, I'll say, 'Mother, can I go to . . .'" (He usually called her "Mom.") They agreed on their special code. The boy felt good because his mother had listened to his dilemma and that he had solved his own problem without her input. Dads can do that too.

## AVOID BEING JUDGMENTAL

It's so important to avoid being judgmental when you're talking to your kids. Never say, "That's a crazy idea," or "I don't think that will work." Be respectful, even if you don't agree. If you disagree, you can certainly offer your thoughts, but be sure to validate what they're feeling as well as what they're saying. They may be telling you something, hoping you'll say no and not approve. One adult recalled as a child hearing his parent say, "Oh, go ahead. I don't care what you do," and thinking, "Oh, I wish you did care."

Just as with your ex, observe your child's body language to see if the nonverbal cues conflict with the words being said. And while you're doing that, take a moment to focus on yours as well. Are you fiddling with your cell phone or reading your e-mail messages? Checking your watch? Edging out of the room? Those are shut-down clues your kid will quickly recognize. If your youngster feels that you're faking interest and really aren't listening, it will be as though you hit the Exit button on your computer program. He or she will say, "Whatever. It's not important." And you'll never know that it was until it's too late.

## FAMILY MEETINGS

Family meetings are an important way to boost communication in your family unit. Everyone, even the little ones, have the opportunity to express what's on their minds without interruption. No one is permitted to be judgmental or make comments about what the other is expressing. While you must have the final say in important matters, if you listen first, you'll learn a lot about what's on your kids' minds.

Chapter 4 describes how to organize and hold family meetings. It's really not difficult and there's a great deal of benefit, regardless if it's to discuss house rules, where to go for a vacation, or how to rotate chores. You may find that your kids may remind you from time to time that there's a need for one. If so, you'll know you've expressed the importance of open communication with your youngsters.

## DON'T TRY TO BE A PERFECT PARENT

Admitting mistakes as you begin to single parent is important as it helps your youngsters understand that, like them, you're also human and that making mistakes (and learning from them) is never ending. It allows your children to feel more comfortable when they mess up and gives them the opportunity to fess up. You may feel frustrated that you can't fix problems when they arise. Accept that some things just can't be fixed, that things won't be like they used to

be, and learn new ways to adjust to these changing times.

## WHAT YOU DO SPEAKS LOUDLY

Remember you're a role model—or as psychologist Ganz Ferrance says, "a subconscious template for your child's behavior"—and what you do is more important than what you say. Kids learn from observing their parents' behavior, even if you don't realize it. So don't get caught with your hand in the cookie jar. Here are some ways to model good behavior:

- Demonstrate honesty by not pulling into a handicap parking place, by telling the truth about your kids' ages when going to the movies or to an attraction, and by speaking up when a salesclerk gives you back too much change.
- Show them how you bounce back from failures by looking for the positive lessons rather than focusing on the negatives or blaming another person.
- Laugh at your own foibles so they know that laughter has healing powers.
- Don't just talk about the dangers of smoking, drinking and driving, using illegal drugs, and riding a bike without a helmet. Show by your behavior that you avoid these potentially dangerous actions.

Show them you practice what you preach. Your actions communicate.

# Chapter 3
# Showing Affection

*When I approach a child*
*He inspires in me two sentiments:*
*Tenderness for what he is,*
*And respect for what he may become.*
—LOUIS PASTEUR

Many wives (or former wives) complain that their husband never said he loved them. He may have made a good living, bought her expensive jewelry, taken her on lavish trips, but despite all that, he never said those magic words: "I love you." He just assumed his wife knew he did. But chances are she didn't. Your kids are no different. It's not enough to assume they know you love them. Why else would you have insisted on dual custody, or driven miles to be with them on your weekend, or called just to hear their voice? But have you ever actually told them?

## TELL THEM YOU LOVE THEM

A forty-two-year-old man lay dying of colon cancer in a hospital bed. "You know," he said to his sister, "Our father never said he loved me."

"That's because his father never told him," she said softly, stroking his forehead.

"Well, I've told my boys," he said. "I've told them often that I love them."

"They've heard you," she answered. "They know you love them. You did good!"

Why is this true story an important one to tell? Because many single dads with kids were raised by fathers who didn't or couldn't show their emotions. You may have heard, "Be a man!" From the time you were five or six, your father may have told you to shake it off when you were hurt and formally shook your hand when you graduated from high school, went off to college, or were successful in any way.

It is possible that your dad occasionally gave in to emotion and smothered you with a bear hug from time to time, but unfortunately, the words "I love you" just weren't uttered because, you guessed it, his dad couldn't say it either. Your dad (and his father) may have felt that showing his children affection wasn't manly, so he shook your hand instead of hugged.

## HUGS ARE NICE TOUCHES

Kids need that reassurance, that hug, that pat on the back, and that kiss. Even though you know your kids know you love them, tell them anyway; they need to hear it. One father tells his kids he needs ten hugs a day and then he gives them back.

Cartoonists Jeff and Bil Keane also understand the importance of hugs. A recent *The Family Circus* cartoon shows a little girl running to greet her daddy. The caption reads, "Daddy! My hugger's empty!"

Your child may not admit that his or her "hugger" is empty, so it's up to you to be sure you keep it filled. Don't think your teenager doesn't need hugs either. We never outgrow that need for affectionate touches. Babies who are not touched and caressed often waste away, which is why many hospital neonatal intensive care units (NICUs) have volunteer "huggers" who hold and cuddle these preemies. Studies also show that our most elderly population, especially those in nursing homes, suffer less depression when they are hugged on a regular basis. (There actually is an organization that sponsors a National Hug Holiday Week geared to increase awareness for volunteer support for the elderly in senior and long-term care facilities. Their Web site is *www.hugs 4health.org*.)

"But I'm not a hugger," you may say, or "My family wasn't into hugs." While that may be true, it doesn't mean that you can't learn. It's easy to master. Besides, when you reach out to hug, pat, or touch your kids, you're getting good touches back, too, and maybe you need them as much as the kids do. Start slowly until you and the kids feel more comfortable with this hug therapy. Give them a pat on the head or cheek as you pass by or gently touch an arm or ruffle their hair. Advance to putting your arm around their neck and shoulders and giving a gentle squeeze. Eventually, you'll probably work your way up to the good old-fashioned bear hug and wonder why you didn't try it sooner.

Don shows his love and affection by giving private time to each of his three kids at bedtime. It takes longer than just tucking them all in and saying a general goodnight, but these private moments with dad offer rich opportunities for a youngster to open up about his or her day, share concerns, or just exchange special thoughts.

## LAUGH A LOT

Although at times you may feel as though you don't have much to laugh about, you do. Laugh at the absurdities in your life as you find yourself playing yet another game of Candyland, hearing the same knock-knock jokes over and over again, when you

### ✔ Tip from the Trenches

Dan suggests, "Take the extra two minutes to comb their hair, and while you're at it, hug them and tell them you love them. Tickle them, smile, enjoy them now. They grow up all too fast anyway. Call them (no more than once a day and only if your ex agrees that she can do the same) when they are with their mother, sending notes if you're out of town, or just cutting out and posting funny cartoons that have special meaning to them. Ask them about their activities. Show you care."

can't figure out how to braid your daughter's hair, when you mess up a meal you're trying to make, or when you're showing your son how to dance and you step all over his feet. Laugh when you can't put the "some assembly required" together or when the refrigerator compressor goes out with a week's worth of groceries inside. Your kids will learn to laugh too, and will learn to use gentle humor when things get tough.

Laughing with your kids creates special bonds in the family and makes good "remember whens." Our family still laughs about the California trip when our "navigator" (no names, please) thought a careless pencil mark on the map was a road called "G16" and directed us through miles of country backroads. We laugh about the excessive green food coloring that made the key lime pie look like a St. Patrick's Day dessert gone crazy and family foibles that now seem funny. We laugh at the recollection of the youngest son, then four years old, who, bored at the dinner table recitation of his siblings saying "I got straight As on my report card," spoke up saying, "I got curvy As."

As long as laughter isn't at any one family member's expense, it is an expression of affection and love for one another, an admission that although we all are imperfect, we are loved.

Laughter is a wonderful stress reducer, too. (More on stress reduction in Chapter 24.) Laughter makes us all feel better. The late pianist and comic Victor Borge once said, "Laughter is the shortest distance between two people."

Laughter is also physically good for you. It boosts the immune system, causes you to breathe deeply, reduces blood pressure, improves circulation, and lifts the weight of depression.

Think about what laughter does for you personally and why we keep going to comedy clubs or watch TV when we know Jay Leno, Bill Cosby, Jerry Seinfeld, Chris Rock, or Ellen DeGeneres have a special on.

There actually are more than one hundred clubs throughout the United States and Canada where health care professionals lead people in what cofounder psychologist Steven Wilson calls "laughter exercise workouts and other activities that encourage playfulness, fun, and natural balance."

According to Wilson (who also founded the World Laughter Tour along with Karyn Buxman, R.N.), "It's important to dispel some myths about laughter. First, there is no medical evidence that anyone ever 'died laughing.' Second, humor is very personal. One individual may laugh at the antics of circus clowns while another laughs at Jay Leno jokes. What's important is that you laugh. Laughter's a physical art that's universal. Thirdly, you don't need a joke to laugh. Actually, only 10 percent of laughter comes from a joke while ninety percent of laughter is from social reasons. . . . We're all born with an ability to laugh and smile," Wilson continued, "So even if you were raised in a serious family with an absence of laughter, I like to say it's never too late to have a happy childhood."

"But there's no doubt that many people suffer from 'sense of humor' abuse," Wilson told us during a telephone interview. "We're taught not to laugh in church or school. In our workshops, we encourage recollections of being criticized about laughter, that we laughed too loud, we cackled, snorted, or were too silly. Our Laughter Clubs offer an environment where there's cheer, where people learn to laugh. We don't use racial, ethnic, or sexist humor. Our humor is uplifting and draws people together. . . . Even an inner chuckle has good physiological benefits."

For more information about Wilson's Laughter Clubs, call 1-800-669-5233 (6140855-4733 international) or check out their Web site at *www.laughterclubs.com*. If you don't feel like joining a laughter club, you can still bring laughter into your home by checking out tapes and DVDs from the video store or the library to enjoy movies that make you and your kids laugh. Depending on your children's ages, it could be cartoons, slapstick humor, or more sophisticated humor.

Cut out funny cartoons from the newspaper or magazines and post them on your refrigerator or in the kids' bathroom. Buy joke books and tell jokes and funny stories at your dinner table. Let your children learn early about the power of laughter. If they can laugh at, as well as learn from, their mistakes, they'll be able to cope with life much easier and be healthier for it. But be sure they understand that while it's okay to laugh with a person, it is never all right to laugh at them.

In her book, *KidStress*, author Georgia Witkin, Ph.D., director of the Mt. Sinai Medical School Stress Program, writes, "Parents should key in to their *child's* sense of humor; don't force a grown-up's brand of funny on them—it won't get a laugh. . . . Understanding a good joke reflects an ability to understand the difference between how people are supposed to act and how they do act. It teaches that unpredictability is funny, not scary. . . . Laughing at change gives children (and adults) a sense of control; they see change as part of life."

You can give your kids a great gift by encouraging them to express their sense of humor and to look for the funny side of things rather than believe, as one girl was told by her mother, that "life is real and life is earnest." Life is also funny at times.

# DON'T TRY TO BUY THEIR LOVE

Although you may want to shower your kids with gifts to show your love, especially if you live away from them, don't overdo it by constantly buying your children toys and clothes every time they're with you. Your ex may feel you're trying to outdo her and it could turn into a nasty competition. You don't need to buy your children's love, nor give presents to show how much you care. The time you spend with them—listening to them, playing with them, and enjoying them for the unique individuals they are—is your gift to them. Let your presence, whether it's in person or from a distance, be your present to them.

# CATCH AND REWARD GOOD BEHAVIOR

You often hear parents complain that all they ever seem to do is yell at their kids and fuss about their misbehavior. Chances are the kids have learned that they get the most attention that way. Try instead to catch and reward good behavior. That's not a new concept, but it's one that works. Rather than yelling at your kids for not putting their toys away, compliment them for putting a couple of them back on the shelf or in the toy box. Just a simple, "Thanks, son. That's a good job," followed by a hug or a pat will make most kids want to earn more praise. If you need to jump-start the effort, look at your watch and say, "Can you put all your trucks away in one minute?" It's unlikely that you'll get a "Nope!" as a response (unless your kid is a teenager). If your teenager is unmotivated, you need a stronger carrot, such as "If you can bring all the laundry down and set the table for dinner, you can watch TV until dinner's ready." Don't think of it as bribery but rather as motivation.

# USE APPROPRIATE PRAISE

No matter your age, you respond to praise if it's appropriate. Having someone tell you that your report is fantastic, when you know you hurried it and didn't even proofread it, is gratuitous. You can avoid doing this with your kids by praising them for being themselves rather than what their accomplishments have been. If you praise your son for his awesome catch in the football game, he may focus instead on the passes he dropped. But if you tell him, "I love you. I'm so lucky to have you as my son," he's unlikely to argue (though he might blush a little). Likewise, show your love for your daughter by telling her how much she means to you rather than how pretty she is.

# ACKNOWLEDGE THEIR FEELINGS

You also demonstrate your love for your kids by really listening to them and acknowledging their feelings. Imagine how you'd feel if you told someone you felt nervous about giving a speech and they said, "That's silly. You'll do great." Rather than being reassured, you'd be frustrated that your feelings were ignored. Your kids are no different. So listen carefully to what they say and what they're feeling. Don't try to tell them they don't feel the way they say they do or that it's silly to feel that way. Their feelings are theirs, regardless of what you think, so accept them, ask why they feel that way, and what could they do to feel differently. When you accept their feelings, just as when you accept them for themselves, you reveal your love, your trust in them, and your support.

# BE FLEXIBLE

Although it's important to have house rules and to be consistent, don't be rigid about it. You're not running a boot camp. Give your kids leeway for special events like a later curfew for the prom or other school activity, or an extended bedtime for a television program. Determine curfews and other guidelines and be sure your kids understand what the extensions are and what happens if they push the envelope beyond that. This teaches them the importance of good communication, compromise, and responsibility—all abilities they'll need as they mature into adults.

# STAY IN CONTACT EVEN WHEN THEY'RE AWAY

Be flexible, even if you only have the kids during certain holidays or summer vacation, by staying in touch with them. Despite the distance, they still need to know that you care and that you want to know about their lives when you aren't together.

You may feel that it's difficult to show affection when you're far away, but you can. It may take more planning than if you saw them more often, but it isn't impossible. Chapter 16, Fathers Afar, offers many tips for staying in touch with your kids, even though distance may separate you.

# GIVE THE GIFT OF YOUR PRESENCE

As you'll read throughout this book, it's important to let your kids know you're thinking of them, regardless if they are with you or not. It's also necessary to keep in touch when they are with you by asking how an oral book report went, showing interest in a science project, and appearing at their sporting, musical, and theater events as much as possible. Even if your son is the equipment manager, not the quarterback, or your daughter has a walk-on role with one line rather than the lead part in the junior class play, be there for them.

Your kids probably won't remember what you gave them for their last birthday, but they'll treasure the fact that you supported them even when they weren't the star. Your presence spoke volumes.

# DON'T GIVE UP

You may wonder at times if it's worth the effort to work so hard to stay close to your kids after a divorce when you have so many time commitments pulling you in a multitude of various ways. But all the men we interviewed said they wouldn't have it any other way.

You may falter when the kids, especially in their teens, sometimes act as though they would rather be with their friends than with you. But don't take it personally. Parents who are not divorced from their partners complain about the same problem. It's normal for youngsters as they get older to want to be more independent and spend time with friends.

Nevertheless, as a parent you have the right to set schedules when you and your kids will be together, such as special holidays, family events, and when it's your time to have them. But be flexible, willing to compromise, and welcome your children's friends into your home. Try to be non-judgmental and supportive of your kids, especially during those difficult teen years when they want to pull away but still need you. It's a "two step forward, one step back" dance that these not-quite-adult youngsters do and they need to know that you're right there in the shadows, ready to "cut in" when they stumble and step on toes.

Show your love for your teenagers by being there—in person, by phone, or e-mail—and listening. Keep lines of communication open. You need to set limits, of course, but listen to his or her side of things too. If your idea of a curfew means your son has to be home by eleven and all of his friends (who have curfews) have to be home by midnight, be willing to compromise. Never say, "I don't care what you do" or "Oh, just do what you want." Kids, even teenagers, want boundaries.

The bottom line is that parenting is difficult and being a single father is even more so. But don't give up. It makes it somewhat easier if you can work with your ex, who may find the same things difficult. But keep communicating with your kids, letting them know that you love them, respect them, and even, most times, like them. Also don't forget to laugh; it keeps you from gnashing your teeth.

# Chapter 4

# Remaining Consistent with Discipline and Rules

*The secret of success is constancy to purpose.*
—BENJAMIN DISRAELI, EARL OF BEACONSFIELD

When you're a single father, it's important to be consistent when dealing with your children, especially in discipline, for two reasons. First, kids need structure in their lives, especially now. Second, if you don't establish this structure and limits now, they'll take advantage of you as well as your ex-wife. "Mommy lets us . . ." is the beginning of their playing one parent off the other. Don't fall for it. Smart parents will remind them, "Rules may be different in Mommy's house and my house, but they're still house rules."

## DISCIPLINE IS NOT A FOUR-LETTER WORD

You may feel rotten when you have to tell your kids no. After all, you tell yourself, you really don't have them with you that much and you don't want to be the bad guy when you have them. But when you give your kids limits, they know you care about their well-being, even if they won't tell you that while they're sulking in time-out or, if they're older, grounded.

It helps if you and your ex can agree on the guidelines so there's more consistency between the two homes. Unfortunately, that's not always the case. But at least you can have consistency under your roof. Be fair, but be consistent. That way they'll know what's expected of them and know just how far they can go without stepping over the line. If they should disobey the rules, never, ever resort to spanking or hitting your kids. That's not discipline; that's being a bully, and it only teaches your kids that if you're bigger you can hit smaller people. Yelling doesn't work too well either, other than frightening your children. It's much more effective to lower your voice when you're angry. You can tell the kids you're disappointed in their behavior when they break the rules, but don't say you're disappointed in them.

## DEAL WITH BEHAVIORAL PROBLEMS IMMEDIATELY

Psychologist Ganz Ferrance advises you to be sure that your kids know your expectations of their behavior. "Let them know up front that you care enough to hold them responsible for their behavior. Structure age-appropriate boundaries and deal with misbehavior immediately so your kids understand cause and effect. Saying, 'Wait 'til we get home' dilutes the message."

"Tell them, 'How I look in public is not important. If you misbehave, we will leave . . .' (the grocery, swimming pool, shopping center, ball game, whatever). Then be sure to follow through."

## DETERMINE HOUSE RULES

Be sure that you're not making rules just for the sake of having rules. Think about what things are really important to you. Do you really care if the kids make their beds or not? Is just pulling up the comforter considered enough? If you like eating popcorn in front of the TV, is it fair to make a rule that kids can't eat in front of the TV? What about telephone and television usage? Have fewer rules, but make them ones that are fair for all and that you consider to be important for safety, respect for others, and encourage responsibility.

Once you've done that, list the house rules and go over them with your children. If the youngsters are old enough, let them have input or ask why they have to hang up their clothes or clear the table. Family meetings are a good way to begin. (Ways to set up these important gatherings will follow later in this chapter.) If your kids are old enough to read, post the house rules in a conspicuous spot. Encourage discussion. You might be surprised to find that your kids come up with one or two rules that they think are important, too.

## CHORES MEAN "WE'RE A FAMILY"

Don't be afraid to assign chores. It says, "We're a family here and we have to work together." They might not do the job as well or as quickly as you can, but pitching in to help around the house gives kids a sense of confidence and a feeling of being grown-up. They feel valued and that boosts their self-esteem. When they're working along side you, they can learn not only the task at hand but also a great deal about respon-sibility, efficiency, and teamwork. It's a great opportunity for you to listen to what's on their minds.

Let them trade chores if they want to, as long as you safeguard that the youngest child isn't getting stuck with the worst tasks. In one family there was a "work wheel," with a variety of tasks such as setting the table, feeding the dog, and taking out the garbage. The inner wheel had the kids' names on it, so on Sunday when the wheel was rotated each child had a new task. The youngest

---

### ✔ Tip from the Trenches

Stan said, "I have a 'job jar.' It's not original as I got the idea from the comic papers years ago. I put all the chores that need to be done on pieces of paper. On Saturday, everyone, including me, reaches in and selects something. I try to keep all the jobs fairly equal."

---

finally complained that the older kids were secretly moving the wheel so each week he was always stuck with garbage duty.

You may think you're doing your kids a favor by giving them no responsibilities when they're with you, but you aren't. You're teaching them to be waited on, and they'll grow up into adults who have no sense of duty or responsibility.

## STRUCTURE BEDTIME AND OTHER ROUTINES

Structure bedtimes and other routines close to those in your ex-wife's house, if possible. But if she lets the little ones stay up until they fall asleep on the floor, you can assign whatever bedtime you think is right, along with a bath and story time, and simply say, "This is how we do it in Daddy's house." Do not say, "Mommy's wrong to let you stay up so late!"

Paul says, "It's hard to be consistent about rules when other extended family members don't respect them. Before my daughter turned four, she used to leave her bed and crawl in with me and I'd let her stay. But when she turned four, I told her she had to sleep in her own bed. She's good about it when she's with me, but when she's with her maternal grandmother, she gets away with it and crawls in with my ex's mother. It's hard to break that sleep habit of hers when the other family members won't be consis-tent as well."

## TRUST YOUR JUDGMENT

This is probably as good a time as any to say that you need to trust your instinct when it comes to raising your kids. For the most part, there's no definite right or wrong. These are your kids; you love them, and most of the time you'll make the right decisions concerning them. If you realize that you've made a mistake, admit it and adopt a new course. But as one size doesn't fit all, you need to remember to be attuned to the fact that each child is unique and has his or her own needs. When you have questions, and you will, go to your favorite bookstore or the local library and get some parenting books that are written from recognized experts, such as the American Academy of Child & Adolescent Psychiatry's excellent reference, *Your Child: What Every Parent Needs to Know: What's Normal, What's Not, and When to Seek Help.* You also can use the Internet, but only rely on Web sites from recognized expert sources, such as universities and the ones listed in Appendix C: Resources in the back of this book. You also can ask your pediatrician, but unless it is urgent, write the question down so you don't forget to ask it at your child's checkup.

Don't be embarrassed that you have questions about child rearing. We all did and still do. Kids are the most complicated beings, and unlike your refrigerator or stove, they don't come with an instruction manual and have no warranty.

## THE FAMILY THAT EATS TOGETHER IS A FAMILY

Mealtimes are another powerful way to establish that you are a family by sitting down at the table (not in front of the television) and enjoying a meal together. Studies have shown that when families sit down and enjoy a meal together, the children are less likely to get into trouble. According to University of Michigan researchers, dinners at home were the single strongest predictor of better achievement scores and fewer behavioral problems—far more influ-

ential than school or church involvement or sports or arts activities. Obviously it's the joining together at the dinner table that makes the magic, far more than what you actually serve.

It's healthier, of course, to eat a home-cooked meal than to constantly grab fast food. Chapter 15 is packed with good and simple meal preparations that make it easy for dad and will appeal to most kids. See The Essential Single Father's Cookbook section for recipes.

Keep the table talk light by asking "How was your day?" or "What was one good thing that happened today?" One father said he and his children sat around long after the meal was over, laughing and telling jokes. It was so much fun that one child said, "After we do the dishes, can we sit down and do this some more?"

If your kids are older, talk about current events and what's happening in the world. Hang a map on the wall so you can illustrate where various countries are and how the world is actually a big family that needs to learn to live together in peace. (A recent study revealed that many of America's high-school seniors not only didn't know where Iraq was, they also didn't know where the state of New York was located.)

## TEACHING MANNERS

"Youth today loves luxury. They have bad manners, contempt for authority, no respect for older people, and talk nonsense when they should work. Young people do not stand up any longer when adults enter the room. They contradict their parents, talk too much in company, guzzle their food, lay their legs on the table, and tyrannize their elders."

No, the above statement was not made by your kids' grandparents, but rather by someone you've no doubt heard of, the Greek philosopher Socrates, in 500 B.C.

Yet there is something you can do to help your kids, both girls and boys, to develop good manners. It will help them get along in life, feel more comfortable in social situations, and because so few youngsters have learned good manners, your kids will stand out in the crowd and be greatly appreciated. William of Wykeham (1324–1404), who was Bishop of Winchester, Chancellor of England, and architect/builder of a large part of Windsor Castle, thought manners were so important that when he created England's Winchester College and New College, Oxford, he made the motto of both Manners Maketh Man. And so they do. So brush up on your manners and teach them to your offspring.

You can make a game of learning manners by role-playing with your children and praising them when they remember to use them. By practicing them in your home (and hopefully your ex practices them in her home as well), these niceties will become second nature to your kids.

In her book *The Family Manager's Guide to Summer Survival*, author Kathy Peel suggests a list of manners dos and don'ts. Italicized information is quoted from her book. Here is a sampling:

- *Practice good introduction manners: Teach your children to stand and shake hands with adults when meeting them for the first time.* Make a game of this at home by introducing your kids to yourself as a movie star or cartoon hero and have them practice standing up, shaking hands with you, and saying, "Hello, Mickey Mouse." (or Spider Man) "It's nice to meet you." Show them how to have a firm handshake without breaking any of the twenty-seven bones in the other person's hand.

- *Teach your child to say "Excuse me?"* [instead of "huh?]* if he doesn't hear what someone is saying.* Again, you can role-play this at home by mumbling so your child will have to either say, "Excuse me?" or "I beg your pardon. Could you repeat that?" Your child's teacher will probably thank you personally for correcting this behavior as most teachers grow tired of hearing students saying "Huh?" no matter how clearly the teacher has spoken.

- *Teach your child to be sensitive to the loner at a party, to invite him or her to participate or to talk.* You may get complaints with this one as your kid probably will say, "But he's a geek. Who wants to talk to him?" Explain that the other person may be shy, not know anyone else at the party, or just not be terribly social. Ask how he'd feel if no one spoke to him at a party and tell him it's an act of kindness and shows good manners. (Now if you can get your teenage son to dance with a girl who's been a wallflower all night, you'll get an A.)

- *Instruct your child to offer kitchen help, to keep his belongings organized, and to tidy up the bathroom when visiting another child's home.* You'll hear praise throughout the neighborhood if your child remembers to do this. It's not being a suck up; it's really good manners. Best of all, it probably will ensure that your youngster gets asked back to that home, and everyone will think you've done such a great job teaching your kids manners. Take a bow.

Mealtime etiquette is important too, even if the odds of your child being served a finger bowl and wondering what to do with it are slight. Kathy Peel suggests that you teach your kids to:

- *Sit up straight* [at the table]. It's not only good manners not to slouch, but it also keeps food from falling on the floor, which makes a mess, unless you have a dog that isn't too picky about broccoli or Brussels sprouts.

- *Keep a napkin in your lap, and don't forget to use it.* This not only prevents your kid from wiping his mouth on his sleeve or pants, but it also catches food if it drops in his lap. Buy some cloth napkins that don't need ironing after they're washed and get your kids used to using them. It's hard to practice good table manners with paper napkins that shred.

- *Keep chair legs on the floor.* The reason for this is far more than just good manners. If your kid tilts back in his chair, the chair can topple over and, despite how hard-headed you may think he is, he can still be seriously hurt. (He also can break someone's antique chair if they're foolish enough to put young kids in such a delicate chair.)

- *Don't start eating until everyone is served.* Sometimes the host or hostess will say, "Go ahead and start while it's hot." That's the only time to dig in before everyone, especially the host or hostess, is served.

- *Ask the person closest to what you want to "please pass" it. Thank him or her for doing so.* This prevents leaning across the table or grabbing for something just out of reach and inadvertently stabbing another guest with your fork. Even if there are only two of you at the dinner table, practice this statement until it becomes rote for you both.

- *Take what you're offered. If you don't like something, politely say "No, thank you" or take a very small portion.* This comes in handy if your child is at a friend's house for dinner and they're serving something he or she considers gross or is allergic to.

Remind your child that "Yuck" is not an appropriate comment and that a small bite of a new food might be a surprise and actually taste quite good. Practice this at your home too.

- *Eat slowly.* You don't need to use a timer or insist on their putting the fork down between bites, but most children (and adults) could learn to eat a little slower. It's better for digestion and even gives an opportunity for conversation.

- *Chew with your mouth closed.* Chomping your food for all to see is not pleasant for the viewers. By all means, promote closed-mouth chewing at your own table and hope that when your kids go out into the world's dinner table they remember what they've been taught.

- *Talk only when you've swallowed your food.* Your kid only has to be hit in the face by partially masticated food once to see the importance of this rule. You might consider starting a "rude rule" and setting fines for everyone, including you, who breaks this and other rules for dinner table manners.

- *Keep elbows and arms off the table.* Remember the saying, "Johnny, Johnny, strong and able, take your elbows off the table?" Even if you don't, it's another of these good manner rules your children should learn now so they don't embarrass themselves when they're older and are being interviewed for an important job. Eating with your elbows on the table looks like you're tired and can hardly hold your head up (even if it's true)—or worse, that you're so starved that you need to be closer to shovel the food in your mouth. Neither vision makes a pretty picture.

- *Ask to be excused when the meal is over.* This prevents your kids from jumping up in the middle of the meal and leaving the table while you wonder if it was something you said or just plain rudeness on their part. You can prevent a sudden disappearing act by insisting on using this table manner.

If faced with a bewildering array of forks or spoons at their place at a dinner table, instruct your children to start on the outside and work their way in toward the plate. That way they can't go wrong. If still in doubt, watch what the host or hostess does.

Also, teach your kids to write thank-you notes for gifts or a special treat from a friend or relative. Buy age-appropriate stationery for them and keep stamps on hand. Few kids today write thank-you notes, or if they do, only scrawl "thanks for the gift." They neglect to say what they plan to do with the gift or tell how much they appreciate being thought of. No wonder grandparents and other relatives quickly become turned off to sending presents to kids who never say thanks. It's not "sissy" for boys to write thank-you notes either; it's good manners. (And, hopefully, you're setting a good example by writing them as well.)

## HOW TO SET UP AND HOLD FAMILY MEETINGS

Although you, as the benevolent dictator of the family, have the final say with your kids, it's important to give them the opportunity to tell you what's on their mind, what they'd like changed, and what responsibilities (and privileges) they feel they should have. The best way to accomplish this is with family meetings.

If your children are four or older, announce that you'll be holding regular family meetings to discuss and make plans for this newly constituted family. If that sounds too formal, call it a "family forum" or "family council." It doesn't matter if you only have the kids every other weekend and some holidays. Do it anyway. The younger ones will feel important and the preteens and teenagers will look forward to the opportunity to express themselves. It's good practice for them to learn how to communicate respectfully and be persuasive. Best of all, you'll fare better by gaining their cooperation and trying to compromise whenever possible on the house rules and regulations.

What's on the family meeting agenda? You can talk about anything and should encourage the kids to give you items they want discussed. A few typical examples include:

- Allowances: how much, when given, what it's to be used for
- Chores: what they are, how they are assigned, and how they are to be carried out
- Activities: what to do, when, and how to do it
- Rules: what they are, why, what happens if they aren't followed
- Complaints: what, how can the situation be fixed or made better
- Meals: what to have, who fixes, who cleans up

Let your kids know that the purpose of your family meeting is to clear the air, to hear everyone's voice, and to help you (the benevolent dictator) make the final decision. The rules are that everyone gets a chance to speak without being criticized or teased. When someone has the floor, no one (including you) can interrupt (filibustering is not permitted).

The results of holding family meetings include:

- Communication within the family improves.
- Good ideas often arise through group discussion.
- You don't make quick and arbitrary decisions without really thinking them through.
- Your kids have the opportunity to understand more fully the other side (yours) of an issue.
- You gain insight into what your kids are thinking.
- Your kids feel empowered yet learn the art of compromise.
- Your kids feel part of the family group, which strengthens their self-esteem.

Although you may feel a little awkward as you conduct your first couple of family meetings, you may be surprised how quickly your kids respond to it as they learn how to express their opinions clearly and, sometimes, forcefully. Don't be surprised if they present a united front when they discuss the importance of an increase in their allowance or the need for a puppy. Family meetings become a special ritual that your kids will long remember and may want to continue even when they become adults.

Chapter 5

# Playing Together

*We do not stop playing because we grow old,*
*We grow old because we stop playing.*
—OLIVER WENDELL HOLMES

When you're having fun as a family, you tend to forget your problems and just enjoy one another. Play time opens communication, allows you to observe your kids without being too obvious about it, and lets you all blow off a little steam. Obviously, the ages of your children make a difference in what and how you play, but don't think that because your kids are preteen or even teenagers that they're too old to play. Kids as well as adults, even single dads, need to include some silliness, fun, and friendly competition in their lives.

## ENJOY YOUR KIDS

"I don't feel much like playing," you may think. "My life's turned upside down, my finances are a mess, and that supposed 'light in the tunnel' looks pretty black to me right now."

That's all the more reason to include some fun and recreation for yourself as well as your kids. However, playing includes so much more than just games. It's when you're being silly with knock-knock jokes, planning an in-house picnic on a blanket, making a tent by tossing a sheet over a card table, painting a room together, creating costumes from the dress-up box and putting on a play, kicking a ball, building a snowman, singing together, or a myriad of other things that you begin to transform as a family, forget the stress you've been carrying around, and begin to let laughter heal.

---

✔ **Tip from the Trenches**

Al reminded: "Remember to include the smaller kids in the fun and never let some of the children gang up on another."

---

Play time doesn't have to be costly either. Jack said, "When my girls were little, I took them to the library for storytelling hour, to outdoor art shows, and to the free concerts in the park. When they got a little older, we went to a movie house that runs old movies at reduced rates. I don't think they ever felt they were missing out on anything and we all had fun."

Stan recalls, "My son became interested in soccer shortly after my ex-wife and I split up. I took an active interest in his sport, eventually becoming an assistant coach, then a coach. He continued to play soccer until he was about thirteen years old, so we had a lot of years playing together."

Stan's son was also a very avid Lego builder just as Stan was when he was a kid. Stan said, "We spent hours together sitting together in the living room of my small apartment building Legos and even invented a game we called 'demolition derby.' We would each build a car out of Legos, making them as tough as we could, and then go to the hallway (which had a wood floor) and raced them toward each other (crashing into one another). We continued to race until one of the drivers came flying out of his car. The other car was the winner."

## DON'T BECOME A "DISNEY DAD"

It's a shame that the delightful amusement parks in California and Florida have become synonymous in the media with the single father who is trying to entertain his children when they're with him. There is nothing wrong with Disneyland and Disney World, but you don't have to bring your kids to expensive theme parks in order to amuse them. Often the things that cost the least—a Nerf football, modeling clay, Legos, toy blocks, and puzzles—are the most enjoyable because there's no pressure on dad or the kids to have fun.

If your kids are older, set up a badminton net, kick a soccer ball back and forth, or toss a football. If you have room in the yard, play croquet. When your kids see you playing and having fun, you not only give them permission to play, but you also demonstrate good sportsmanship through your behavior (hopefully). Although you may have a stack of papers on your desk that need your attention, right now it's important to give your kids your full attention. If you're just going through the motions, they'll know it, whether you're playing catch or building a tower with dominoes.

Don't be surprised if when you're playing with your kids that they open up and start telling you what's on their minds. Listen attentively; that precious moment may not return any time soon. According to a 2006 study by the American Academy of Pediatrics, "Some of the best interactions occur during downtime—just talking, preparing meals together and working on a hobby or art project, playing sports together, or being fully immersed in child-centered play."

## QUIET TIMES ARE GOOD TIMES

Playing also includes some quiet time where you can listen to different types of music, read, or even just talk. Mike, a single dad, fondly remembers watching a sporting event on television with his then three-year-old daughter just quietly cuddled up in his lap. She was with her daddy so all was right in her world.

Other quiet activities you can do together as a family include putting together jigsaw puzzles (be sure to buy age-appropriate ones so the younger children don't lose inter-

est or become frustrated), reading aloud, watching a video, or telling a story with each person picking up where the last one left off. You also can lie on a blanket in the yard and take turns announcing what you see in the clouds as they pass by.

Arts and crafts are also a great way for you and your kids to work together on a project, and you don't have to be an artist or even especially creative. It also offers the kids the opportunity to express any fears or worries, either on paper or in a play.

Michael's kids, ages four and five, put together an imaginative circus that they presented for their grandparents, aunts and uncles, and cousins. The four-year-old jumped through a paper hoop. "I'm a lion," she growled.

Then the five-year-old put a red poker chip on his nose. "I'm a clown," he informed the cheering crowd. And what was his grand finale? He picked up two stuffed animals and attempted, without success, to juggle them. But both kids took numerous bows, got tremendous applause, and were proud of their efforts. They had busied themselves for a couple of hours planning and rehearsing their act and everyone enjoyed their creative output.

## ARTS AND CRAFTS AND WHY THEY'RE IMPORTANT

Kids are creative at any age. All you need to create an art center in your home are a few plastic bins and containers for:

- Dress-up clothes, which could include an old bathrobe, a necktie (good use for some of your awful Christmas ties), a variety of hats, beads, scarves, jackets, and, of course, some makeup. Ask the women in your family to donate bed jackets, lacey blouses, old crinolines, earrings, and other items that might make a good addition to a costume. (And don't panic if your son comes in looking like a dancing girl. It only means he's having fun.)

- Crayons (fat ones, if your children are toddlers)
- Paper (colored construction or plain white)
- Clay (some stay soft after use; others harden when exposed overnight to air)
- Scissors (safety ones with blunt ends if your children are small)
- Cellophane tape
- Watercolors or colored (washable) felt tip pens
- Stickers of all kinds
- Colored chalk (useful for drawing pictures on your driveway)
- Buttons

Where do you find this treasure trove of art supplies? They're available at a teacher's supply store, stationery shops, dollar stores, and at retail chain stores such as Wal-Mart, Michaels, and Target. If you're not certain or need suggestions, talk to your children's teachers.

# CREATE NEW MEMORIES THROUGH PLAY

Playing also includes carrying on some family traditions that are still viable in your single-dad relationship with your kids, as well as creating new rituals and meaningful events that mark this new family you and your children are creating. It gives your children a sense of still belonging to a family—dad's family—and hopefully their mother will be doing the same when she has the children with her. This means creating memories for your children while at the same time show-ing them that you love them very much and that they are important to you.

If you have your kids during Halloween, for example, go all out decorating the house and yard. Decorate cookies, create your own costumes, and serve a special Halloween dinner with bones (drumsticks), witches' brew (lemonade), and ghosts (ice-cream sundaes) for dessert. If you don't have your kids with you then, send them Halloween cards and gift boxes filled with Halloween candy, stickers, cupcakes, and accessories for costumes, along with a disposable camera so they can take photos and send it back to you. If they have a digital camera, they can download the pictures and e-mail them to you.

## Create Celebrations
Create your own celebrations, such as the Second Wednesday Wingding, Spring Bounce, National Pickle Week, the Christmas Past Party, or anything else that tickles your funny bones. Encourage your kids to think creatively, be silly, and have fun. The 2006 American Academy of Pediatrics report states that "Undirected play allows children to learn how to work in groups, to share, to resolve conflicts, and to learn self-advocacy skills." It's a different kind of play when the kids make up (and change) the rules, rather than following the adult-created league rules. There's less stress and more laughter.

## Enjoy the Outdoors
Follow the example of Connecticut, a state that recently initiated a No Child Left Inside program to encourage kids to enjoy the outdoors. Take your kids hiking to a picnic area, visit a state park, go bird-watch-ing, or look for wildflowers. According to Richard Louv, author of Last Child in the Woods—Saving Our Children from Nature Deficit Disorder, most of our kids suffer from

"nature deficit disorder" today because they spend too much time indoors playing computer games or watching TV and are disconnected from the outdoors.

What's more, many community zoning laws forbid kids and parents from building tree houses, planting vegetable gardens, or otherwise "destroying" the planned development's prescribed environment as they enjoy the wonders of outdoors. Whereas their parents and grandparents played outdoors in the neighborhood until the streetlights went on, most kids today are fenced in by fear and security walls. By going with your kids to explore the great outside and enjoying the beauties and wonders of nature, you can reduce your stress as well as that of your kids, a wonderful benefit of play.

### Follow Their Interest

Follow your kids' interests. If one of your children enjoys stamp collecting, ask questions. Buy a large map of the world so you can locate the countries (before their names change). Don't be surprised if your child teaches you some things about each country that you didn't know before.

Another youngster may opt for chess or knitting. While you may not be very good at chess, play anyway and praise your youngster every time he or she checkmates you. And while you may not want to take up knitting, you can still show an interest by asking your daughters (or sons) where to find patterns and how long it takes to knit a sweater or vest, and by admiring their handiwork and wearing the tie or socks they make for you.

The important point to remember is that you and your kids may have dissimilar interests, but you can learn to enjoy, or at least be interested in, their activities and hopefully they will enjoy some of the things you're interested in. It's all part of playing

well with others. You don't want to get a failing grade, do you?

## KNOW THEIR FRIENDS

One way to get to know your children's friends is to get involved in activities with them. Some dads said they were involved in their daughter's Brownie troops so they not only got to know her friends, they also met some of the other parents of these friends and had an idea what their values and ideas of parenting were, which was helpful when their daughter wanted to go to the friend's home to play.

Others made sure their home was the one their kids' friends wanted to come to by letting them make popcorn and having plenty of soft drinks available along with some appropriate DVDs. There often were soda spills or a few kernels of popcorn buried under the couch seat cushions, but they knew where their kids were and who they had as friends.

Just be sure that you don't overschedule the kids. They need some downtime too.

---

✔ **Tip from the Trenches**

Stan says "The opportunity to enjoy your kids in their youth goes by way too quickly. Try to use a third-party event (sports, scouting, youth groups through your church or synagogue, theater, or whatever the child's interest are) to do [activities] together. In our situation, I have coached baseball/soccer for my son and soccer for my daughter and my ex has been the team mom for virtually every season I have coached. Between all the sports and for both kids, it has been nearly fourteen seasons."

Rushing youngsters from soccer to swimming practice then home for homework is neither quality time nor play time. Be sure they really want to be on a particular sports team before you sign them up, and make certain you have some idea who their teammates will be as they'll be spending a great deal of time with these peers. We know of too many kids who stay on a team because they think that's what their parents want them to do. One stayed with football for two years longer than he really wanted because his dad was one of the coaches and he didn't want to disappoint him by quitting.

## PLAY TIME HAS VALUE

Play time is when kids can relax, even if they're running around playing cops and robbers, jumping rope, or tossing a football back and forth. Real play time differs from organized sports and other activities because there are no strict rules, other than those the kids themselves create, and there aren't any adults telling them what to do. Play teaches our children to be independent, to take turns being the leader and follower.

Never underestimate the importance of play, especially for your younger children. According to the 2006 report prepared by the American Academy of Pediatrics, for healthy development and to use their imaginations fully, children need "spontaneous free play, whether it's chasing butterflies, playing with 'true toys' like blocks and dolls, or just romping on the floor. . . ." The report continues, "Perhaps above all,

play is a simple joy that is a cherished part of childhood."

In the above-mentioned report, the American Academy of Pediatrics recommends that:

- Free play should be promoted as a healthy and essential part of childhood.
- Overuse of "passive entertainment," including television and computer games, should be avoided.
- All children should be afforded ample, unscheduled, independent time to be creative, to reflect, and to decompress.
- Spending time together talking and listening can help parents serve as role models and prepare their children for success.
- Parents should avoid conveying an unrealistic expectation that every child needs to excel in many areas to be a success.

Actually, according to psychologists Elena Bodrova and Deborah J. Leong, coauthors of "Why Children Need Play," published in the September 2005 edition of *Scholastic Early Childhood Today*, there is "a link between play and the development of cognitive and social skills that are prerequisites for learning more complex concepts as children get older. For example, play is linked to growth in memory, self-regulation, oral language, and recognizing symbols. It has been linked to higher levels of school adjustment and increased social development . . . to increased literacy skills and other areas of academic learning." And you thought it was merely child's play, didn't you?

# Chapter 6

# Celebrating Rituals and Customs

*This passing moment
is all we can be sure of;
It is only common sense
to extract its utmost value from it.*
—W. SOMERSET MAUGHAM

Over time, most families develop certain ways of doing things, as major as the ways in which birthdays and holidays are celebrated (or not celebrated) to as minor as bedtime routines and when dinner is served. These rituals become guidelines so everyone in the family knows what to expect. But once the parents divorce and each sets up his and her household, routines may of necessity change. You may drop specific routines and customs because they no longer seem to work for you or because they cause a flood of memories you'd just as soon keep buried, at least for a while.

The best of plans often crumble, creating conflict and chaos during a child's birthday or holidays. What happens when one parent's scheduled time with the kids occurs over the other's birthday, the child's birthday, or a holiday?

If the kids are lucky and their parents can communicate and compromise, their folks may switch dates, have a separate celebration close to the actual date, or celebrate that holiday with their child on alternate years. Some parents even put aside their mutual hostilities or frustrations with one another and agree to cohost the event for the sake of their children.

This latter course of action, however, is only helpful to a youngster if the parents can truly behave themselves and not resort to sarcasm or snide remarks. Kids are more perceptive than we usually give them credit for, and they, even young ones, can quickly decipher the meaning behind comments and body language. They'll resent your pretending to be nice when you're really throwing daggers at each other.

## CREATE NEW TRADITIONS

Every family has its traditions that it cherishes, and children carry the memory of those traditions throughout their lives. Although every family has its own traditions, it's sometimes better (and more fun) to create new ones than to try to revive one that meant a lot when your family included your now ex. Trying to struggle through the old tradition without her might make her absence more difficult for the kids. Here are some tips for creating new traditions:

- Be creative. Celebrate birthdays by having cake for breakfast or hide the presents and make the birthday boy or girl go on a treasure hunt looking for them.
- Open Christmas presents the night before if your ex will have the kids Christmas day. (Santa has often been known to come early when requested.)
- Rather than trying to follow their mom's tradition of making Christmas cookies, start a new tradition like driving around to see Christmas lights or anything that makes your time with them special and different.
- Celebrate Boxing Day (celebrated throughout Great Britain, New Zealand, Canada, and Australia) on December 26.
- If you're Jewish, celebrate Hanukkah one or more of the eight nights you have the kids.
- If your ex and her extended family have the kids for first night Seder on Passover, hold a second night Seder and make it original for you and your kids by asking them to act out parts or write their own prayers.
- Grill steak for Thanksgiving dinner rather than fixing a turkey and have make-your-own sundaes instead of pumpkin pie for dessert.
- Go fishing with the kids and catch and eat fresh fish instead of turkey for Thanksgiving. (Be sure to have a frozen pizza handy in case the fish aren't biting.)

✔ **Tip from the Trenches**

John says, "Allow both parties to enjoy the holidays with the children. Evaluate honestly who has the best schedule for the kids and allow the children to enjoy the events. We split the holidays fairly, generally alternating lunch and dinners. One year we split up Christmas Eve/ Christmas morning. We sometimes determine who has the most family members, cousins, etc., in town that year, and then make the decision."

- Take a trip together to a children's museum, a national park, or other special locations on or near Saint Patrick's Day.
- Pick a day and create your own holiday for it. Name it after a cartoon character, movie star, or sports figure, and create your own traditions, foods, and decorations for it. Be silly, have fun, and create special memories for your kids. You'll be surprised when they're adults to learn how much some of these celebrations meant to them.

Rituals can be as silly as eating a backward meal, starting with dessert, one day a week or as sentimental as making valentines or thank-you cards when someone does something nice for another. It can be all of you snuggling in your bed on Sunday morning to read the comics, or, with older kids, watching the news and then discussing important issues at dinner. It can be a picnic on the last day of school or renting a beach cottage for Father's Day.

The important thing to remember is that whatever you come up with, it should be fun, let you enjoy special foods and decorations, include lots of laughter, and make new memories for you and your kids.

## HANDLING LIFE CYCLE EVENTS

Life cycle events are the occasions that imprint our lives, such as birth, confirmation, bar/bat mitzvah, graduation, weddings, and funerals. Most life cycle events are happy ones, but when you're a single dad, each emphasizes the fact that now you are half of the couple you used to be. Nevertheless, that former tie connects you to the function and requires you not only to attend but to do so cheerfully and be supportive of the individual who is being honored. This is easy if you and your ex (and her family) have remained somewhat friendly despite the divorce. It is more difficult, but equally necessary, if there has been bitterness and friction since the divorce. Being the mature person you are, don't ruin the happiness of the day for those involved.

### First Communion

In the Catholic Church, the First Communion is usually held when the children are eight years old. It is a spiritual ceremony in which the class, as a group, is welcomed into the church. Families usually host some type of reception afterwards. Hopefully you and your ex, along with your families, will attend even if you are not Catholic. If your child is having a First Communion, it's rather obvious that he or she is being raised Catholic. Don't do anything to suggest that you are not supportive of this special moment in your young child's life.

### Confirmations

Many religions hold special ceremonies for youngsters called confirmation. It can mean different things depending upon the religion—a sacrament, the coming of an age to be counted as a mature member of the congregation, the solidification of the youngster's relationship with the Christian faith, or graduating from religious school. In Judaism, confirmation takes place around age fifteen or sixteen and is a group ceremony for the entire confirmation class, marking the transition to adulthood for the teenagers and allowing them to proclaim to the gathered congregation that they are voluntarily accepting the laws of the Torah and the Jewish faith.

Regardless of the particular religion, confirmation is a special time for your children, even if they'd never admit it, and of course they'd like both of their parents to witness the moving ceremony. Don't stay away. Even if it isn't your religion, it is now that of your children and you don't want to lessen its significance.

### Bar/Bat Mitzvahs

This is a coming-of-age ceremony for Jewish boys and girls who are thirteen years old in which the child reads in Hebrew from the Torah and can be counted in a *minyan*, the minimum number of adults needed for specific parts of religious services. It also means that they are considered old enough to be responsible for their own actions. Hopefully their parents—you and your ex—can also remember your responsibility

---

**✔ Tip from the Trenches**

Dan suggests, "If you like to write, you might want to try this tradition. I have written to my two girls since they were babies . . . poems, letters, cards, thoughts of what they are doing at that moment in time, things they say. I finish the note or whatever, I postmark and mail it to them, but only to be opened later in life when they will be able to appreciate it or have questions as to what they were like or what they liked."

---

to your child and put away your differences so this meaningful religious occasion can indeed remain a special memory.

Every rabbi has far too many lurid tales of parents who ruined the ceremony for their child by refusing to share the pulpit with each other or help pass the Torah from one to the other and then to their child. We recently attended a very different bar mitzvah ceremony where the boy's mother, stepfather, father, stepmother, and an assortment of stepbrothers and half brothers all took part in the event. It was a beautiful ceremony filled with love for this youngster and a tribute to the parents who were able to join together, despite their many differences, in creating a special moment for their child.

### Graduations

Graduations are another life cycle event where parents are called to join in celebration of their child's accomplishments, be it from kindergarten, high school, college, or graduate school. Unfortunately, for some dads it (along with a wedding) is the only time they plan to be in the same vicinity as their ex.

Stan admitted that he and his ex still had an acrimonious relationship. "Even her e-mails were filled with venom. I saw my son every weekend from the time I moved out when he was six, but we never fought in front of him and I never talked badly about his mom."

### Weddings

It's often said that weddings, like funerals, bring out the worst in people. You may have always assumed that you would walk your daughter down the aisle. But a stepfather has entered the picture and now your daughter's mom (your ex) wants him to do the honors. Your daughter's torn. What's a dad to do?

Ask your daughter if she really has a preference, but be prepared to step aside if she decides she really would like her stepdad to have the honors. You could agree to a compromise and have both of you escort her, though that might look as though you both were forcing her to wed. Instead, consider having him walk her halfway down and then handing her off to you so you are the one to deliver her to her groom (and get the last kiss).

If your ex is getting married, allow your kids to attend, even if you really may not want them to. It's their mother and it's important for them to share in this important occasion in her life. Bite your tongue if you think her new husband-to-be is a creep because, after all, he will be your kids' stepfather and, who knows, you may find yourself eventually enjoying his company. Besides, when you remarry, you'll want your kids to be involved at your wedding as well. Yes, what's good for the goose is also good for the gander.

### Funerals

The death of a loved one creates a myriad of emotions—loneliness, despair for questions no longer able to be asked and answered, anger, and fear of who will handle things now. Death and the ensuing funeral throws families together and unites people who perhaps haven't even seen each other in years.

Yet, hopefully, death is the stranger in the midst who is able to reconcile individuals, even for one brief moment, as priorities are put into place and everyone involved realizes that his or her time on earth is limited.

When an interviewee's mother had a beloved aunt die at age ninety-four, she was surprised to see her former daughter-in-law sitting in the back of the temple during the memorial service. "I went up to her

afterwards, and thanked her for coming. It meant a great deal to me—and said a lot about her—that she had come to pay her respects."

Remember that your kids may have been very close to members of your ex's family—aunts, uncles, and grandparents—as well as their stepfather, stepsiblings, and steprelatives. Make it easy for these relatives to come to the funeral, wake, shiva, or reception afterwards. Respect the finality of the occasion as you would want it respected for your family. If the deceased was one of your ex-in-laws, you might consider attending if you think it would not upset your ex.

## SPECIFIC PERSONAL OCCASIONS

Children should be with their mother on Mother's Day and with their father on Father's Day whenever possible, even if that doesn't coincide with that parent's legal custody time. If that isn't possible because the parent lives out of town, the other parent should be sure the children have some type of contact such as by phone or e-mail.

If your children are too young to shop on their own, put your differences with your ex aside and take the kids with you to buy a card and gift for their mother on Mother's Day, on her birthday, and on Christmas or Hanukkah. By ignoring the occasion, you make your children feel sad that they weren't able to celebrate their other parent's special day and they may grow to resent that you didn't help them.

If they're old enough to shop on their own, remind them in advance that their mother's birthday is coming up or that it soon will be Mother's Day. Why? Because it's important to them and makes you look like a good guy. Remember: TOYK (think of your kids).

Chapter 7

# Acknowledging That Daughters Are Different

*He who has daughters*
*is always a shepherd.*
—SPANISH PROVERB

Single dads of boys tend to have it somewhat easier than single dads of girls because they probably remember, to some degree, what it was like being a young boy. If you have daughters, however, you probably usually left the "girl talk" and emotional stuff to your wife. But now that it's just you, you'll find that problems and other issues don't just arise when it's your ex's turn to have the kids. Chances are these awkward situations and topics will fall into your lap, even if it's during the one weekend you have the girls.

## EMOTIONAL GAMUT

Although this chapter will give you numerous tips on how to handle many situations—how to do a little girl's hair and help older girls cope with cliques, bullies, mean teachers, pimples, cramps, and wandering boyfriends—you'll have to be prepared for the unexpected. You can fortify yourself by remembering that 1) girls usually tend to be more emotional than boys and often cry easily, even if they don't want to, 2) they often just want to verbalize to unload and don't expect (or want) you to tell them what to do, and 3) they want you to take them seriously.

If you think that's a lot to remember, here's one more important point: You are the first man in your daughter's life, and as such you have a tremendous influence on how your daughter thinks about herself, her body, and her relationship with boys (and, in the future, men). Therefore, think before you comment on women you see on TV or in the mall, especially about their weight, size of breasts, or body type. If you have pre-teen or teenage sons too, squelch that type of comment from them as well. Your daughter may take that type of a casual remark to heart, worry about it, and then personalize

it. As you'll see later in this chapter, girls are extremely susceptible to developing a distorted body image, and that can quickly lead to serious eating disorders or other body-image issues.

## BREAKING THE CODE IN YOUR DAUGHTER'S CHATTER

As a single father, you'll probably spend more time as the only male adult around your daughter than you ever did before the divorce. You'll quickly become aware that girls are far more verbal than boys. They not only start to talk earlier than little boys, they talk more, frequently putting their thoughts, ideas, and feelings into words, lots of words.

### Stop, Look, and Listen for the Meaning Behind the Words

If you stop listening with only half an ear and give your daughter your full attention, you'll realize there's more under the surface of the words you're hearing. Girls talk about how they feel about their relationships with other people, their teachers, their friends, their coaches—everything. Boys may only shrug and say, "He's okay."

You may sometimes wish there were a stop button to turn off your daughter's constant chattering. But that's how girls work things out. When you start listening and not interrupting to give your opinion, you may learn a great deal about Daddy's little girl. You may learn, for example, that when she's talking about a teacher or coach, she's really telling you that she's afraid of failing and disappointing you. It may be the girlfriends she's chattering on about have formed a "we're in it and you're not" club, a common occurrence especially with middle-school-age girls. She's embarrassed

## ✔ Tip from the Trenches

MG says, "As far as daughters being different . . . well, they are, although they
should be treated just like a son in many
ways. Take them to events, expose them
to all the things you do and know about
life and want your children to be exposed
to and know. Be sure to get involved in
the girly stuff too. Go shopping, pick out
clothes with her, and let her know that
she can count on you to be there for her.
But always be a parent. Set rules and
guidelines that must be followed and do
not spoil for poor behavior. . . . I think
being a Dad is the most important thing
you can do for your daughter."

to let you know that she was left out. While
her mom may understand because she probably experienced these types of situations as
a young girl too, it's hard as a dad to identify
with these emotions. Saying, "To heck with
them. You have other friends," only underscores your lack of comprehension of the
depth of her feelings.

### Give Your Full Attention

Give your daughter your full attention
when she's talking. Stop looking at your e-
mail or the baseball scores on your Blackberry or watching the TV game with half
an eye. Act as though you're interested,
because if you're not, your daughter will
sense it and stop talking to you.

Her silence also may mean that she is
frustrated that you keep trying to "fix"
everything rather than just listen to her as
she decides what to do. Ask her why she's
not talking to you anymore. Let her know
that it hurts you and then promise to make
a safe and nonjudgmental environment for
her to open up to you. Listen to her ideas

and don't be surprised if they're good ones.
Let her talk out her dreams and never, ever
suggest that they're impossible for her to
achieve.

### Understand the True Meaning of Your Daughter's Greeting Cards

Along with listening, carefully read
the greeting cards you receive from your
daughter. They're not just a "grab and buy."
According to Keith Yocham, product manager at Hallmark Cards, research reveals
that daughters carefully select the cards they
send to their dads. "They want to bridge the
gap and get closer to their fathers and they
use a Father's Day card to say what they feel.
But frustration and disappointment can follow when a daughter does not get the reaction she had hoped for from her dad." She
tends to think that she hasn't been heard
and that her feelings are not reciprocated.

Dr. Gilda Carle, a relationship therapist
and professor at Mercy College, says, "The
irony is, dads don't have a clue that there is
a problem, or that something more is hoped
for because no one ever tells him."

Consider yourself told. Rather than just
scanning the card's text and tossing it aside,
Hallmark suggests your reading the card
aloud and then allowing the words to open
the door to a special conversation with your
daughter.

According to Dr. Carle, daughters don't
necessarily want a hug-and-kiss fest, nor are
they expecting a great display of emotion
or tears. A few minutes of personal conversation, a few seconds of eye contact and
a smile, and a comment or two about the
message in the card are what they are looking for. Those are the treasured moments
that daughters (of any age) long for.

# HANDLING HAIR

In 1967, Broadway rocked with a love-rock musical that demanded the end of the Vietnam War. It was called *Hair*. Now, forty years later, "hair" is still demanding attention, especially with single dads. In fact, more than half of the single dads we interviewed who had daughters mentioned problems dealing with their girls' hair. Here is their advice:

Michael admits, "Hair has always been my nemesis. My four-year-old daughter has very long hair and apparently, I am neither great at brushing it nor a graduate of the seminar that all women seem to have taken that explains how to do these elaborate braids, ponytails, etc. Two words of advice on this subject: headbands and clip-on bows. If you can't figure these out either, then head off to the nearest Supercuts and somehow convince your ex-wife that short hair really is in."

Sam adds: "Brushing girls' hair is a very sensitive and confusing issue. Make sure you do it when the hair is wet as that makes it much easier and buy a very soft brush. Hard bristles will make this more of an adventure that it already is."

From Jack: "I was so desperate trying to make my two daughters' hair presentable that I took them to a hair salon and threw myself at the mercy of one of the stylists. Thankfully, she took pity on me and showed me some tricks."

John proudly explained that he "learned to braid hair first thing. Now I can do 'piggies' [pigtails], pony's, etc."

Joel says, "My daughter is in the middle of two sons, age eight. I used to spend a lot of time on her hair. Oy vey. It was tough in the winter coming out of the pool. We cut her hair for ease of care and made sure she shampooed and conditioned it after every visit to the pool."

Matthew suggests, "I would advise all single fathers with girls to learn how to plat [braid] hair and remember that all women need longer than we think to get ready."

Obviously, learning to do their daughter's hair was a challenge for most of the single fathers of daughters that we interviewed. However, there is help out there. You can use the search engine Google (*www.google.com*) and type in "How to Braid Hair." There are sites that explain how to do a French braid, cornrows, twist, and simple braids without pulling too hard and breaking the hair.

Ray Stover, a hair stylist for forty-two years, suggests using a detangler cream rinse or spray to take the knots out. "You can use that or a styling gel for girls with tight ringlets, but you need to use a special wide-tooth comb that is available at the drug store." Stover said, "Never try to brush curly hair as it becomes frizzy. At night, it helps to put curly hair in a pony tail so it doesn't become super tangled during the night." He suggested conditioner and a big-toothed comb for African Americans' hair to make it more manageable, but suggests leaving cornrows to the women who "know how to do it best because they learned from their mothers." Never, ever decide to cut your young daughter's hair without your ex's permission.

What about the other hair, the hair under your daughter's arms and on her legs? Don't be surprised if when she's in middle school she learns from her peers that she should shave it off. If she approaches you about this, buy her a razor and some shaving cream and show her how to gently move the razor against the hair. Be sure she puts the razor away if you have younger children in the house.

## NUDITY: YOURS AND HERS

When the kids are toddlers or under five years of age, it's easy to toss them all in the tub and bathe them at once or have them all shower with you. But once your daughter reaches four or five, she may begin to want more privacy, especially if her brothers tease her about her lack of a penis or she sees yours and wonders why she doesn't have one too. If you're a widower, your daughter may not have a woman in her life for comparison and she may need reassurance from you that her genitalia is perfectly normal, that it's one of the differences between boys and girls. If she asks why you have pubic hair, explain that adults have it, and when she's grown up she'll have pubic hair too.

Most experts say daughters should not see their father naked after the age of five as it can be traumatic for a child, especially if she has some knowledge of sexual intercourse. Wrap a towel around yourself or throw on a bathrobe. If she barges in when you're showering, calmly tell her you'd like some privacy and will be right out.

If your young daughter asks you questions about sex, answer them using proper terminology such as penis, vagina, vulva, testicles, and labia. If you use baby words like *pee-pee*, *gerdie*, or *wee-wee*, she won't know what the pediatrician is talking about if the doctor asks her questions, and she'll feel silly when she uses the baby words and her friends know the correct ones. Besides, according to Deborah M. Roffman, M.S., in her book *But How'd I Get in There in the First Place?*, "How we respond to our children's natural curiosity about sexual parts and functioning, and about gender differences, will teach at least as much as any particular factual information we may impart. . . . Language is a potent conveyor of attitudes and values, not just information."

But when you're answering her questions about sexual matters, be careful not to give more information than she wants or needs. Remember the old story about the child who asked where she came from, and after hearing a lengthy dissertation about sperm and eggs and ending with labor pains and the actual birth, the little girl said, "Oh, Cathy comes from Syracuse. I just wondered where I came from."

On the other hand, when your daughter is nearing puberty, she may ask more specific questions. Don't just assume that your ex has explained the birds and the bees. Some women (like men) are uncomfortable talking about sex to their children. If you and your ex can communicate with one another, you can compare questions you've received (along with your joint answers). It may be that your ex has already discussed this with your daughter and your daughter is just checking to be sure you offer the same information.

## MASTURBATION

You may have thought the M word just described a male activity. But girls, even toddlers and those of preschool age, do it too and for the same reasons little (and big) boys touch themselves—they're curious about their bodies and, admit it, it feels good.

Don't overreact if you see your preschool-age daughter masturbating. Instead of yelling and telling her it's dirty, or making her feel guilty about touching her genitals, remind her that that part of her body is private and that if she wants to touch it it's okay but that she should do so in private, in her bedroom or in the bathroom. Also, be sure she knows that no one should touch her without her permission.

According to the American Academy of Child & Adolescent Psychiatry's book, *Your Child: What Every Parent Needs to Know: What's Normal, What's Not, and When to Seek Help*, "If your child masturbates openly, inserts objects into her vagina to masturbate, acts out sexual intercourse during play, or tries to touch the genitals of others, these may be signs of sexual abuse." If you ever suspect your child has been sexually abused, talk to your ex, if you can, and your child's pediatrician. Remember that in cases of sexual abuse the abuser often is a family member.

Girls of every age, as well as women, masturbate, even though your ex may never have admitted it. Women as a rule tend not to discuss masturbation despite the fact that it's a perfectly normal act, and most women have done it at least once in their lifetime, if not a lot more. If your daughter asks you about it, tell her that it is nothing to be ashamed of.

## YOUR LITTLE GIRL IS GROWING UP

Your daughter will begin to mature physically, or undergo puberty, between the ages of eight to fourteen (a bit earlier in African-American girls). Your daughter's breasts will begin to form. She'll then develop coarse hair under her arms and in the pubic area. About two years after her breasts begin to develop she'll begin to menstruate, discharging a half-cup or so of blood from the vagina each month. This is caused by the lining of the uterus sloughing off because no egg has been fertilized. Although your daughter's periods will probably be irregular the first year or so, eventually they'll become fairly regular, appearing anywhere from every twenty-eight to thirty days and lasting two to seven days. She may have cramps right before her periods start.

Read the next section to learn about the importance of having sanitary pads at your house in case your daughter starts menstruating while she is with you. Be prepared.

Be sure your daughter understands what menstruation is so she doesn't suddenly wake up one morning and find blood on her sheets and think she's dying. If you're uncomfortable explaining it to her, there are many books available at your pediatrician's office, the bookstore, or library to help you both. Encourage her to ask questions and do your best to answer them. You also can enlist the help of a female relative.

It's difficult to discuss puberty without beginning to talk about sex with your daughter. Be sure to include more information than just the physical side of sex. Explain the emotional aspects of it as well when she becomes a preteen, and let her know that when a boy says "If you love me, you will," it's okay for her to say, "No, I'm not ready."

### ✔ Tip from the Trenches

MG suggests: "Get involved with your daughter's friends and activities. They want and need us to be involved and really like seeing us there for their events. I am often asked by my daughter to attend Brownies. And I do. Children will remember if you were not there for an important event. Get involved in school events like Career Day or High Interest Day or volunteer for library and/or field trips so you can get to know her friends and their parents as well."

# HOW TO BE PREPARED IF YOUR DAUGHTER STARTS MENSTRUATING AT YOUR HOME

When asked what he would do if his eleven-year-old daughter began menstruating the weekend she was at her dad's house, one highly successful attorney blanched, stammered, and finally blurted out, "I'd call my mother."

It's a fact of life that girls are beginning to get their periods earlier and earlier, often as early as ten years of age. While girls often follow their mother's history, you may not want to ask your ex just when it was that she began menstruating. Better to be prepared beginning when your daughter turns about nine, or even earlier if she is overweight.

Have an open discussion about menstruation with your daughter before she begins so she knows that she can tell you if she gets her period when she's with you. (She may think that you don't know anything about it.) Also, be sure she knows what menstruation is. There are many good books to help you talk to your daughter about all the facts of life. See the Selected Reading appendix in the back of this book for recommendations. Although your daughter may have discussed these issues with her mother,

she may be interested in getting the man's viewpoint too—or she simply needs to know that she doesn't need to be embarrassed around you.

Be matter-of-fact about the menstruation process even if you feel a little awkward talking about it at first. It's a normal occurrence and usually takes place somewhat regularly on a monthly basis, although some girls (and women) remain irregular until menopause, never knowing if or when to expect a period. When girls first begin, however, they may be irregular, having their first period and then not another for a few months.

Some girls have mild to severe cramps when they are menstruating. If you and your ex can't compare notes, call your pediatrician and ask if there's some mild medication to help your daughter. Don't anticipate that she'll have cramps each time or let it constantly be used as an excuse to get out of school or physical education, although occasionally cramps are severe enough that she'll just want to crawl into bed with the heating pad. If you're in doubt, ask her.

If you don't have female friends or relatives, go to your pharmacist and ask for what you need to prepare for a daughter who may soon have her first period. Sanitary pads have adhesive to help them stick to her underpants, and tampons are not suggested for preteen girls. When she discovers that her peers are using tampons, she'll decide and either get them herself or casually mention to you or her mother that she wants tampons, not pads.

Whether your daughter uses pads or tampons, have her wrap the soiled items in toilet paper and put them in the garbage can and not try to flush them in the toilet (regardless what it says on the package) because they stop up the plumbing.

---

### ✔ Tip from the Trenches

Matthew, who has sole custody of his two daughters, advises: "It is important to be open about puberty and learn about sanitary napkins. It is important that they and you are not embarrassed about girl stuff. On the other hand, do not try to become their mother. Involve aunts and other female relatives, if possible."

## WHERE TO FIND TRAINING BRAS (AND WHY THEY'RE SO IMPORTANT)

Getting your preteen daughter a training bra may make no sense to you, but it's important to her, especially if she's late to develop. (Remember that what's considered normal is a process spread over a six-year period.) Your daughter wants to feel like the other girls and probably is embarrassed to still be wearing undershirts. If you feel strange going to a department store lingerie shop to find her a training bra, ask a female relative or friend to take over.

If it's just you and you daughter, explain to her that an expert female fitter will come into the dressing room with her. She'll have a variety of bras for your daughter to try on as it's important to have the right style and size and that it be a perfect fit, even though she may need new ones in six months. Tell her that the woman is a professional doing her job, like a physician, and that she understands that your daughter might be a little self-conscious at first. Don't tell her not to be embarrassed because it's perfectly natural to feel a little strange when we do something so intimate the first time. Once you've prepared her, then bite the bullet and act like a confidant man: Speak quietly to the salesperson in the lingerie shop and say, "My daughter is looking for a training bra. Can you help her find one that fits?" Then let the saleswoman take over, sit down in one of the chairs they thoughtfully provide, and pat yourself on the head. Well done, dad.

## HOW TO HELP YOUR ADOLESCENT DAUGHTER BETTER UNDERSTAND HER BODY AND EMOTIONS

If you and your ex share custody of your daughter, or you have your daughter only on weekends, it's probable that your ex has listened to and explained what's it's like to be female to your daughter. But don't figure that that puts you out of the equation. Chances are your daughter may still have questions when she's with you and wants the male point of view. If you squirm or stammer, she'll think something's wrong with being curious about what's happening to her. Do your homework and read some of the age-appropriate books listed in the back of this book in the Selected Reading appendix before the questions come. If you have your daughter full time you have your homework cut out for you. But it's probably one of the most important cramming sessions you can do. In her book *Embracing Your Father: How to Create the Relationship You Always Wanted with Your Dad*, Dr. Linda Nielsen writes that girls "whose dads reach across the awkward gaps to maintain contact are usually more self-confident, self-reliant, and successful in school and career." Doesn't that encourage you to pass the test?

While most guys are reasonably comfortable with their daughters as little girls, they begin to panic when puberty arrives. Hopefully you have accessible female role models for your daughter—her grandmother, aunt, or the wife of a good family friend. Be sure these women are giving the proper message to your daughter: that women are smart, valuable, and intelligent. If it's just you and your daughter, admit to her that you may not know all the answers, but for any that you don't, the two of you working together can find the information she needs.

Tom shared his thoughts about his fourteen-year-old daughter: "My relationship with my daughter is, I think, very straightforward and we understand each other pretty well. Yes, the emotions are difficult for both of us, but I just flatly admit it and carry on from there."

What a great gift this dad has given to his teenage daughter, that of trust and respect. It can't help but boost her self-confidence, which is so important to all children.

Matthew, who has sole custody of both daughters, said, "I think that like all fathers, I would rather my daughter, who is now thirteen, kept her interests to riding horses or other pursuits that don't include boys. And, like most fathers I meet, we do not just mean now, but until they have reached at least twenty-five!"

Again, a good example of how important it is for kids to know their father trusts them and respects their judgment. This youngster's self-esteem must soar.

Other comments from single dads included George, who said, "My daughter is definitely fast approaching puberty. Some of my concerns are what kinds of friends will she have or what kind of group will she hang out with?"

Frazier said, "My first thought is to leave talks about puberty up to my ex, but the reality is that I feel I have to start sooner rather than later and it is up to me to communicate. I am not sure what my ex will say and convey. My one daughter is eight and I am starting to ask her questions to find out what she is aware of and what knowledge she has. I will need to start having one-on-one conversations when her sister is not around and we won't be interrupted.

"My oldest daughter is eight and I feel these next four years are critical in developing from her study and personal habits to how she views herself and the world around her. That being said, when I am with the girls I try to have as much quality time as possible knowing the time they will listen to me is finite."

Dan added, "I believe one's concerns about puberty can be minimized a bit with healthy communication that starts years earlier. My eleven-year-old has always been a bit of a flirt, even since kindergarten. There was one particular boy there that she really liked and said she was going to marry. Now it's a different boy, a different ring, but the same butterfly feelings in her tummy."

Dan continued, "Just like with smoking, drugs, sex, applying sunscreen lotion, or the necessary shots kids have to have growing up, we talk about things. We've been talking about the dangers of smoking for four or five years. School provided sex education class, but that's not enough. We were talking about that even before. The class provided another opportunity to bring up the subject without sounding strange."

## CLIQUES

Some of your pubescent daughter's issues are probably similar to those of boys entering puberty—pimples, physically developing earlier or later than her friends, feeling awkward at times, and having strange emotions due to surging hormones. In addition, however, girls often tend to have social difficulties in which other girls, some of whom may have been former friends, delight in a female version of "piling on," or shutting out others from their group. If your daughter is the one shut out, it can be very painful for her and challenging for you. Your first thought is probably to storm into the "club house" on your high horse and tell those other girls off.

But cool down, dad. Your job isn't to try to rescue or protect your daughter from her peers. Instead, wipe her tears, listen to her,

✔ Tip from the Trenches

Andy suggests, "It's important for you to help your daughter feel comfortable in her own skin. Tell her you have faith in her ability to make good decisions about her actions."

and ask how she plans to handle the situation. Let her describe to you what she considers her various options, rather than your telling her what she should do, or worse, what you would do. She may decide to go it alone for a while or create her own group and ignore the ones who are rejecting her. She may be thinking about going to her former friends and trying to rekindle the friendship. Listen and be supportive of her decision.

If, however, your daughter is a victim of what the Annals of the New York Academy of Sciences calls "cyberspace violence," where adolescents are victimized by personal attacks, deception, and private information aired in chat rooms, online messages boards, e-mails, or instant messaging, contact the school and the other parents, if you know who's responsible. Teach your own children that this type of harassment and humiliation is not only cruel, it may also be illegal.

## MAKEUP AND PROVOCATIVE CLOTHING

Probably nothing makes a dad more uncomfortable than seeing his little girl putting on makeup, wearing a low cut T-shirt and tight jeans, and holding hands with some creepy looking boy, or worse, a muscular hunk. Why? First, you know your daughter is growing up, and second, you remember what you were like as a boy and you don't trust him one iota.

Hopefully, even if you and your ex don't share custody, you have been able to agree on when can she start wearing makeup and if she should go out wearing sexy-looking outfits. Yes, times have changed and girls are wearing makeup at a younger age than even ten years ago. Clothing styles have changed as well. The skirts are shorter and tighter, the tops are skimpier, and the belly button is often quite evident. But it's up to you when your daughter is with you to be sure she understands what is proper to wear. Hopefully her school has a dress code or, even better, a uniform. But if not, you'll have to be the clothing cop. Exposed belly buttons are fine for the beach but not appropriate for school, church or synagogue, or going out for dinner with Grandma.

Sometimes moms and dads don't agree on how their daughters should dress. According to Frazier, "This is an interesting question. My ex would rather our daughter dress like a twenty-year-old; I would rather she dress her age, which is eight. By being divorced, I can give my opinion and not have to hold back. I am not trying to tell my daughter that her mother is wrong, but instead frame it in that there is another way to look and another perspective to consider. I want to avoid criticizing her mother, although I am sure her mom is more than willing to criticize me."

Sometimes dads have to use the father veto when it comes to appropriate choices in clothing. And, it's okay to say no here, just as it is when necessary in other situations.

Dan has two daughters, ages eleven and nine. He shares custody with his ex. He says, "My older daughter and I have had disagreements on her dress. She likes to wear tight fitting shorts, if she can get away with it. I believe it is an issue of her wanting to be thinner than she is. We have discussed the dangers of certain eating disorders. (This is probably what I worry about most.) My eleven-year-old daughter knows I won't let her go out in public in tight clothes.

"The other day the girls and I were at the mall and passed by the Victoria's Secret store. My older daughter asked what type of clothing the mannequin was wearing. Of course, being the communicative parent, I said 'that's underwear.'

"'Well, it doesn't look like underwear and it doesn't look comfortable,' my daughter said. (It was a thong.) I agreed and we walked passed. Soon after, I thought I was out of the woods. She stated that she would never wear underwear like that. 'You promise?' I said, and we shook on it. If I had had a contract, I would have had her sign and date it. Of course, then the nine-year-old said she'd never wear that kind of underwear either. I believed her too, until we saw the camouflage pair in the window that she thought was cool. But we did have a good discussion about different types of underwear and why women are concerned with showing no panty lines."

George has fifty-fifty shared custody of a son and an eleven-year-old daughter who, he says, "is somewhat overweight. She is starting to be concerned about her clothes—and as for what she likes/wears, I think the weight issue works in dad's favor here as some of the types of clothes that I would not want her wearing do not really fit her well, so she doesn't really want them. Some of it works, though, and I have had to say no to some things already, especially as we shopped for back-to-school clothes recently. The schools have pretty strict rules about clothes too, so that also helps."

But even if you're willing to go along with the makeup and outfits, chances are you and your ex may disagree on when your daughter should be able to start dating. You are probably thinking maybe when she's twenty-five while your ex is a little more realistic.

## DATING AND SEX

When it comes to dating, talk to your daughter to learn why she wants to start dating and what her idea of dating entails. Does she want to go on a date because all of her friends are going out on dates? Does her idea of a date mean going to the movies with a friend who's male, being picked up at the house and getting something to eat and then seeing a movie, or is it going to his friend's house party and just hanging out? Beware the latter, because she may be getting into a situation that's totally over her head or one that at least you'd like to think she is too young for. By keeping communication open with your daughter, however, you'll know where she's going. If you don't, you will have no clue. And yes, either way, you'll worry. That's what dads do.

Tom says, "As for boyfriends, I used to worry more than I do now. I realize that she is strong and competent and quite capable of taking care of herself."

Matthew adds, "Many fathers are not aware of their daughters' boyfriends and this is a situation as a single father I wish to avoid. I have always allowed the girls to bring their friends to our house because that way I can, at least, monitor who they go around with and adjust my approach accordingly. Because I have acknowledged my daughter's new boyfriend's existence, she confides in me and I can monitor the relationship. It is important that if she breaks up with him, (which at this age is inevitable) I can support her or at least understand her behavior when it changes."

Single dad George says, "As for dating—wow! I haven't thought too much about it since she is only eleven, but it will come. But not before she turns sixteen. My rule."

And from Frazier: "I kid that she cannot date until she is thirty-five. But kidding aside, I think it is okay for her to date in her teens, but in a supervised manner."

Psychologist Ganz Ferrance reminds us, "Daughters seek out familiarity when they start dating. She'll expect to be what the men in her life think she and other women should be." So be careful what you say about other women, especially their bodies. If you rave about sexy women in skimpy outfits, she'll feel she needs to dress that way to impress guys, too.

Never bury your head in the sand and assume that your "little girl" (that is, your teenage daughter) would never experiment with a sexual relationship. According to the National Campaign to Prevent Teen Pregnancy, the National Center for Health Statistics, and the American Social Health Association:

- Half of all teens have had intercourse by the time they're sixteen.
- Every year, three million teens get a sexually transmitted disease (STD).
- More than half of all teens, ages fifteen to nineteen, have engaged in oral sex.
- The United States has the highest teen pregnancy and birth rate in the developed world.

If your daughter is between the ages of twelve to fifteen (depending on her development), it's time to coordinate that dreaded conversation with your ex on who's going to initiate the sex talk. Don't think if you talk to your daughter (or son, for that matter) about the importance of safe sex you will be putting ideas in her head. The ideas are already there! Try to remember what was on your mind when you were that age. It's fine to tell her to just say no, but if hormones overrule her head, you want her to be safe, not only from an unwanted pregnancy but also from sexually transmitted disease. So what's a dad to do? Keep listening to your daughter and urge her not to rush into a sexual relationship. If she is sexually active, stress the importance of safe sex and that she can always have an open conversation with you. (Yes dads, this is a hard thing to do, but knowledge is power, and at this age often she may be having an adversarial relationship with her mom and will be open to your advice.) If she's interested in considering birth control pills, you can suggest (and hopefully her mother will agree) that she see a gynecologist. If, on the other hand, you find condoms in her room, it's time to accelerate the above conversation, offer advice if asked, and pray a lot.

## HPV Vaccination

Recently, there has been a great deal of discussion in the media about an injection (three, actually) that may minimize your daughter's chances of getting cervical cancer if given before she becomes sexually active. The shots vaccinate her against HPV, a sexually transmitted virus that can cause cervical cancer. This presents an emotional challenge for you and your ex and shows why it's vital for you both to be able to discuss something that pertains to your daughter's future well-being. It's bound to be an emotional discussion, with no real right or wrong answers, because the injection is relatively new at this writing and the long-term effects may not be known at this point. Also, it isn't 100 percent effective. As with all medicines, there may be some side effects. You and your ex should talk to either your daughter's pediatrician or a qualified gynecologist before making your decision. If there's a family history of cervical cancer, it might sway you in the affirmative.

## HOW TO RECOGNIZE IF YOUR DAUGHTER HAS AN EATING DISORDER

Although boys develop eating disorders as well, more than 90 percent of eating disorders occur in females, even in girls as young as six or seven. In fact, studies show that almost half of American elementary-school students between the first and third grades want to be thinner and that half of nine- and ten-year-old girls report that they feel better about themselves if they're on a diet. Fifty percent of girls between the ages of eleven and thirteen see themselves as overweight.

There are three major types of eating disorders of which you need to be aware, one of which is difficult to recognize, but it's vital for you to know about all three of them as, untreated, they actually can cause death. Eating disorders actually have the highest mortality rate of any mental illness.

The disorders include anorexia nervosa (low body weight and distorted body image), bulimia (binge eaters who then vomit or overuse laxatives), and obesity (20 percent or more above normal, healthy weight).

### Anorexia

Anorexia nervosa is a psychiatric disorder in which the individual has an obsession with food but refuses to eat much of it because she fears being fat. The American Psychiatric Association's *Diagnostic and Statistical Manual of Mental Disorders* (Fourth Edition) lists the following paraphrased criteria:

- Refusal to maintain body weight at or above a minimally normal weight for age and height.
- Intense fear of gaining weight or becoming fat, even though presently underweight.
- Self-esteem is unduly influenced by body weight and denies being seriously underweight.
- Missing at least three consecutive menstrual cycles.
- No known physical illness that would account for the weight loss.

What causes anorexia nervosa? Although there are many theories, one of the major causes is the pressure girls are under from peers, teachers and coaches, the media, and even her immediate and extended families to be "nice and thin." Girls see popular emaciated actresses on TV and ads in newspapers and magazines with anorexic models and perceive that it's the way they should look. Girls as young as five are often overheard saying that they're on a diet. In fact, if you were to stop ten women on the street and ask if they're on a diet (probably not a good idea to try this), at least nine would probably say they were.

According to a Yale study by Frances F. Conte, reported in *Eating Disorders and Adolescents: Conflict of Self-Image* for the Yale-New Haven Teachers Institute, "In almost 50 percent of anorexics, some traumatic event precipitated the onset of the disorder. Among those that have been reported to trigger anorexia in a predisposed adolescent are: death of a loved one, divorce, illness of a parent or family member, or romantic rejection which the adolescent believes was the result of being overweight."

Sometimes the disorder is triggered by a casual comment by a parent, teacher, or coach. Tom, a divorced father admitted to trying to lift his seven-year-old daughter up. "My goodness, you're getting so heavy," he said. His daughter translated that innocent comment to mean that her beloved daddy thought she was getting fat, while he only meant that she was growing up and is no longer a toddler that he could easily carry around. Did that cause her to have an eating disorder? Not specifically, but it could have become the tipping point along with some other factors in a susceptible child. Researchers are beginning to consider that this potentially fatal disease may have its roots in genetic makeup and brain chemistry imbalances.

### Bulimia

Individuals with bulimia are binge eaters, obsessively eating great amounts of food such as a quart of ice cream, a loaf of peanut butter and jelly sandwiches, or an entire cheesecake. They stuff themselves in secret and then experience great guilt over the fact that they don't seem to have control over it. After binging, they rid themselves of it by purging either by vomiting, enemas, diuretics, or taking laxatives to cause diarrhea. It's difficult to recognize if your daughter suffers from bulimia because most of the signs—vomiting or diarrhea—take place in private in the bathroom. Sadly, girls who are bulimic are often willing to share their tips for vomiting with their peers, and there are even "pro-mia" (for bulimia) and "pro-ana" (for anorexia) Web sites where people with eating disorders can compare notes on how and where to purge better.

### Obesity

Obesity, the third major eating disorder, is an epidemic in America and predisposes kids to diabetes and heart disease. According to the January 2004 *Archives of Pediatrics and Adolescent Medicine*, about 31 percent of American teenage girls and 28 percent of boys are somewhat overweight, while an additional 15 percent of American teen girls and nearly 14 percent of teen boys are obese (20 percent or more above normal, healthy weight).

Obesity is caused by too much food, too much sugar and fat in the diet, along with too little exercise. It's a classic Catch-22. These kids don't feel like exercising because they're too heavy, and they're too heavy because they eat too much of the wrong things and don't exercise. Obese children have difficulty finding trendy clothes to wear and feel left out of peer activities, tend to experience more depression than their normal weight peers, and tend to be shunned or teased by their peers.

You have somewhat more control if your child is obese than you do with the other two eating disorders. You can contact a nutritionist at a local hospital or university or the American Dietetic Association (*www.eatright.org*) to get professional advice on how to prepare healthier meals for your kids. You also can join with your kids in turning off the TV and computer games and going outside to play and exercise together.

## SUBTLE SIGNS OF EATING DISORDERS

It's easy for you to deny that your daughter may have an eating disorder. Your daughter will also refuse to admit that she has an eating disorder and insist that she is just watching her weight. You, of course, want to believe that. If you can communicate with your ex, you should discuss these changes. But if she also struggles with anorexia, chances are she'll tell you that you're exaggerating and that your daughter is just fine.

The subtle signs of an eating disorder like anorexia are difficult for most men to recognize, especially if your ex also had an eating disorder and you think all women talk about their weight constantly, subsist on celery and tomato lunches, and exercise hours each day. You may not have noticed that your ex occasionally sneaked food, a lot of it, sometimes eating a box of candy bars or a gallon of ice cream in one sitting. So you may think your daughter's eating habits are normal, but they're not, and they could prove fatal.

## Signs of Anorexia

A person with anorexia does have overt symptoms of her disease, other than just losing too much weight.

- Her hair becomes dull and thin.
- The hair on her arms and face becomes soft and downy, almost like fur.
- She always is cold, due to the extreme loss of body fat.
- If she's begun menstruating, her periods stop.
- She may love to cook and will prepare wonderful meals but won't eat any of it.
- She'll pick at her own food, move it around on her plate, and even spit out bits of it into her napkin, hide it under a potato skin (upside down so you can't see that the potato wasn't eaten), or slip it to the dog.
- She'll become compulsive about exercising in order to burn up what few calories she does eat.
- She'll run, often as much as twenty miles a day.
- She may do hundreds of sit-ups and pushups at night while everyone else is sleeping.
- Many young women with anorexia are involved in gymnastics or ballet, activities where they not only burn off more calories but are praised by their coaches and dance instructors for keeping their weight down.

## Signs of Bulimia

Although the signs of bulimia are more difficult to recognize, you may observe that she:

- Gets up from the table immediately after a meal and heads for the bathroom
- Tends to have dental problems caused by the stomach acid bathing her teeth when she forces herself to throw up
- Refuses to eat (fasts) when she feels she has binged too much
- Diets publicly
- Is overly concerned about body image
- Exercises excessively
- Upsets her body's chemical balance from the constant vomiting, which can trigger heart attacks

## Signs of Obesity

It's not too difficult to recognize when your child is obese. Don't write it off as baby fat. Obesity, being twenty-two pounds over her normal weight, is traumatic emotionally for a youngster as well as being dangerous to her physical health.

- Exercise is exhausting so she finds excuses not to get involved.
- Obese girls have an 80 percent chance of developing breasts before their ninth birthday and menstruating earlier than average.

For dads who need to find help for their daughter (or son) with an eating disorder, talk to your pediatrician to find an eating disorder specialist in your area who deals with children with eating disorders. You also might contact the International Association of Eating Disorder Professionals (IAEDP) at 1-800-800-8126. A list of centers located throughout the country and in Canada can be found in the Resources appendix in the back of this book. Always research a program and get references before having your child begin treatment there.

For kids with weight issues, Weight Watchers has specialized programs for youngsters. There also are summer camps specializing in weight reduction, but be sure to get references from parents who have had their children enrolled.

## THE IMPORTANCE OF ROLE MODELS

If you don't have female family members who can serve as confidants and role models for your daughter, look around. There are many organizations, such as Girl Scouts and Big Sisters, whose leaders can become good role models for your daughters. Encourage your daughters to become involved in activities such as athletics, ballet, gymnastics, theater, music lessons, and so on where coaches and directors can serve a similar purpose. Stay involved, and be sure the coaches' values are the same as yours. Keep communicating with your daughter so if she has any problems she will share them with you.

### Take Your Daughter to Work Day

Take your daughters to work in April on Take Our Daughters to Work Day. Let them see what the women you work with do, especially if they are in nontraditional jobs. If your daughter shows interest in a so-called traditional man's job, encourage her. Let her know that you have confidence in

her ability. You might even find a woman who is in one of these nontraditional professions and let her shadow her rather than going to work with you so that she sees that she can be whatever she wants to be.

## NOT THE LADY OF THE HOUSE

While it may be tempting to think of your daughter as the little lady of the house, when she's with you, don't do it. It puts too much of a burden on a child and she may resent it or feel overwhelmed. While it's important for her and her brothers to have specific chores when they're with you, dole out the jobs fairly and don't make them gender specific, with your daughters doing the cooking and dishes while your sons mow the lawn and take out the garbage.

You are the adult in your home; your kids are just that—kids. Let them enjoy their childhood, even as you prepare them all for added responsibilities as soon as they are old enough for them.

Give your daughters your unconditional love and let them know that you have confidence in them and their decisions. Listen to them, love them, and learn from them. No man can offer his daughters a more valuable gift.

# Chapter 8

# Raising Sons, Not Little Men

*You don't raise heroes, you raise sons
and if you treat them like sons,
they'll turn out to be heroes,
even if it's just in your own eyes.*

—WALTER SCHIRRA, SR.

## ACH SPORTSMANSHIP

ough many coaches do teach true
tsmanship on the playing field, some
feel that as long as the players shake
ls after the event, anything goes during
game. It's up to you as your son's dad
plain what sportsmanship is—by your
example.

hink about the sports you play. Are
emonstrating true sportsmanship even
your son isn't watching?

o you throw your golf club when you
to the rough or miss a putt? Do you tap
all a little to give it a better position
you think no one's looking?

o you say the tennis ball is out when
know it really is in? Do you throw
racket when you're disgusted that you
d the ball?

hat about when you play baseball,
all, or go bowling? Think about
xample of sportsmanship you model.
are all supposed to be games. It's
o be competitive, but you're supposed
e fun as well. Be sure that's the les-
ou're teaching your sons. Don't think
n hide bad sportsmanship. Someone
nd to leak the truth to your kid and
over will be blown.

## NDLING FEELINGS

so much that your son doesn't know
handle his feelings, it's just that he's
many that they overpower him. From
through the teen years, when he
a mistake, he's angry, humiliated,
ustrated; a hundred more emotions
to him at the same time, mixing
urning hormones. No wonder he
ack or rolls his eyes at one moment
s up the next. He's a volcano ready
de.

William S. Pollack suggests in
*Real Boys*, that "When your son is
don't hesitate to ask him whether he
to talk." Chances are he won't, not t
But if you take him outside to throw
football around, he might open up. Eve
if he doesn't, he'll know that you're there
for him, if and when he's ready. Of course,
he might be ready just when you're ready to
dash out the door for a meeting, but if that's
the case, shut the door and let him open
up to you.

## ROUGHHOUSING: WHEN IT'S TOO MUCH

You may be tempted to roughhouse with
your young son, especially if you don't have
rotating custody and only see him on weekends or during the summer vacation. Worried that his mom may make him a sissy, you
may wrestle or box with your six-, seven-, or
eight-year-old, perhaps hitting a little harder
than you meant to or tackling hard when
you're playing touch football. It won't make
him tougher, just frightened of you. Remember that right now he's still only a boy and
you're taller and outweigh him. By being
too rough, you may turn him off to contact
sports and he'll find excuses not to play with
you anymore. What's more, one day soon
he'll probably be bigger and heavier than
you and may want to pay you back. While
it's okay to "be a guy" and enjoy some horseplay with your boy, don't be a bully.

## COMMUNICATION SKILLS KNOW NO GENDER

It's too bad when a father and son have
strained or no real communication between
them, other than talking about sports or the
weather. But it need not always be that way.

Don't be afraid to tell your sons you love them, that you're proud of them, and that you think they're smart. They need to hear it. Even if it's not in your nature (perhaps because your dad didn't do it with you), do it anyway. You may feel awkward at first when you say it, but the more often you tell them and sup-port it by your actions, the more comfort-able you're going to be. Don't worry about making a "sissy" out of them. You're going to make them self-confident as they grow into manhood, and they'll be able to show their sons and daughters their love and affection. That's a great gift to give to your sons.

## ROLE MODELING

Like it or not, you are your son's role model, the template for what he can and will become. How you handle adversity, disap-pointment, and even success teaches him the "man's way" of doing things. You may not even be aware that your son is model-ing you, nor he conscious that he is doing so. Dr. Ganz Ferrance tells of a custodian at a university who had lost the use of his left arm. The dangling arm threw his gait off, so he had a very distinguishing walk. The man's son came to the university and, although the boy had full use of both arms, everyone knew immediately that he was the custodian's son because he unconsciously mirrored his dad's walk. Talk about follow-ing in your father's footsteps.

So when you make promises, be sure you can keep them so that he learns that a man's word is his bond. Call to let him know if you're going to be late picking him up from an afterschool event or from his mom's house. Show by your own behav-ior that honesty is the best policy, even if it sometimes creates repercussions in that you have to pay a penalty. Demonstrate

your belief in people by complimenting wait staff on good service, praising the endeavors of fire and police workers, and never criticizing his teachers or coaches. If you have questions for the latter two groups that have contact with your child, make an appointment and speak to them privately. It goes without saying that you should never criticize your child's mother. You may have been burned by your ex-wife, but she is still your son's mother.

Matthew B. said, ". . . even though I have strong words for my child's mother, it is wise to never talk bad about the other parent in front of the child, regardless of what has happened. As fathers we have to set an example of self control and we always have to take into consideration the feelings of our little ones, because it's not their fault, ever." Good advice.

Here are some tips for how you can be a strong ally for your son:

- Be a good role model for your son when you win as well as when you lose. Let him see you congratulate the winner with honest conviction, rather than storming off muttering about the scor-ing not being fair.
- Praise your son when he does well and support him when he fails at something. Never focus on the one C grade when he brings home a report card with all As but one. Don't do as one father did when his son came home filled with excitement to report that he had been elected vice president of his class: "Only vice president?" his father said. "Who got president?"
- Work at communication with your son, even if it doesn't come easily.

# REDUCE VIOLENCE IN YOUR SON'S LIFE

You may think there is no violence in your son's life. You may say, "I never yelled at his mother in front of him regardless how much we disagreed. I never even spanked him." That may all be true. But does he hear you cursing when someone cuts in front of you when you're driving or when your favorite sports team looks like they've never played the game before? Always be mindful of the influence you have on your kids, even when you think they are not listening or looking. They always are.

### Video Games and Media

Be aware of the television programs your children are watching and, if they're old enough to go to movies by themselves, what they're seeing. We're always amazed when we're at R-rated movies and see parents with elementary-school-age children in tow. Seeing violence in the media, regardless if it's fictional or on-the-scene war coverage, makes a strong impression on kids and after a while makes them think that violence is routine. A woman beaten and raped, a man stabbed, another with his head blown off, or people being tortured or maimed become run-of-the-mill visuals to your sons and daughters. Is this the picture of life you want for them?

Add to the violent scenes already described the video games that make killing fun and a challenge to see who can bump off the most knights, terrorists, or monsters. It's all the same. It is currently estimated that 60 to 90 percent of the most popular video games have violent themes. And if there's any doubt that our kids are plugged into violence, actually listen to the lyrics of the music they're hearing.

Although you can't be with your son (or daughter) every minute of the day to cen-sor what's being seen or heard, you need to discuss your concerns with them. Studies have shown that kids who constantly see violence in movies, videos, and television and those who hear violent and sexy lyrics in their music tend to react more violently to various situations and to have sex earlier than those who do not.

No matter how hard your son (or daughter) begs, do not put a TV or computer in his room. Keep both screens where you can keep an eye on what your kids are watching and, in the case of the Internet, to whom they are "speaking."

### Bullies

If your child's teacher tells you he or she is concerned about your son's aggressiveness, don't blow it off by saying "boys will be boys." Hitting others is a sign of being a bully, not a hero. It may endear him to other bullies, but this behavior will isolate him from the kind of kids you'd like him to associate with. Talk to your youngster to try to understand his motivation. Discuss other ways in which he can express any anger he feels and be sure that you aren't overdoing your own teasing or making fun of him. It may be a sense of frustration, of feeling he has to prove to you that he's "macho," or of something even he doesn't recognize. Don't delay in getting help from a school counselor, social worker, child psychologist, or your minister, priest, or rabbi. Violence in a child isn't normal; get help.

If your son is the one being bullied, don't urge him to fight back or belittle him if he doesn't. Violence often gets out of hand with devastating results. Encourage him instead to try to use humor or to walk away from the situation. It's hard to do, especially when the bullies embarrass him at school, or worse, post comments or photos on the Internet. He may pretend to be sick so he can stay home from school and not have to

face his tormentors. He'll need your strong support during this period as he'll lose any sense of self-confidence, and bullies tend to smell that fear just as a predatory animal does. Contact your son's school and urge them to have programs discussing the problem of bullying and make their school adopt a zero tolerance for bullying policy.

## BOYS NEED OUTLETS FOR THEIR ENERGY

Boys have a great deal of energy and need outlets to expend it in healthy ways. Encourage your son to get involved in sports, to find one or more that he enjoys. He doesn't have to be a star, nor should you expect it. But it's important that he sample enough different activities in order to find what he likes. It may be a team sport, such as basketball, hockey, soccer, or football, a solo sport where he also competes against his best times, such as swimming or track, or a team sport where he competes as an individual, such as wrestling, golf, tennis, or gymnastics.

Be supportive if your son decides that he really enjoys dancing, such as ballet, hip-hop, jazz, or tap. Don't write dancing off as being too girlie. It's very hard physical labor. If you don't think so, watch the movie *White Nights* with Mikhail Baryshnikov and Gregory Hines.

If you've forgotten what it's like to be a young boy, there are many excellent books, such as Michael Gurian's *A Fine Young Man: What Parents, Mentors, and Educators Can Do to Shape Adolescent Boys into Exceptional Men*, Cheryl L. Erwin's *The Everything Parent's Guide to Raising Boys*, and William S. Pollack's *Real Boys: Rescuing Our Sons from the Myth of Boyhood*, available for you to read. If you let yourself think back to your boyhood, you may remember being scared,

embarrassed, teased at time[...] ing, and very vulnerable. [...] changed that much over the [...] is probably experiencing ma[...] confusing emotions that you [...] standing and encourage con[...] him know that being mascul[...] ing off energy is more than [...] guy. It's being caring, gentle, [...] tive, and nurturing. Be his rol[...] watching you.

## COPING WITH MIXE[...] MESSAGES IN ATHLE[...]

"Okay," you may say. "I've taugh[...] 'love thy neighbor as thyself.' H[...] kid, working on becoming an Ea[...] helping old ladies across the st[...] singing in the church choir. My e[...] supportive of these teachings. Nov[...] for football and the coach is tellin[...] 'smash the quarterback on the oth[...] Really hurt him.' Even in practice, [...] to be mean, tough, angry, and to tac[...] he means to 'crush the other guy.' [...] mixed message from what his mom[...] have being telling him."

We posed this problem to psycho[...] pist Barbara Montague. She said it's i[...] tant to talk to your son about the dicho[...] between being gentle at home and [...] friends and being rough on the playing [...] "Ask him if he wants to play the sport,[...] advised. "Leave it up to the child." It ma[...] that he's playing hockey, football, or bas[...] ball because he thinks you want him to. [...] if he really likes it and wants to play, th[...] "give him permission to play the sport mo[...] aggressively, as his coach desires, as long [...] he plays by the rules."

## TEA[...]

Alth[...] spor[...] still[...] han[...] the [...] to e[...] own[...]

you[...] wh[...]

hit[...] th[...] wh[...]

yo[...] yo[...] m[...]

h[...] t[...]

T[...] c[...] t[...] s[...]

Don't be afraid to tell your sons you love them, that you're proud of them, and that you think they're smart. They need to hear it. Even if it's not in your nature (perhaps because your dad didn't do it with you), do it anyway. You may feel awkward at first when you say it, but the more often you tell them and support it by your actions, the more comfortable you're going to be. Don't worry about making a "sissy" out of them. You're going to make them self-confident as they grow into manhood, and they'll be able to show their sons and daughters their love and affection. That's a great gift to give to your sons.

## ROLE MODELING

Like it or not, you are your son's role model, the template for what he can and will become. How you handle adversity, disappointment, and even success teaches him the "man's way" of doing things. You may not even be aware that your son is modeling you, nor he conscious that he is doing so. Dr. Ganz Ferrance tells of a custodian at a university who had lost the use of his left arm. The dangling arm threw his gait off, so he had a very distinguishing walk. The man's son came to the university and, although the boy had full use of both arms, everyone knew immediately that he was the custodian's son because he unconsciously mirrored his dad's walk. Talk about following in your father's footsteps.

So when you make promises, be sure you can keep them so that he learns that a man's word is his bond. Call to let him know if you're going to be late picking him up from an afterschool event or from his mom's house. Show by your own behavior that honesty is the best policy, even if it sometimes creates repercussions in that you have to pay a penalty. Demonstrate your belief in people by complimenting wait staff on good service, praising the endeavors of fire and police workers, and never criticizing his teachers or coaches. If you have questions for the latter two groups that have contact with your child, make an appointment and speak to them privately. It goes without saying that you should never criticize your child's mother. You may have been burned by your ex-wife, but she is still your son's mother.

Matthew B. said, ". . . even though I have strong words for my child's mother, it is wise to never talk bad about the other parent in front of the child, regardless of what has happened. As fathers we have to set an example of self control and we always have to take into consideration the feelings of our little ones, because it's not their fault, ever." Good advice.

Here are some tips for how you can be a strong ally for your son:

- Be a good role model for your son when you win as well as when you lose. Let him see you congratulate the winner with honest conviction, rather than storming off muttering about the scoring not being fair.
- Praise your son when he does well and support him when he fails at something. Never focus on the one C grade when he brings home a report card with all As but one. Don't do as one father did when his son came home filled with excitement to report that he had been elected vice president of his class: "Only vice president?" his father said. "Who got president?"
- Work at communication with your son, even if it doesn't come easily.

## REDUCE VIOLENCE IN YOUR SON'S LIFE

You may think there is no violence in your son's life. You may say, "I never yelled at his mother in front of him regardless how much we disagreed. I never even spanked him." That may all be true. But does he hear you cursing when someone cuts in front of you when you're driving or when your favorite sports team looks like they've never played the game before? Always be mindful of the influence you have on your kids, even when you think they are not listening or looking. They always are.

### Video Games and Media

Be aware of the television programs your children are watching and, if they're old enough to go to movies by themselves, what they're seeing. We're always amazed when we're at R-rated movies and see parents with elementary-school-age children in tow. Seeing violence in the media, regardless if it's fictional or on-the-scene war coverage, makes a strong impression on kids and after a while makes them think that violence is routine. A woman beaten and raped, a man stabbed, another with his head blown off, or people being tortured or maimed become run-of-the-mill visuals to your sons and daughters. Is this the picture of life you want for them?

Add to the violent scenes already described the video games that make killing fun and a challenge to see who can bump off the most knights, terrorists, or monsters. It's all the same. It is currently estimated that 60 to 90 percent of the most popular video games have violent themes. And if there's any doubt that our kids are plugged into violence, actually listen to the lyrics of the music they're hearing.

Although you can't be with your son (or daughter) every minute of the day to cen-

sor what's being seen or heard, you need to discuss your concerns with them. Studies have shown that kids who constantly see violence in movies, videos, and television and those who hear violent and sexy lyrics in their music tend to react more violently to various situations and to have sex earlier than those who do not.

No matter how hard your son (or daughter) begs, do not put a TV or computer in his room. Keep both screens where you can keep an eye on what your kids are watching and, in the case of the Internet, to whom they are "speaking."

### Bullies

If your child's teacher tells you he or she is concerned about your son's aggressiveness, don't blow it off by saying "boys will be boys." Hitting others is a sign of being a bully, not a hero. It may endear him to other bullies, but this behavior will isolate him from the kind of kids you'd like him to associate with. Talk to your youngster to try to understand his motivation. Discuss other ways in which he can express any anger he feels and be sure that you aren't overdoing your own teasing or making fun of him. It may be a sense of frustration, of feeling he has to prove to you that he's "macho," or of something even he doesn't recognize. Don't delay in getting help from a school counselor, social worker, child psychologist, or your minister, priest, or rabbi. Violence in a child isn't normal; get help.

If your son is the one being bullied, don't urge him to fight back or belittle him if he doesn't. Violence often gets out of hand with devastating results. Encourage him instead to try to use humor or to walk away from the situation. It's hard to do, especially when the bullies embarrass him at school, or worse, post comments or photos on the Internet. He may pretend to be sick so he can stay home from school and not have to face his tormentors. He'll need your strong support during this period as he'll lose any sense of self-confidence, and bullies tend to smell that fear just as a predatory animal does. Contact your son's school and urge them to have programs discussing the problem of bullying and make their school adopt a zero tolerance for bullying policy.

## BOYS NEED OUTLETS FOR THEIR ENERGY

Boys have a great deal of energy and need outlets to expend it in healthy ways. Encourage your son to get involved in sports, to find one or more that he enjoys. He doesn't have to be a star, nor should you expect it. But it's important that he sample enough different activities in order to find what he likes. It may be a team sport, such as basketball, hockey, soccer, or football, a solo sport where he also competes against his best times, such as swimming or track, or a team sport where he competes as an individual, such as wrestling, golf, tennis, or gymnastics.

Be supportive if your son decides that he really enjoys dancing, such as ballet, hip-hop, jazz, or tap. Don't write dancing off as being too girlie. It's very hard physical labor. If you don't think so, watch the movie *White Nights* with Mikhail Baryshnikov and Gregory Hines.

If you've forgotten what it's like to be a young boy, there are many excellent books, such as Michael Gurian's *A Fine Young Man: What Parents, Mentors, and Educators Can Do to Shape Adolescent Boys into Exceptional Men*, Cheryl L. Erwin's *The Everything Parent's Guide to Raising Boys*, and William S. Pollack's *Real Boys: Rescuing Our Sons from the Myth of Boyhood*, available for you to read. If you let yourself think back to your boyhood, you may remember being scared,

embarrassed, teased at times, afraid of failing, and very vulnerable. Things haven't changed that much over the years. Your son is probably experiencing many of the same confusing emotions that you did. Be understanding and encourage conversation. Let him know that being masculine and burning off energy is more than being a tough guy. It's being caring, gentle, communicative, and nurturing. Be his role model. He's watching you.

## COPING WITH MIXED MESSAGES IN ATHLETICS

"Okay," you may say. "I've taught my son to 'love thy neighbor as thyself.' He's a good kid, working on becoming an Eagle Scout, helping old ladies across the street, and singing in the church choir. My ex is just as supportive of these teachings. Now he's out for football and the coach is telling him to 'smash the quarterback on the other team. Really hurt him.' Even in practice, he's told to be mean, tough, angry, and to tackle like he means to 'crush the other guy.' What a mixed message from what his mom and I have being telling him."

We posed this problem to psychotherapist Barbara Montague. She said it's important to talk to your son about the dichotomy between being gentle at home and with friends and being rough on the playing field. "Ask him if he wants to play the sport," she advised. "Leave it up to the child." It may be that he's playing hockey, football, or basketball because he thinks you want him to. But if he really likes it and wants to play, then "give him permission to play the sport more aggressively, as his coach desires, as long as he plays by the rules."

# TEACH SPORTSMANSHIP

Although many coaches do teach true sportsmanship on the playing field, some still feel that as long as the players shake hands after the event, anything goes during the game. It's up to you as your son's dad to explain what sportsmanship is—by your own example.

Think about the sports you play. Are you demonstrating true sportsmanship even when your son isn't watching?

Do you throw your golf club when you hit into the rough or miss a putt? Do you tap the ball a little to give it a better position when you think no one's looking?

Do you say the tennis ball is out when you know it really is in? Do you throw your racket when you're disgusted that you missed the ball?

What about when you play baseball, handball, or go bowling? Think about the example of sportsmanship you model. These are all supposed to be games. It's okay to be competitive, but you're supposed to have fun as well. Be sure that's the lesson you're teaching your sons. Don't think you can hide bad sportsmanship. Someone is bound to leak the truth to your kid and your cover will be blown.

# HANDLING FEELINGS

It's not so much that your son doesn't know how to handle his feelings, it's just that he's got so many that they overpower him. From preteen through the teen years, when he makes a mistake, he's angry, humiliated, and frustrated; a hundred more emotions pour into him at the same time, mixing with churning hormones. No wonder he talks back or rolls his eyes at one moment and tears up the next. He's a volcano ready to explode.

William S. Pollack suggests in his book, *Real Boys*, that "When your son is hurting, don't hesitate to ask him whether he'd like to talk." Chances are he won't, not then. But if you take him outside to throw the football around, he might open up. Even if he doesn't, he'll know that you're there for him, if and when he's ready. Of course, he might be ready just when you're ready to dash out the door for a meeting, but if that's the case, shut the door and let him open up to you.

# ROUGHHOUSING: WHEN IT'S TOO MUCH

You may be tempted to roughhouse with your young son, especially if you don't have rotating custody and only see him on weekends or during the summer vacation. Worried that his mom may make him a sissy, you may wrestle or box with your six-, seven-, or eight-year-old, perhaps hitting a little harder than you meant to or tackling hard when you're playing touch football. It won't make him tougher, just frightened of you. Remember that right now he's still only a boy and you're taller and outweigh him. By being too rough, you may turn him off to contact sports and he'll find excuses not to play with you anymore. What's more, one day soon he'll probably be bigger and heavier than you and may want to pay you back. While it's okay to "be a guy" and enjoy some horseplay with your boy, don't be a bully.

# COMMUNICATION SKILLS KNOW NO GENDER

It's too bad when a father and son have strained or no real communication between them, other than talking about sports or the weather. But it need not always be that way.

Just because your grandfather may not have communicated well with your father, nor he with you, doesn't mean that you can't change that dynamic today. Ask (or e-mail, if you live away) your son what the best thing was about his day. He may look at you in surprise and say, "Huh?" But he also may tell you, although you'll have to listen carefully.

If he says, "Nothing was good," don't just say, "Oh," and let the subject drop. Instead, gently ask him what is going on. Then listen. You may be flabbergasted at what he's dealing with at school—teachers who expect him to sit still for hours at a time, a coach who ridicules him in front of the entire team, a foreign language class where everything is Greek to him despite the fact that the class is Spanish, and the girl he adores from afar won't give him the time of day—literally.

Be supportive. Never tell him how he should feel, but listen to how he does feel.

Ask him how he plans to handle the various situations he describes and what steps each will take for potential success. If you

> ✔ **Tip from the Trenches**
>
> Stan admits, "My son and I are not 'talkers.' This has always been an issue for us, and continues to be an issue even today (he's now twenty-two years old). As a result, we had long periods of either quiet or simple banter. Deep conversations were rare. This is an area where I wish I had behaved differently. Even though it would have meant that I needed to leave my comfort zone, I should have tried to be more communicative (on a substantive level) with my son. I try to do that now with my ten-year-old . . . but it's damn hard."

struggled with some of the same problems as a boy, this might be a good time to share some of your personal humiliations so he can realize that even this shall pass, despite it seeming to be earth-shattering at the time. If you, his secret hero, had bad days too, then he'll begin to develop the confidence that he can overcome his as well.

At all times, protect your son's fragile self-esteem. As one saying goes: "There are two things you can give your child: roots and wings." If you can plant the seed that you are confident in his ability to work things out, it will grow within him, giving him the confidence to tiptoe to the edge of the branch and fly. Nourish that precious seed now by working to improve your communication skills with your son today.

## DON'T BE CRITICAL OF WOMEN

Be careful not to poison your boys against women in general. You may not even be aware of doing it, but when you say disparaging things such as, "Just like a woman" or quote Alan Jay Lerner's lyrics from his hit musical, *My Fair Lady,* "Why can't a woman be more like a man?" you belittle women and let your sons think there is nothing wrong in doing it as well.

Don't call household tasks "women's work" either or assign them only to your daughters. Keeping your home reasonably clean does not require a specific gender.

## BIG BOYS DO CRY

Hopefully you know and accept that it's okay for big boys to cry, but sometimes boys need to hear that their dad cries too. Let your son know that you also cried when your beloved family pet died and when frustration built up and you felt like a failure before getting a second wind and trying again. Let him know that you also cry when happy, when you see your kids perform and your pride in them overflows with happy tears.

Remind your son of Washington Irving's message: "There is sacredness in tears. They are not the mark of weakness, but of power. They speak more eloquently than ten thousand tongues. They are the messengers of overwhelming grief, of deep contrition, and of unspeakable love."

# REMEMBERING PUBERTY

Chances are puberty was not the favorite time in your life. You seemed to have lost control of your body as it started doing strange things, and most likely no one—except the guys in the locker room—told you what was happening, and who knows how accurate those stories were.

Don't wait too long to tell your son about the changes that will go on in his life. Puberty is a process that occurs gradually, and the date it begins varies from boy to boy. So don't put this discussion off. Begin as early as when he is eight or nine.

## Wet Dreams

The actual name for this experience is nocturnal emissions. It's the discharge of semen while the boy is asleep, and it occurs from ages ten to fourteen. If he doesn't know what it is, a youngster can worry that something is wrong, that he's sick or gay, and that he got stains on his shorts and sheets. You need to assure him that it is a perfectly normal occurrence, as are the vivid dreams accompanying it, and that the stains will wash out with stain removers.

## Erections

You may have been surprised as you changed your son's diapers when he was an infant that he usually had an erection. As a toddler in the bath or whenever he was naked, his hand went right to his penis. As you know, that never changes, but you need to let your son know that when he is eleven or twelve he may begin to have spontaneous erections, even without stimulation. It may be embarrassing when he is in front of his class giving a report or standing in the school hallway talking to a girl. Let him know that it is perfectly normal. Tell him what you did to "hide" the evidence.

## Masturbation

How you view your son's masturbation may be related to how your parents viewed your masturbation. If they punished you or called it "dirty," you may be distressed when you find your son playing with himself.

Masturbation is normal; some guys do it, some guys don't. The important thing to remember is not to reprimand your son if you discover him doing it as it can have lasting effects on his self-confidence and feelings about intimacy. Suggest to him instead that it is a private act and recommend that he reserve this activity for when he is in the bathroom or in his bedroom.

## Pubic Hair

As girls develop pubic hair when they reach puberty, so do boys, although not until they are between the ages of eleven and fourteen. Boys also will begin to have some hair on the face, underarms, chest, and legs. It varies in amount.

## Voice Change

A boy's voice usually begins to change and deepen around age eleven, though it still is perfectly normal for it to be delayed until age fifteen. During this period, the voice cracks occasionally, which can be embarrassing. On the positive side, explain to your son that it means he is getting older and growing up. You might even reward him with some dad time to make him more comfortable with everything that is happening to his body, such as getting some weights and working out with him, letting him walk the golf course with you and your friends, or teaching him how to cast with his grandfather's fishing rod. It's a light introduction into a man's world and you can welcome him into it gently.

### Penis Size

This is a constant concern of boys (and men) everywhere. Indeed, the penis and scrotum start to grow larger and thicker beginning at about age thirteen, and it takes approximately two years for them to reach full adult growth. Although boys tend to compare one another's prowess, be sure your son realizes that there is a great deal of variation both in when development begins and the final result. Reassure him that size doesn't matter.

# DATING

As with girls, there is no specific age that a boy should start dating. Some may be shy and just like girls as friends and enjoy group dates, while others feel more confidant and want to spend time with just one girl. Don't push your son into dating someone until he feels ready as girls can be dreadfully cruel and shatter a young boy's delicate confidence.

Tell him what dating was like for you and how hard it was to cope if a girl turned you down. Let your son know that you are willing to be his driver if he is too young to drive, so he can invite a girl to a movie or sporting activity.

Put restrictions on his going to parties at kids' homes when the parents are out of town or when there is drinking or drugs. How will you know? Either let him have the party at your home while you're there or call the parents of where the party is and be certain they will be home. Does that make you a wimp? Not at all. You could be held legally responsible if there is trouble, whether it's an accident because of the drinking or a girl claiming that she was raped. One of your responsibilities as a dad is to be sure your son becomes a responsible citizen too.

# Chapter 9

# Raising Your Child with Special Needs

*It is a wise father who knows his own child.*
—SHAKESPEARE

You may find it difficult to accept the fact that your child has special needs, regardless if the problems are physical, developmental, neurological, or a smattering of more than one. You may have pictured having that "perfect child," whatever that means, and when yours is diagnosed with a disability or chronic illness, you feel devastated.

First there's denial. "The doctor or tests must be wrong." That soon is replaced by a sense of anger, of thinking or saying "Why me?" and of frustration that you can't fix it because that's what men do—fix things. You feel overwhelming grief, which isn't surprising because you have suffered a loss, the vision you had for your child and his or her future. You have the right to mourn.

Perhaps you and your ex disagreed with the diagnosis or treatment in some way when you were still married and that caused a rift between you both. Maybe the strain of dealing with your child's problems became the tipping point, stress so heavy that an already fragile marriage couldn't remain unbroken under the burden. Possibly your child's special needs were just an added factor that ended the marriage and now both you and your ex must handle those challenges separately, but certainly not alone.

Your child also may have developed a challenging problem after your divorce and you have to bite your tongue to keep from asking your ex what she did wrong, or you have to respond to her asking the same of you.

## REAL MEN DON'T DODGE RESPONSIBILITIES

If you left because you just can't deal with illness of any kind, think again. This is your child and he or she needs your love and support, and not just financial support. Don't dodge your responsibility to your youngster just because you and your ex don't see eye to eye. You may think it isn't manly to have a kid with disabilities, but you've got it wrong. Being a man means not dumping the burden on your ex. Look beyond your child's disability and focus on what you can do to make your kid's life more satisfying.

## MAKE AN EFFORT TO COMMUNICATE

Despite the fact that you and your ex may have difficulties communicating on almost all other subjects, make a special effort to talk at least on this one subject for the sake of your child. Accept that each of you may respond to your child's problem differently. One of you may try to ignore the problem as if that could make it disappear while the other gathers all the available information as though having all the facts and latest treatment reports could alter the reality. Try to keep the conversation focused on your child rather than blaming each other for what you might perceive as the other's fault, guilt, or even your ex's overprotecting the youngster.

## REACH OUT TO OTHERS WALKING IN YOUR SHOES

Know that you don't need to travel this journey alone. Whether your child has cancer, autism, Down's syndrome, diabetes, epilepsy, mental retardation, spina bifida, cerebral palsy, cystic fibrosis, developmental delays, pervasive developmental disorder, traumatic brain injury, Tourette's syndrome, or is visually impaired, has a hearing disability, attention deficit disorder (ADD), attention deficit hyperactivity disorder (ADHD), or some other challenge, there are other parents struggling with the same issues you are at this particular moment. Reach out to them and let them help guide you on this troubled path. This is no time to be embarrassed or too proud to ask for help. One day there will be another dad struggling with the same problems with which you've learned to cope and then you can give him a helping hand.

To find a parent of a child with the same disability as yours, contact the National Information Center for Children and Youth with Disabilities (NICHCY) at 1-800-695-0285 or e-mail them at *nichcy@aed.org.* You also can visit Parents Helping Parents at *www.php.com.* If there is a national association dedicated to your child's particular disability, contact them and ask if they have parents (especially dads) with whom you could confer. Remember, however, that a layperson's experiences are just that, an individual's personal experience with the disability. Your child's problem may not be exactly the same or the disorder may be at a different stage. On the other hand, you may learn some coping tips to help make life a little easier for you and for your child.

## ACCEPT LIMITATIONS

Be realistic about your child's limitations, then focus on and enjoy the things he or she can do. While your dreams of his playing football as you did or your daughter being a cheerleader may be dashed, open your eyes to new possibilities. Don't be blinded by your fear of your child's future. "Can he learn?" "Will he be able to go to college?" "Will she ever have friends?" "Will people reject her or make fun of her?" "Will she ever be able to marry?" No one can predict the future, so try to take each day as it comes.

## FIND INFORMATION AND SUPPORT

The good news is that you can find a great deal of information on the Internet. The bad news is that much of the information is old or just plain incorrect. Stick to the official Web sites of the disability's national, state, or local organization or those of recognized academic institutions or medical centers. Remember that much of the information you'll find is general and that for many disabilities and diseases there can be a vast spectrum ranging from mild to severe. Your child may be at the lower end with a mild affliction rather than at the far end as a worst-case scenario.

Attend support groups, providing they don't just end up as "poor me" sessions. In fact, if it's a constantly complaining group, you'll end up feeling worse, so leave and find a more positive bunch of people. Stress is contagious. Effective support groups, on the other hand, help you understand that you aren't the only one trying to cope with your child's special needs. Because they've gone through the same issues, their members understand your anger, frustration, and occasional depression without being judgmental. They can offer encouragement and may be able to share some tips that can be helpful. What's more, support groups offer social interaction, and you may meet some other dads (and single moms) that you'll enjoy having a beer or a cup of coffee with after the meetings.

If your ex can't or won't attend, e-mail her a memo of the high points or send her copies of the latest bulletin handed out. Encourage members of your extended family (and hers) to come hear a speaker or any other discussion that may be helpful. By educating other family members, including those of your ex, they may be more willing to help with child care and will feel more comfortable when they know what to expect. Remember that your child is part of their family, too.

## LEARN THE TERMINOLOGY

When your child has special needs, you enter a world with a bewildering new language. The terminology may be confusing, and doctors, therapists, educators, and other specialists may speak in acronyms (such as IEP, which stands for "individualized education plan" or IFSP, which stands for "individualized family service plan") or in medical jargon that sounds like a foreign language. Actually, much of it is taken from Latin, Greek, and German.

In her article, "You Are Not Alone: For Parents When They Learn That Their Child Has a Disability," written for the National Dissemination Center for Children with Disabilities, Patricia McGill Smith tells parents "not to be hesitant to ask what it means," when introduced to new terminology. "Whenever someone uses a word that you don't understand," she says, "stop the conversation for a minute and ask the person to explain the word."

"Don't be afraid to ask questions," she continues, "because asking questions will be your first step in beginning to understand your child . . . write down your questions before entering appointments or meetings, and write down further questions as you think of them during the meeting." Her other suggestions include:

- Get written copies of all documentation from physicians, teachers, and therapists regarding your child.
- Buy a three-ring notebook in which to save all information that is given to you.

- Always ask for copies of evaluations, diagnostic reports, and progress reports.
- If you're not a naturally organized person, get a box, label it, and throw all the paperwork in it.
- Don't be intimidated by the professional people with whom you come in contact. They are there to help you.
- Don't be afraid to show your emotions. It's not a sign of weakness to show how you're feeling.

## SHARE INFORMATION WITH YOUR OTHER CHILDREN

If your child with special needs has siblings, by all means clue them in to what's happening. They may fear that they too will catch whatever the other child has. You need to reassure them that this can't happen and that their sibling needs their love and support. Try to get them to talk about what bothers them. They may feel guilty, worrying that they could have done something to cause their sibling to have this disease or disorder. They may feel embarrassed by their sibling or are upset that their friends tease them about their sibling.

When Elaine was writing a book for the American Cancer Society, geared to parents whose children have cancer, one of her interviewees said, "The worst mistake we ever made was not to tell our son's brother that his sibling had cancer. We thought we were sparing him. Instead, he resented all the time and attention we spent with our ill child and, of course, was devastated when his brother died. My advice: share with the siblings. They're part of the family too."

Give your kids time to express their feelings and frustrations. Let them know that these are normal reactions and that thinking things can't make something happen and that it doesn't make them bad for thinking them. This is no time to emotionally close off to any of your kids. If you can't shake your anger or bitterness, you should consider seeing a professional mental health counselor or a rabbi, priest, or minister.

## ACCEPT REALITY

When your child has special needs, you need to face reality. There are some things you can change when life deals you a bad hand, but there are some things you cannot. The task we all must accomplish is to learn which things we can change and then go about doing just that. Read and memorize the Serenity Prayer below, as you may find it helpful to settle you when you feel you're having trouble coping:

*God, grant us grace to accept with serenity*
*The things that cannot be changed,*
*Courage to change the things which should*
*be changed,*
*and the wisdom to distinguish the one from*
*the other.*

—REINHOLD NIEBUHR

## FIND PROGRAMS FOR YOUR CHILD

Regardless of where you live, assistance is available to help you with whatever problems you're having. The National Dissemination Center for Children with Disabilities (*www.nichcy.org*) has information in both English and Spanish on:

- State agencies serving or concerned with children with disabilities
- Disability-specific organizations
- Organizations for parents

- Where to have your child evaluated
- Information about a specific disability
- How you can find another parent whose child has the same disability as yours
- Where you can talk to a group of parents concerned with the same disability your child has
- Specific information about Individuals with Disabilities Education Act (IDEA), our nation's special education law, and how it benefits your child

There also are support organizations for children whose siblings have specific disorders. Ask about them so your kids know that they aren't the only ones who struggle with a sibling who has special needs and so they can learn ways to cope and interact with their sibling.

## DECIDE HOW TO DEAL WITH OTHERS

You and your ex may not agree on how much you want to tell other people about your child's special needs. She may want to talk about it to anyone within listening distance, while you feel it's a private matter. You may resent other people feeling pity for you or your child or get angry with the way they react to your youngster. You may be frustrated when well-meaning friends tell you of "miracle" cures or medicines to consider. Try to remember that many people react oddly to physical, emotional, or mental problems because of a lack of understanding. They don't know what to say or they ask hurtful questions without meaning to.

Try to decide ahead of time how you will deal with these thoughtless individuals and don't waste too much of your valuable time or energy focused on why people act as they do. NICHCY suggests that you focus instead on your youngster, who is your child first and foremost. The special needs may make him or her different from many children, but this does not make your child less valuable, less important, or less in need of your unconditional love and parenting.

Include grandparents and other members of your and your ex's extended family in helping them to understand what your child can and can't do so they don't baby your youngster or tell a youngster with Tourette's syndrome, for example, that he could stop his tic if only he tried. The more comfortable your family members feel with a child with special needs, the more help they can give you.

# PART TWO

# DADDY DETAILS: NEW DAY-TO-DAY CHALLENGES

# Chapter 10

# Making Your House (or Apartment) a Home

*It was the policy of the good old gentleman
to make his children feel that home was
the happiest place in the world; and I
value this delicious home-feeling as one
of the choicest gifts a parent can bestow.*

—WASHINGTON IRVING

Y ou may wonder how you can possibly recreate this "delicious home-feeling" as a single parent. But you can, and many single fathers have done just that. To make a house, apartment, or condo a home you need to fill it with love, laughter, respect, and joy. It has nothing to do with the cost of your furnishings, and not even your address. It has to do with you and your ability to create this atmosphere of unqualified love for your children.

Dan recalled, "I guess everyone's story is different, and yet, perhaps, the same. When I moved out, I left the house with nothing but my clothes and a few favorite books. After a bit, I was able to secure several folding chairs, a living room chair, and a few odds and ends including that odd pillow case that matched nothing the ex had or wanted, etc. My priorities were strictly with the kids. I went to a model home that was selling the furniture and bought the kids bunk beds, pillows, etc. I hit garage sales and flea markets for glasses, cups, dishes . . . things I felt could be washed at 12,000 degrees to make them my own, if they didn't melt. And if they did, I was better off without them."

Dave's story was similar. "My first place was a trailer," he said. "No working a/c or stove. It had broken windows and one working toilet and shower. Naturally, it was infested with bugs and was as dirty as the ground outside. I cleaned and cleaned— wouldn't let the kids come over until the windows were repaired and the bugs gone. They grow up too fast on their own. I wanted to spare them any bad memories if I could. I then bought a cheap microwave and a microwave cookbook and learned to prepare nearly everything in that fashion. Another handy item is a slow cooker. You turn it on in the a.m. and by the time you return in the evening, your 'chef bored-are-wee' is prepared."

## CONSIDER THE NEIGHBORHOOD

Although your finances will have a great deal to do with where you set up house, keep in mind your kids' safety and whether there are other children in the apartment complex, condo, or neighborhood. Try to relocate in the same school district as your ex, if possible, so your kids can remain where they are in school. It gives them a sense of stability and also helps with car-pooling schedules or bus routes. They're also more likely to know the kids in the neighborhood already if they're in their school district as opposed to trying to make friends with kids who go to a different school.

## FURNISH YOUR HOME

Don't fall for the temptation to keep your living space bare to show the world that she got everything, even if it's true. Your kids need to live in a real home with you when you have them, not an empty shell or something akin to camping out. If your new dwelling isn't a furnished one, you'll need to beg, borrow, or buy some furniture, the amount dependent on your means. It doesn't have to be fancy or expensive either. Many secondhand shops offer slightly used furniture that you can get rather inexpensively. Try to buy pieces that serve more than one purpose and that offer storage opportunities, such as a foot locker that can hide out-of-season coats and also be a coffee table, or a three-drawer file cabinet that becomes both a night stand and a place to keep your important papers.

Finding time to shop may be more of a problem for you than the cost of the furniture. But most furniture stores are open on weekends and evenings, so tear yourself away from the TV you've probably already purchased and go hunting for what you need. Some stores have complete sample rooms and can offer you the option of buying the entire room of furniture as shown or just one or two selected pieces.

If you're uncertain what to get or don't trust your decisions, ask a friend or relative to go with you. Stay away from fads and loud prints as they may not travel well from the store to another domicile. Many men opt for leather (real or fake) furniture because it feels good and wears well, unless, of course, a little one gouges it with a pencil or pair of scissors. Corduroy and heavy velvet fabrics hold up well, especially when dark, so spills don't show. Most furniture stores now have a microfiber fabric that is comfortable and stain resistant, especially after being treated with a special coating. Always sit in chairs and on couches to make sure they're comfortable.

Your first purchase should be beds (and good mattresses) as you'll spend most of your time at home sleeping. A bed can also be used as a couch if you put it against a wall and put pillows in back. Let your kids have input on what kind of sheets they want as this will make them more comfortable in their second home. Make your next purchase a table and chair set. It can be used in many ways, for mealtime, a game table, a desk for your kids' homework, and

---

## ✔ Tip from the Trenches

Jack said, "The important thing to remember is that furniture and other supplies are sometimes only a phone call away. A friend, coworker, or relative may have a spare bed, some unused kitchen items, something in their garage or basement that they're not using and would be happy to loan or give to you."

---

a gathering spot for you and your children to talk. Remember, you are creating a home for your kids, not a bachelor pad.

## DO-IT-YOURSELF HOME DECORATING

Empty walls shout "lonely." Perhaps that's why cavemen decorated the walls of their ancient dwellings, to add a little warmth and comfort to the place. You can find paintings, posters, and framed prints at garage sales, secondhand shops, galleries, and museum gift shops. Artwork does help to turn a dwelling into a home.

Pete said, "Let your kids draw pictures and be sure that you have photos of your children hanging prominently throughout the home. Ask your ex for a few photos, (take some of your own, or use one of the inexpensive photo shops found in many malls). The latter often has costumes your kids can dress up in for the pictures and that should bring a smile to your face, even when the kids aren't with you."

Consider a do-it-yourself project as well. It not only will help to fill your at-home hours when you don't have the kids, but you also might find some activity that you really enjoy. Wander through a craft or hobby shop or sign up for a class in pottery, oil painting, or wall painting. Home Depot and Lowe's both offer classes in painting, hanging wallpaper, and building shelves. If you have any home improvement question, their staffs are friendly and willing to help answer questions. Crafts shops such as Michaels also offer a variety of craft and hobby possibilities.

## GIVE THE KIDS A SPACE OF THEIR OWN

Although it would be great to have separate bedrooms for each of your kids when they're living with you, it may not be possible. But even if they have to use bunk beds or a trundle in the same room, allot each of them some private space.

Be sure there's a dresser, cabinet, basket, or shelves and some closet space (with available hangers) where your kids can unpack, whether they live with you for a week or a weekend. No one enjoys living out of a suitcase or backpack as though they are only guests when they're with you. You can keep some clothes, jackets, toothbrushes, and toiletries for them at your home that are the same as they have as their mom's. However, a couple of dads we interviewed said that their kids brought those items with them to the dad's house. Offer each child a drawer, footlocker, or any type of box that can be locked where he or she can lock up any treasures to keep them out of a sibling's reach.

Jack said, "I let my two young daughters pick out paint colors for their room and the three of us painted it together. It was a mess, but we had fun doing it. Although the girls don't keep separate wardrobes at my house, they do keep a few toys there."

Other dads said they encouraged their kids to select posters and otherwise decorate their room so they felt it was really theirs. Also, especially for younger children, allow and encourage them to have a photo of their mother in their room. Kids get lonely sometimes for the parent who isn't there, and being able to look over and see their favorite picture can help them to get through those times. This may seem like a difficult thing for you to do if you harbor any bad blood with your ex, but remember, you're an adult and this isn't about you, it's about your kids.

### Let the Kids Help Decorate

As your kids will spend some time with you, enlist them as decorators, at least for their space. Ask their opinions on their bedspread or comforter, pictures for the walls, rugs, or whatever needs sprucing up. Chances are they've never had the opportunity to do that before and will find it exciting to be included. You may even be pleased with some of their ideas, but even if you're not, you actually may find yourself becoming very attached to the easy chair they selected for you in Green Bay Packer colors just because you always feel their presence when you're sitting in it.

## CREATE A HOMEWORK AREA

Don't let your kids try to convince you that they can do their homework just fine in front of the TV. While they might be able to complete it, chances are it won't be their best work and they won't remember anything they were supposed to learn by doing it.

Homework is your child's responsibility and you need to show them how to discipline themselves to do it and do it correctly. Your responsibility, on the other hand, is to provide a place for them to work. It can be on the kitchen or dining room table. In fact, many kids like to do their homework there while their parent is fixing dinner so they can ask questions if they need help.

It's possible to buy inexpensive desks at secondhand shops or at unpainted furniture stores, and desks or tables with flat surfaces are preferred because you need a lot of space to spread out textbooks and notebooks, especially if more than one kid is doing homework at a time or if you're joining them by paying bills while they do their homework and school projects.

## GET REAL DISHES

Why should you spend money buying real dishes when paper ones don't have to be washed? While paper plates are great for picnics and cookouts, real families eat off of real plates. You want to make your kids feel as though they are home when they're with you. Chances are they eat off real plates when they're at their mom's house. (Of course they do; it's probably the same china you both spent hours deciding on before registering them for wedding gifts.) You don't have to buy expensive bone china either. You can buy a decent set of matching dinnerware at Wal-Mart, Target, Sam's Club, garage sales, Goodwill, or the Salvation Army stores.

Even if you're used to paper napkins (or worse, none at all), setting your dinner table with matching plates and silverware lets your kids know that you think they're important enough to make a real home for, even though it may only be on every other weekend or a week or two during the summer. It shows you love them in a very important nonverbal way. Some dads said they used permanent press napkins that they tossed in the machine with the rest of the laundry. In the long run it was cheaper than constantly buying paper napkins.

## ASK FOR HELP

Whether your previous house was ready for the cover of a magazine or just had basic decorating, chances are you didn't have too big a hand in the design decisions. No one expects you to be an expert in selecting fabrics, paint colors, or window treatments. Don't panic. Most department stores have interior decorators that can help you, often without charge if you purchase some of your furniture there. You also can leaf through home catalogs like Ikea or Pottery Barn for ideas. If you have friends whose homes seem cozy to you, ask if they would be willing to help you put your place together. If you're more high end in the interior design arena and want to hire a decorator, just remember to never hire a decorator without seeing some of his or her work and knowing exactly what the fee will be. Also, even though this is technically a bachelor pad when the kids aren't there, remember that it is a family home when they are with you, so try not to get too off-the-wall with single-guy stuff.

## IS THERE SPACE FOR A PET IN YOUR LIFE?

You should probably get used to juggling your kids' needs before you take on more responsibility, especially a living thing that needs to be walked, fed, combed, have water changed, taken to the vet, costs you money, and needs to be provided for if you have to go out of town.

The kids may try to convince you that cats are a cinch to take care of because they don't take up much space, don't need to be walked (just require a litter box), groom themselves, and don't bark—and aren't kittens adorable? Don't get tempted. Although cats are easier to care for than dogs, they also usually live for fifteen or more years. What's more, a study by the American Society for the Prevention of Cruelty to Animals (ASPCA) revealed that the average cat costs the owner approximately $640 per year, a figure that includes food, litter, supplies such as a scratching pole, brush, and toys, and of course, the vet bills. And that's for a healthy cat. The price goes up when you have to get special diet food for them, along with medications for fleas, hairballs, worms, and kidney and bladder infections.

Also, pets such as dogs, cats, hamsters, mice, and gerbils have been known to nip or actually bite their young owner, which means a hurried trip (and long wait) to the emergency room, walk-in clinic, or pediatrician's office.

Still not convinced? Buy an orange goldfish. If it dies, you can easily buy a replacement.

On the other hand, a number of fathers interviewed for this book said that they had bought their kids a dog or cat to play with when they came to dad's house. Russ, however, said "My former wife and I also share custody with our standard poodle. The dog goes back and forth with the kids. I think having a dog can help distract the kids from the changes in their lives when their parents divorce."

As long as your apartment or condo stipulates that pets are allowed, if you do agree to have the pet come along with the kids, be sure to stock up on the same food (pets can be fussy and refuse to eat a new brand), and buy a leash, a basket or bed for the pet to sleep in, some pet toys, and make sure you know the name of the vet in case one is needed so you'll know where to go and what shots the pet has already had.

## FOCUS ON SAFETY

You may not have thought much about safety issues when you bought or rented your house, condo, or apartment, but you need to take special precautions to insure your kids' safety. It's not only important to be sure your neighborhood is a safe one, but also that your home is safe as well.

### Bathroom Safety

You may have heard that the bathroom is the most dangerous room in the house. Why? Think about it. The fixtures are made of hard porcelain, the shower may be in a bathtub (another hard surface), and the floor is often tile. Hard surfaces and water make for a slippery slope.

- Use bath and shower mats and be sure they have a rubber backing so they don't slip. You should wash them every month and when they lose that rubberized backing, throw them out and buy new ones.
- Most hardware stores and pharmacies, along with Target, Wal-Mart, and Kmart, have adhesive strips that you can put in the bottom of your tub or shower to keep people from slipping.
- Use paper cups or plastic glasses so if they're dropped you don't have chards of glass all over the floor.
- Never leave a baby or toddler alone in the bathtub to go answer the phone. Small children have drowned in only an inch of water (as well as in a five-gallon scrub bucket or even a toilet). Let your answering machine or voice mail earn its keep at bath time.
- Check the hot water heater to be sure the water isn't scalding if a child turns it on first. Ask your plumber about antiscalding devices, or lower the temperature on your hot water heater to 120 degrees Fahrenheit.
- Keep your medications out of the bathroom and in the kitchen on a high or locked shelf. Steam in the bathroom makes some medicines lose their potency (and a child is less likely to lock himself in the kitchen with forbidden medication).
- Keep toilet-bowl cleaners, mouthwashes, and shaving lotions locked up.

- Take the blade out of your razor (if you don't use an electric razor) and never leave it lying on the counter by the sink.
- If your teenage kids use an electric hair dryer, remind them to never fill the nearby sink with water and to keep the dryer away from a filled tub.
- Remind your teenage daughters to be careful with their curling iron if there are toddlers in your home as well. According to the U.S. Consumer Product Safety Commission, "in an average year, 7,700 children under the age of five need to be treated in the emergency room after burning themselves on a hot curling iron."

## Kitchen Safety

- Put knives up high enough so little ones can't get at them, or put them away altogether.
- Place cleaning supplies in a locked cupboard and never under the sink if you have younger children. Toddlers can move quickly when your back is turned, and many of the cleaning supplies are dangerously toxic.
- Always turn pot handles away from the edge of the stove so curious little hands can't grab them.
- When using electrical appliances, be sure the cords don't dangle off the countertop as a young child can pull on them and get clobbered with the fry pan, coffee pot, or toaster.
- Wipe up grease and other spills as soon as they occur so no one slips.
- To prevent food poisoning, refrigerate meat, poultry, eggs, seafood, custards, creams, milk, and milk products as soon as you're through eating.

## Stair Step Safety

- If you live in a two-story or more building, put safety locks on the windows or sliding doors that lead to a balcony or pool. Screens alone will not prevent a fall.
- Use safety gates to keep toddlers from falling down stairs.
- Be sure the stairs are well lit.
- Keep the stairs unobstructed. Don't pile toys and laundry on the steps.
- Be sure the stair treads aren't slippery. Never wax your stairs.
- Check that the handrails are in good repair.

## Furniture Safety

- Avoid glass tabletops that can break if a child jumps or falls on them.
- Protect sharp edges on furniture by purchasing rubberized guards for them.
- Put safety locks on dressers with heavy drawers that can be completely pulled out.
- Fasten tall bookcases to the wall.
- Avoid heavy lamps that can be toppled if a youngster pulls or trips on the cord.

## General Safety Tips

- Never mix bleach and ammonia. The combination creates dangerous fumes.
- If you have guns in your home, unload them and store the guns and ammunition under lock and key in different places, regardless of the ages of your kids. Don't think your teens won't touch them. According to the Harvard Injury Control Research Center, the majority of youngsters who died from intentional and unintentional firearm injuries in 2004 (the most recent year's statistics) were teens.

- Never leave glasses with alcohol sitting out after you go to bed. Kids may get up before you and drink the remaining alcohol, which could be toxic to a child.
- Never transfer turpentine, bleach, spot removers, or other chemicals into food containers such as bowls, jars, or milk or soft drink containers as kids may think it's something to drink.
- Return all medicines and household cleaning supplies to a safe and locked place immediately after using. If you set it down for just a moment to answer the phone, you might forget and leave it for your young kids to pick up. This includes vitamins, over-the-counter medications, and herbal remedies.
- When your shirts or suits come back from the dry cleaners in thin, plastic bags, immediately tie knots in the bags and throw them away. They are very dangerous if a youngster puts them over his or her head.
- Install safety guards in all unused electrical outlets. (They're available in hardware stores, pharmacies, and children's shops.) Remain watchful, as one enterprising youngster of a father we interviewed took a screwdriver, pried the guard out, and then stuck the screwdriver in the outlet.
- Never leave a child of any age alone in a pool. Even teenagers can get a cramp and panic. Always have a locked fence around a pool if you have small children. But remember, toddlers are drawn to water and can drown in as little as one inch of water found in a scrub bucket. Preschool and elementary-age youngsters also have been known to pull a pool chair over to the fence and climb over. Put safety locks on sliding doors leading to a pool.

### Safety Council Reminders

The National Safety Council warns that accidents are the largest single cause of death to children under fifteen and most accidents involving children happen at home. They suggest:

- As kids often like to help dad in the workshop, keep them at a safe distance when you're operating power tools.
- Don't let your kids play in the car. It's easy for a child to disengage the parking brake or slip the transmission lever out of Park and cause the car to roll down an incline. Never leave car keys in the ignition.
- Fire fascinates kids. Keep matches and lighters out of the reach of toddlers and warn elementary-age children of the danger in playing with them.

## EXPERT SAFETY ADVICE

Dr. Rohit Shenoi, a physician with Texas Children's Emergency Center and professor of pediatrics at Baylor College of Medicine, stresses, "Drowning is a silent killer that can strike even older, more experienced child swimmers. Among children ages one to nine, drowning is the second leading cause of death next to automobile accidents. A near drowning can result in brain damage."

"Most children drown in pools. Eighty-six percent of children who drown were being supervised, usually by a family member, according to research by SAFE KIDS," said Susan Hirtz, manager for Texas Children's Center for Childhood Injury. "In major metropolitan cities, the apartment complex pool is the site of many drowning tragedies."

Safety advocates are also seeing a rise in the number of children who use doggie doors to access the swimming pools.

"Children will see their pets use the doggie door to get outside and will use it to get to the pool," said Hirtz. (You might consider putting a screen hook on Fido's door when the kids are with you, as long as you remember to take the dog for a walk so it doesn't have an accident because you've locked the door.) Hirtz added, "I strongly recommend fencing be put up all the way around the pool. Parents cannot rely on vigilance alone." Hirtz said she's also heard of children who have drowned in large beverage coolers. They go head first into the cooler and can drown in the water left by the melted ice.

Other safety suggestions that are highly recommended include:

- Keep your local poison control phone number by all phones.
- Use night lights in the halls, bedrooms, and bathrooms as kids who have two homes may forget where the bathroom is when they wake up in the middle of the night.
- Don't let your children stay in the yard when you're mowing the lawn or ride on the mower with you. The mower can run over stones, glass, and other sharp objects and shoot them like missiles. Children riding lawn mowers can fall off and be run over and seriously injured.
- Don't let your toddler have popcorn, hard candy, or nuts as these items can easily be inhaled into the windpipe and cause choking.
- Keep balloons away from small children as they can bite off a piece and choke.

- Remove the doors from unused refrigerators, lids from trunks, and tops of large picnic coolers (or put locks on all of them), as kids think these are great hiding places and can get trapped in an airless environment.
- Keep matches locked up as kids are fascinated with them. Have practice fire drills so you'll all know what to do and where to meet if a fire breaks out. Also, have fire extinguishers and fire alarms in good working order.
- Don't smoke, but if you must, don't smoke around your kids. Secondhand smoke is dangerous to young (and adult) lungs.
- If your kids (regardless of age) are bike riding, using skateboards, or in-line skating, be sure they wear a helmet that fits properly. You should wear one as well.

## What to Do When Accidents Happen

Although the above may seem like an overwhelming list of precautions, following them can make your home safer for your children. Be prepared for the unexpected by taking infant and child CPR and first-aid courses from the American Red Cross. You can find their number in your local telephone book or by visiting *www.redcross.org*. It's also a good idea to keep a first-aid kid kit handy.

But despite your best efforts, accidents can still occur. When accidents do happen, follow these few but important instructions: keep calm, use emergency numbers by the phone, use CPR (that you previously have learned), if necessary, and tell your ex as soon as possible.

# Chapter 11

# Juggling Your Day

*One hundred years from now, it will not matter*
*What my bank account was, how big my house was,*
*Or what kind of car I drove.*
*But the world may be a little better*
*Because I was important*
*In the life of a child.*
—FOREST WITCRAFT

To paraphrase a well-known saying, "A man can work from sun to sun, but a single dad's work is never done!" The constant juggling act required by parents with kids, work, chores, social life, and more chores is always tricky, but it's especially so when you're a single dad. How much of the routine did you used to do? Were you the one in charge of bath time? Were you the "story at bedtime" dad? Did you just come home from work, help with a few things, and then park in front of the TV until it was dinnertime?

It really doesn't matter though, because either way there's a big adjustment to be made. You are now front and center and doing it all. The days you have the kids you now need to juggle getting up in the morning (no more sleeping in), getting them dressed, fed, and to school, while at the same time trying to do the same for yourself and still get to work on time. The mantra of most single dads: "It's not easy."

As Dan, a single dad with two daughters, remarked, "Juggling your day begins when you decide to get the divorce. It requires planning, a sense of humor, planning, and more planning. And did I mention planning? From the beginning, understand that you will make mistakes. Shake them off and try again. If no one cries, it's a good day."

## PLANNING IS EVERYTHING, BUT LEAVE TIME FOR SURPRISES

Begin your day the night before. That means creating routines that let everyone know what is expected of them. Here are some tips for saving time in the mornings:

- Do bath or showers the night before and have regular bedtime hours.

- Make lunches the night before, other than sandwiches that tend to get soggy overnight.
- If your children's school has a free breakfast and/or paid lunch program, consider using it to give you more free time with the kids before taking them to school.

## ROUTINES HELP

If your children's school doesn't require uniforms, lay out the kids' clothes the night before. If they're old enough, let them have a say, but only offer two choices, not everything in their closet. This eliminates arguments and tears in the morning when your child feels she must wear a certain outfit that is in the clothes hamper and you have

> ✔ **Tip from the Trenches**
>
> Michael admitted, "I'm a big fan of Lunchables and Smucker's Uncrustables. All you have to do is put them in the lunchbox. I take no credit/blame for nutritional info. I just know it is better than their bringing a Happy Meal every day."

no time to wash it. Taking responsibility for selecting the next day's outfit empowers your youngster, making him or her feel somewhat grown-up. If there's a uniform, be sure they have it—not that it's a surprise in the morning—and that it's clean and ironed, if necessary.

## BE PREPARED FOR THE DAY

Be sure all homework is done before the kids go to bed. If they try to finish it in the morning it causes too much stress, for them as well as you.

Pack the car with whatever you need the next day. Lay out your own clothes the night before as well, and organize your keys, wallet, and briefcase. Set a good example.

Also, lay out everything your kids need to take with them in the morning, such as completed homework, books, signed permission slips, sports uniform, and Scouts uniforms.

Have a specific spot by whatever door they use to catch the school bus or get to your car for their book bags and lunch boxes. Some dads put coat hooks on the wall with a cubby below to hold everything.

## SUNRISE SERENADE

Start with a solid morning routine. No matter whether your ex-wife used to sleep in and morning time was your responsibility or you used to sleep in and she took care of it (which means right now you are really hanging on by a thread), the morning routine is never easy. But it is the most important part of the day. Just as your mom always said breakfast was the most important meal of the day, the way your morning starts will dictate the way both you and the kids feel the rest of the day. When you start the day off with an argument over food, clothes,

homework, teeth brushing, or anything, large or small, you and your children will feel grouchy all day.

It doesn't really matter if you're a huge breakfast person or someone who can get by with a cup of coffee, you can't blow breakfast off with your kids. They're more active at school than you are at work, and a good breakfast gets their brains going and gives them vital energy for the day.

Eggs are a great, easy breakfast and the kids can help as well. Make scrambled eggs with cheese on top, some toast, and a glass of milk and you have just given them a nutritious breakfast to get their day started. Pancakes can be easy (though sticky with younger kids), but there are some good frozen varieties that you can toast or heat up in the microwave. Try not to rush them through this process, and don't eat in the car. (As Mom always said, "It's bad for the digestion.") Cereal, especially oatmeal, is all right as an option, but try to add some protein with it such as Canadian bacon or a hard-boiled egg (made the night before).

It makes life a lot easier if you get yourself ready first, preferably before the kids get up. Shower, shave, and maybe even have a cup of coffee and glance through the paper in complete tranquility. Then you're set, except for the hard part of getting the kids up in the morning and then getting them breakfast, dressed, and out the door in time for school.

Dan suggests, "Wake them up in stages, not when it's almost time to leave. Just like you, they need time to wake up. With my girls, I used movie quotes in the morning. 'Bambi, it's time to get up.' Later, it might become, 'Bambi, you must get up.' '*Finding Nemo*' works just as well."

With older youngsters, especially teens, you can give them a clock radio so they can become responsible for getting up in the morning. But check on them in the beginning because they probably will turn the alarm off and go back to sleep.

Don't let any of your kids watch TV in the morning. While TV could be helpful in getting them up, it can cause problems when it's time to leave and their favorite show isn't over yet.

## JUGGLING THE UNEXPECTED

When you have a sudden emergency at your job and have to work late or a meeting runs over, now there's no one at home to fill in for you without getting a relative, friend, or a baby sitter to step in. Of course, if you have a reasonably friendly relationship with your ex-wife, you can occasionally ask her to help out, as long as you don't overuse the privilege.

### Emergency Plan

The best emergency plan is one that you've thought about ahead of time and figured out all the details of what will work best for you in different scenarios. Ask yourself what-if questions. What if I have a flat tire and am delayed in picking up the kids from daycare? What if my youngster runs a fever the day I have to make an important presentation? What if my ex has an emergency out of town when she's supposed to have the kids? Create backup plans now so when you have to juggle, it goes more smoothly.

See Chapter 12 on child care for more tips on finding good child-care help, and make sure to keep a couple of baby sitter's phone numbers programmed into your cell phone for those last-minute emergencies.

### Sick Kids

If your child gets sick, however, sick time is kid time. Make your child the priority. Work will and must wait. Divorce, sadly, is so frequent today that most employers have a number of divorced employees, many of whom have children. Businesses are finding ways to adapt to workers' occasional absences due to a child's illness. Check with your company's human resources department to see if they have any programs that can help you. In many fields you might be able to work at home on days that your child is sick, or some have services for children who are sick but not contagious.

If you have family in town, ask if you can call on them in case of an emergency. Don't take advantage though, especially if they are your ex-relatives. As they are still related to your children, however, they may be pleased to feel needed and it may help them to see you in a better light.

## HANDLING GROCERY SHOPPING AND MEALTIME

Although Chapter 15 will give you specifics on making mealtimes less stressful, here is one suggestion from Dan for juggling what goes into making those nutritious meals: "Shop for groceries without the kids the night before you get them back and work from a shopping list. That way your refrigerator is full when they arrive and it's empty when they go to the ex's. It helps avoid spoilage and you don't end up buying things you really don't want in the house but gave in to prevent a scene in the grocery store when little Johnny wants 'frosted cavity makers.' This also allows you to spend quality time with your children, having fun in the park, at a movie, or playing a game of Monopoly instead of having a stressful shopping experience."

If you have freezer space, consider buying meat and chicken in bulk and dividing it into smaller serving-size packets. Then when the kids come, you can put one of the packets in the refrigerator (never on the counter) when you leave for work and it will be thawed when you get home. You can do the same with large packages of vegetables.

## YOUR NEW NEIGHBORHOOD

As you probably have moved to a new house, condo, or apartment, you possibly haven't had time to get to know your neighbors or their children. Yet by doing just that, you will know whom to call when it's your turn to have the kids and they'd like some peer time. A caveat: be sure you really are comfortable with any neighbors whose home your kids will be visiting. Get to know them before your child is unsupervised in their home. You want to make sure they don't

> ### ✔ Tip from the Trenches
>
> Paul suggests, "If you can afford it, pick a location for your new home that is near to your ex, in order to establish the triangle of work, her house, your house. Times to and from work and school will be similar to how they were when you were married. (If the children ride the bus home, it could be bus A for Mom, bus B for Dad.)"

have unlocked guns around, and look for subtle clues that might suggest drug or alcohol use. Most accidental shootings occur during the daytime when dad is sleeping in front of the TV or outside raking leaves and Johnny sneaks in to the den to show his new friend his dad's cool gun. These days you can't be too careful, so always get all of your answers before you allow your child to spend time in other people's houses.

As many communities have little, if any, public transportation, many single dads also become their kids' chauffeurs. Try these tips:

- Leave early so you don't feel rushed.
- Avoid heavy traffic areas. Learn alternate routes to save time, enjoy scenery, and to help you stay alert. When you drive the same route every day, week in and week out, you often find yourself at a location without remembering how you got there.

## CONQUERING LAUNDRY DUTIES

You may not know much about doing laundry. Chances are when you were married, your underwear, knit shirts, and socks just magically flew from the laundry bin and back to your bed or dresser, clean and nicely folded. You may have taken your dress shirts to the dry cleaners, or possibly they too were transformed from dirty to clean seemingly by elves and hung back in your closet for another day's wear.

Now that you're a single dad, you not only have your own laundry but your kids' laundry as well. What's a guy to do? It's really not that hard and you don't need an advanced academic degree to figure things out. Below are just a few tips from single dads who have mastered the task:

- Don't wait for dirty clothes to pile up. If you do, the task becomes overwhelming.
- Use only "color safe" bleach, not chlorine bleach.
- Before washing, check all laundry (particularly shirt fronts and knees on pants) for stains or anything in the pockets.
- Teach your kids to put their dirty clothes in the laundry bin you have thoughtfully placed in their room.
- Start doing the same with your own.
- If you run out of detergent for the washing machine, avoid the temptation to use one made for dish washing. Their chemical makeup is vastly different.
- If you or your kids have allergies, look for "scent free" detergent.
- Use a stain removal stick for spots.
- Separate the clothes, putting whites in one pile and dark clothes in another, and wash separately
- Put the detergent in the washer first and push the button to let the water in. Then add the clothes. If you pour detergent directly on your clothes, it will bleach spots on them.
- For blood stains, soak the items in cold water, then wash in cold water. Hot water sets the stain.

- Never wash brightly colored shirts, socks, or sweatshirts with anything other than other brightly colored items, unless you want to wear pink jockey shorts and T-shirts. The dye in red and other colored clothes runs and colors everything in that wash pink.
- It's a good idea to wash new colored towels by themselves the first couple of times.
- If you take clothes out of the dryer as soon as they're finished, you'll prevent most wrinkles.
- Socks always tend to disappear in the washer. Buy a little nylon zipper bag to put them all in or pin them together with safety pins. Nevertheless, somehow the socks thieves still manage to steal one or two socks out of the washing machine. That's why we always buy at least three pairs of the same kind of socks, so for a while you'll still have at least one matching pair.
- Always empty the lint trap on the dryer between loads. Otherwise, you'll undermine the efficiency of the dryer.

✔ **Tip from the Trenches**

Michael E., a single father with full custody of three-year-old triplets, two girls and a boy, commented: "Do all girls change their clothes a lot? My girls change their dresses about every five minutes. The boy doesn't."

## BALANCING YOUR PERSONAL LIFE

It's hard to make time to do everything you must—giving full focus to your job, grocery shopping, cooking, paying bills. But schedule regular home time with your kids as much as you can. You can always pay bills as you watch TV once they're in bed or while they're doing their homework. Be with them, in the present, even if that means playing Candyland or Scrabble three times in a row and having to tape your football game to watch later. If, however, your kids really enjoy the football game too, then pop some popcorn and curl up on the couch with them. Streamline your chores and have the kids pitch in so you can spend more time with your family.

If you have more than one child, arrange to spend some time alone with each child. It can include playing catch, a computer game, or Old Maid; talking about a movie or sports event; raking the leaves; or even baking cookies. Children with both parents at home often have to compete for time and attention, not only with siblings but also with their parents. Now that it's just you, take advantage and enjoy some one-on-one time. See Part Three for more tips on your personal life, such as dating and keeping active.

## ASK FOR HELP

You don't have to do everything yourself. It doesn't mean you're not a good parent if you ask others to lend a helping hand. If you have family or friends who are willing to pitch in with car-pooling or child care from time to time, do so. You can thank them by returning the favor, having a barbecue for all your helpers, or just taking time to write a "couldn't do it without you" note.

Ask other single dads for their tips from the trenches. You may be able to trade ideas. Don't forget that single moms face many of the same juggling issues that you do, so don't think of them as the enemy. Invite one or two to have coffee with you and ask how they've handled trying to be one or two places at once. Even if they don't have any suggestions, it's a great pickup line!

## REDUCING STRESS

Handling stress with all this juggling is very important with your new responsibilities. That includes eating properly, keeping your weight down and exercising, meditating, and utilizing other relaxation techniques. Your kids watch what you do, and if you blow off exercise, eat fast food, and let yourself go, they'll copy your actions. Chapter 25 offers many tips on ways to find a form of exercise that you'll enjoy at least enough to keep at it, as well as how to reduce stress in your life while helping your kids reduce it in theirs.

## BE FORGIVING

It's so easy to get caught up with all your time and responsibility juggling that you never give yourself the opportunity to forgive yourself and your ex for everything that contributed to the divorce. In his book *Dare to Forgive,* Edward M. Hallowell, M.D., says that "If you are going to forgive, you first have to admit to yourself, if not to others, that you have been hurt."

You may not want to admit that you've been hurt, or maybe you don't even realize that you have been hurt, especially if the divorce was primarily your idea. Nevertheless, you and your vision of what your life was going to be have suffered a loss, and that is painful. You need time to grieve and, yes, to forgive. Hanging on to anger and resentment only causes you more pain. As Hallowell says, "Forgiveness is a gift you give yourself."

So come out of your cave and begin to enjoy your new life. It may not be the one you planned or dreamed of, but it's where you are at this point, so dabble your toes in these new waters.

## THERE'S NO "U" IN PERFECTION

Stop trying to be the perfect dad. There is no such creature. All of us goof up at times, drop the ball at others, or even say things we wish we could take back. Remember that even the best jugglers in the world occa-sionally drop a ball or two. What do they do then? They pick up where they left off and start again.

When you try for perfection, you're set-ting yourself up for failure, so just be the best dad you can be and you'll be success-ful. Before you know it, you'll be surprised how well you've learned to juggle. It's a skill, like any other. And, just for the fun of it, you can really learn to juggle. The kids will be amazed and will want to learn too. It's a great way to impress dates and, best of all, it's a wonderful way to reduce stress.

# Chapter 12

# Securing Competent Child Care

*At work, you think of the children you left at home.*
*At home, you think of the work you left unfinished.*
*Such a struggle is unleashed within yourself.*
*Your heart is rent.*

—GOLDA MEIR

Your need for competent child care really depends on how often you have the children as well as their ages. But even if you only have them on weekends, the occasion might arise that you need to be away during the day or evening, so you should think ahead and have at least a few names listed in your contacts under "baby sitters."

Hopefully you have a relative or two in town who might be willing to fill in for a few hours if you need to be away, but never try to persuade someone who really doesn't want to stay with your kids. He or she may not like kids, may not have patience with kids, or may be concerned about handling the responsibility.

One single dad, who has his kids 50 percent of the time, says he and his ex agreed that if either of them needed a sitter when they had the kids, they would first ask the other.

If you only see your kids on weekends or other short periods of time, chances are you won't be using child care too frequently. Nevertheless, you need to be aware who your ex is using and how to get in touch with them, as well as what daycare or aftercare programs the kids are in. Emergencies do come up and you may find yourself with the kids for a longer period of time. If you can keep your kids with the child-care providers they're used to, it will help them have an easier adjustment.

## AFTERSCHOOL CARE

If your children are of school age, they're in school during the greater part of your workday. After school there are many programs, not only those run through the school itself but also at the Y, Boys and Girls Club, churches and synagogues, and sports, arts, and science recreation centers. If using an afterschool program that is not located at the school, the trick is to find another parent who would be willing to take your kids along with his or hers to the afterschool program in return for your picking the entire group up after work and delivering them to their respective homes. Lacking that, check with your local high school or college guidance department to see if they can recommend a responsible student who could pick up your kids and take them to the afterschool program.

If your kids are not of school age, you either need to find a qualified daycare center (one that is properly licensed and has trained daycare personnel), have a sitter who comes to your home (or a nanny who may or may not live in your home), or take them to someone's house to be looked after, probably with one or two other children. With the latter choice, check to see how many children are being cared for and learn what your state's requirements for licensing are.

Take care in selecting any type of daycare for your children, especially those for youngsters of preschool age. Your kids will be spending many impressionable hours with these adults. According to the National Association for the Education of Young Children (NAEYC) there should be "a minimum of two adults for every eight infants, [for every] fourteen two and three-year-olds, and [two adults for] no more than twenty-four and five-year-olds."

## WATCH LIST FOR DAYCARE CENTERS

- Carefully eyeball the area to be sure it is clean and safe. Is there a sturdy fence around the play area with a locked gate? (To keep kids in and strangers out.) Are the bathrooms clean with plenty of soap for washing little hands? Is there leftover food sitting around? Are the toys, swings, and slides in good condition?

- What percent of the staff has received Red Cross or other qualified first-aid training?
- Are there adequate toys for all the kids, including blocks, toy dishes, dolls, trucks, and dress-up clothes?
- Are there adequate books for the children to read and to have read to them? What type of art projects do you see on the walls?
- Ask to see the schedule of planned activities (so the children aren't plunked in front of the TV all day).
- What is their policy about late pickups if you have to work late?
- Do they have a summer program?
- Are there qualified substitutes for teachers who may be ill?
- Request a sample menu to be sure a healthy lunch is provided (if they provide lunch) rather than your having to pack a lunchbox.
- How does the daycare center insure that kids are picked up only by those who are on the secure list?
- If grandparents and other relatives and friends are included, be sure to have them listed. Try using a secret code word that anyone permitted to pick up the kids would know.
- Trust your gut reaction; it's usually right.

The good aspect of having your pre-school kids in a daycare center is that they learn to socialize, share toys without (too much) fighting, and become more independent because neither you nor your ex are there hovering to help. On the other hand, because there are other kids there your kids are likely to pick up more germs, but then that helps boost their immunity to bugs. Visit a daycare a couple of times before you make your decision. Hopefully it will be a decision that both you and your ex will make together and one you both can feel good about.

## HAVE AN EMERGENCY PLAN

Regardless what type of child care you arrange, you also have to have an emergency plan when the sitter is sick or on vacation. Stan recalls, "I was fortunate in that my ex-wife didn't work much (a bone of contention in and out of our marriage—but one which actually eased my burden of workday child care). Spur of the moment child-care needs were difficult simply because of the time it took me to get from work to home. That being said, there were some occasions when my son would have a day off from school and his mother could not care for him (because of other commitments, sickness, and so on). On those occasions, I would sometimes bring him into the office with me—loaded with toys, coloring books, games, etc. I found that I could usually get an hour of work in before he needed attention (i.e. entertaining). So, thirty minutes of attention, then another hour of work. He always found it fun coming in to work with me—especially going to lunch."

For some lucky dads, their company has seen the importance of providing daycare for its employees and even has a "sick child" room for kids that don't feel well but aren't contagious. Others recognize their employees' (male as well as female) responsibilities in regards to their children and make allowances for personal days so their workers can stay home to care for a sick child.

## WHERE TO FIND CHILD CARE

Mary Poppins just dropped in by way of her umbrella. In the real world, however, finding qualified child care is more difficult. One of the best ways to find reliable and competent (not necessarily the same) baby sitters is by asking friends who have children around the ages of yours, whose lifestyle is similar to yours, and who share your values about parenting including discipline. In many communities there are agencies that screen prospective sitters and can furnish you with contact information, but always do your own interviewing as well.

You also can run an ad in the newspaper, but be sure to be up-front. If you have a giant dog or pet boa constrictor, mention it along with the fact that only nonsmokers should apply, that driving is required, and that cooking may or may not be part of the job.

Does your child have special needs? Would you like someone who is bilingual? It might be a good way for your kids to learn Spanish, French, or one of the Chinese dialects. Do you prefer a female or a male?

Ask friends and acquaintances who also have child care what they pay in order to get an idea what your "Mrs. Doubtfire" will cost, but don't put the figure in the ad. You don't want someone applying just because you pay better than most in your community.

Either ask prospects to call you in the evening or have them e-mail you, mentioning their qualifications and contact information. The latter gives you the opportunity to call them, rather than the other way around, and also tells you that they can read and write. Don't laugh. Unfortunately, many adults can't. It won't do you any good to leave them notes of what you'd like them to do if they can't read it or are unable to write down a phone message for you correctly.

## INTERVIEWING TECHNIQUES

Although you can do preliminary interviews on the phone, you will want to meet the individuals in person. That way you can see how they dress, tell if they smoke or have alcohol on their breath, and observe how they interact with your kids. Your questions on the phone should include:

- How did you learn about this position?
- What are your child-care qualifications?
- How long was your last job and why did you leave it?
- Can you tell me a little about yourself?
- What are the names and contact information of three references, including the former employer or last person whose children you cared for? (Preferably all of these should be people for whom this individual has done child care.)
- What is your availability in a typical week?

## FOLLOWING UP ON REFERENCES

Always follow through in checking references, with one caveat. Obviously, the names the prospect gave you are his or her friends, relatives, or satisfied ex-employers. It's unlikely that the potential baby sitter would share the name of her last boss who found her rummaging through the jewelry box with a bottle of his favorite cabernet by her side, or the one before that who discovered that she put the kids in front of the TV while she talked on the phone all day.

Elaine once hired a woman who had a reference who raved about her. After discovering that the woman, who lived with them and helped to care for her five small children for a number of months, was an alcoholic, she called the original reference back.

"Why didn't you tell me that she was an alcoholic?" Elaine demanded.

"If I had," the reference responded, "you wouldn't have hired her. I knew she needed a job!"

## LISTEN TO YOUR INSTINCTS

If you're comfortable with what you've heard, both from the prospect and her references, invite her to your home to see your kids.

- Does she seem comfortable with them or does she overwhelm them with chatter and inappropriate hugs?
- Does she seem apprehensive when you mention the routine, show her the books the kids like to have read to them before going to bed for a nap, or describe what they eat for lunch?
- Ask her about how she disciplines youngsters in her care. Does she believe in

speaking softly but carrying a big stick? You don't want someone who spanks your kids or who is verbally abusive to them.

Excuse yourself for a moment and eavesdrop to hear what she says to the kids and what they say to her. Kids tend to be very intuitive. They seem to know instinctively who really likes children and who doesn't. Does she ask them what games they like to play and engage them in conversation or does she sit on the chair, anxiously picking at her cuticles, waiting for your return?

When you ask questions, write her answers down in a notebook so you can refer to them later if needed. In his book *The New Father: The Single Father*, author Armin A. Brott offers a few of the following suggested questions, but you may have others:

- What age(s) of children have you cared for?
- What would you do if . . . ? (Give several examples of things a child might do that would require different degrees of discipline.)
- When would you hit or spank a child? (If the answer is anything other than "Never," find yourself another candidate.)
- How would you handle . . . ? (Name a couple of emergency situations, such as a gashing head wound or a broken arm.)
- What are your favorite things to do with kids?

You'll have many more questions for each candidate, including specific ones if you have a child with special needs. Be sure to ask the person if he or she has questions for you as well.

# FINANCIAL CONSTRAINTS

There's no doubt that child care is expensive. But you're looking for someone to look after very special people in your life—your children—and to keep them from harm's way. Whether you're looking for someone to come in one evening so you can go to the movies, stay with your kids while you're away overnight on business, or to be in charge from when the kids get out of school until you arrive home, you want the very best person you can afford. Even if you have to cut expenses elsewhere, take time to find a qualified and caring individual for your kids.

In addition to paying your child-care provider for her services, you'll also have to register with your state tax department, file reports, fill out forms, and pay all the required taxes. If it all seems overwhelming—and it can—check with an accountant to be sure you're crossing all the required t's and dotting all those little i's. Unfortunately, ignorance of the law is not a defense. Remember that if the individual you hire is an alien, be sure he or she has a valid green card, which permits the person to work in the United States.

# ALTERNATIVE CHILD-CARE OPTIONS

Some high-school students have taken a certified baby-sitting course and might be good for a few hours of baby-sitting, but most high-school students probably aren't mature enough to handle the responsibility of caring for children overnight or for a lengthy period. A middle-school student might be a good "dad's helper," which means amusing or playing games with your kids while you are still home. Never trust a young person to watch your toddler in the swimming pool. They could be easily distracted.

You may also be able to barter for child-care services with a friend or neighbor by trading a service you can offer, such as carpooling for them on the weekend, tutoring their child, helping with computer questions, or having their child over one night a week so those parents have a free night. Be creative.

# GRANDPARENTS AS SITTERS

Although your parents or your ex's parents may be more than willing to baby-sit your kids, be sure they are physically and emotionally able to do so. Keep these questions in mind:

- Are they agile enough to run after a toddler?
- Is their hearing good enough to know when the baby's crying or your kids are fighting?
- Do they have the energy and patience to keep up with active children, answer the same question five times, or break up squabbles between siblings?
- Will they panic easily if your child has a nosebleed or cuts a hand?
- Are they willing to follow the new rules of child rearing that include time-outs instead of spanking and reasoning rather than a "because I say so" ultimatum?

If grandparents (or other relatives) watch your kids in their home, be sure there are no safety issues. Pills left out on a bedside table (or in Grammy's purse) can be tempting to a toddler. Extension cords that seemingly run on for miles also can seem like a toy to a curious little one. If the grandparents live in a high rise, be sure there are safety locks on sliding doors that lead to balconies. If they live in a home with a pool, be sure there are safety locks on their doors as well as a secure fence around the pool.

Are there cleaning supplies under the sink, sharp knives on the kitchen counter, or guns around? Do the grandparents have a pet that may not be used to kids pulling on its tail or ears and may bite or snap? Check out your children's environment whenever they are in a new location and be proactive when it comes to their safety.

Whether the grandparents are your parents or your ex's, be sure they understand that speaking negatively about either of the children's parents is verboten. They need to listen to their grandchildren and be their ally, but unless the children are in danger (such as from your ex's boyfriend's unwanted attention or temper or either parent's drinking or illegal drug use), they are to stay neutral. As Thumper's mother told him in the movie *Bambi*, "If you can't say something nice, don't say anything at all." Good advice, especially coming from a rabbit.

# Chapter 13

# Concentrating on School Matters

*What you teach your own children
is what you really believe in.*
—CATHY WARNER WEATHERFORD

Your school-age kids spend more day time in their school environment than they do with either you or your ex. Therefore, it is vital for you to consider the school another partner in your children's lives.

## KEEP THE SCHOOL INFORMED

School is children's work. Therefore, it's important for you to get to know your kids' teachers, coaches, administrators, and other school personnel as soon as possible if you haven't previously. Don't consider it an invasion of your privacy. They need to know that you and your wife have divorced (but obviously not any details). Let the school understand that you intend to be included in all school matters dealing with your kids. That includes teacher-parent conferences, sports day, receiving regular bulletins and the school directory so you can contact some of their friends' parents, and getting a copy of their report cards. If you live out of town, the school may ask you to help with the cost of postage, but it's worth it to stay in touch with your kids and their school life.

Yes, it also means that you may need to volunteer to read to the class, carve a pumpkin or two, or judge a science fair, but the time you spend as a volunteer for your kids' school will pay big dividends for you, the teachers, and, most importantly, your kids. It underscores the fact to them and to all the school personnel that you really care for your kids and are interested in all phases of their lives. If you have a special expertise that the class might enjoy hearing about, tell the teacher.

## MEET THE TEACHERS

Paul picks up his daughter from school on Fridays. "Even though I live two hours away, I like to pick her up at school when I get her for the weekend because it gives me the chance to talk to her teachers and to let them know I'm interested in how she's doing. They've been very cooperative and I think it's because they know I care."

Tom, a school administrator and single father, says, "My most important message to single dads is to stay as involved and supportive as possible with your children's schooling. I recommend regular communication with your ex-spouse about the academic and social aspects of schooling. Most schools will cheerfully comply with your requests to send print or e-mail to both houses. It is also very important to attend parent–teacher conferences as a couple and to focus on your common interests—your kids—not your own issues. If you think that your situation is a strain on your child, make an appointment with the school counselor and address it on an adult level."

Attend the parent-teacher conference with your ex, even if it's difficult for both of you, rather than insist on separate meetings. The overworked teacher will greatly appreciate the effort so she doesn't have to schedule two conferences for the same child because the parents cannot be in the same

> ✔ **Tip from the Trenches**
>
> Frazier offers, "Take an active position. If your ex doesn't tell you when school conferences are until the night before, call the school counselor and schedule your own meeting. Then request that, in the future, all notices of school activities come to you as well as to the kids' mother."

room with one another. Besides, that way you'll know that you both heard the same thing and won't get into a "But the teacher told me that . . ." shouting match.

## PTA AND YOU

Join the PTA, and if you have time, sign up for committees and volunteer for the fair, book sales, and other fundraisers. You need to be active in the school PTA for two reasons: First, your involvement will help make the school better financially, educationally, and physically. Second, your kids will know that you're taking time to be involved to make their school better in every way, such as getting the candy machines removed, the playing fields cleaned up, the fence around the schoolyard built, and school rooms painted. Their teachers will get to know you as an individual, not just as your kids' father. Your contributions to the school will please the teachers and administration, and it can't hurt your kids to have that reflected glory.

## UTILIZE SCHOOL COUNSELORS AND OTHER SCHOOL PERSONNEL

School counselors used to be called guidance counselors, but the name was changed because they do far more than just guidance. Those at your children's school are there to help your kids with personal issues and emotional stress, but they can't be of help if they don't know what's going on. Obviously, you should never divulge the gory details of what caused the divorce, only that it has occurred and how you think your kids are reacting. Also alert the school counselor and other school personnel (such as the school nurse, bus driver, coaches, and

**✔ Tip from the Trenches**

Dan suggests, "Talk with your child's teacher. Explain that you are divorced (or newly widowed) because school counselors may be able to help your child adapt better, such as providing tips for homework at two homes, etc. This was useful to me. The teachers knew when the kids were with me and helped me make some allowances."

teachers) if there is serious illness or a death in the family, including that of the family pet. Never minimize the loss of a beloved pet, but especially when it happens while your kids may be trying to cope with your divorce.

Be sure your kids' coaches and other school personnel are also kept aware of any home issues that may be creating distractions in the classroom or on the playing field, such as you or your ex moving to a new home, either of you getting remarried, or losing your job.

## HANDLING HOMEWORK

Dan, a single father of two, stresses, "Homework must be done at both homes. If your kids are old enough to be at home alone, encourage them to start before you get home from work. Some elementary schools have special afterschool programs (usually about twenty to fifty dollars a week) and they have scheduled homework time. Let your kids save the tougher assignments for when you or your ex come home and can help."

Try to coordinate your rules about homework with those your ex has so that one of you isn't saying, "Do it as soon as you get home," while the other says, "Get it done before bedtime." Remember that although they'd never confess it, kids like structure in their lives. It helps reduce stress when that structure is as similar as possible between their two homes.

## DON'T EXPECT PROBLEMS, BUT BE WATCHFUL

Although you shouldn't expect your kids to have problems in school, be alert for signs that your kids are being bullied, teased, seem depressed, or are using alcohol or illegal drugs. Middle-school and high-school years are difficult times as kids are struggling with hormones, cliques, bullying, and other issues. They want to be independent while at the same time keeping one foot on home plate, just in case they want to feel safe. Keep your communication open with your children, but if you're concerned about a potential problem, bring it to the school personnel's attention.

## AFTERSCHOOL PROGRAMS

You and your ex may need to check out possible afterschool programs for your kids if you both work or if you have your kids full time. As mentioned in an earlier chapter, there are many different types, such as sports programs, the Y or JCC, Boys and Girls Club, theatre programs, and private organizations. Check out the personnel qualifications and safety issues as carefully as you would any type of child care. In addition, ask the following questions:

- What are the hours?
- What happens if I am unavoidably late?
- What activities do you offer (and are they ones that might interest your kids)?
- Do the kids just sit and play computer games or watch TV or are there physical programs as well?
- Are the kids separated by age?
- What type of discipline do you use when it's necessary?
- Is there a quiet place where kids can do homework?
- What type of snacks are available?
- Are you open during teacher planning days and school conference days when schools are closed but parents have to work?
- Do you offer transportation from school, and if so, how are your drivers screened for safety?

Before you sign your kids up for a particular afterschool program, stop by and watch what's going on. If it's a basketball program, for instance, do all the kids get a chance to play or only the more skilled players? If your child is a beginner, do you really want him or her sitting on the sidelines while the others have fun? What are the other kids like? Do you see bullying? Are the counselors really involved or are they off to the side talking to each other? Listen to what your child has to say after the visit. If he or she doesn't have a good feeling, don't force it. There are a lot of other afterschool programs that may be a better fit.

# Chapter 14

# Becoming Doctor Dad

*The best doctors in the world
are Doctor Diet, Doctor Quiet, and Doctor Merryman.*
—JONATHAN SWIFT

Regardless of how often you have your kids with you—an occasional weekend, half of the time, or full time—chances are at some point you'll have to play doctor, that is, determine what course of action to take for an illness or accident while you also reassure your child that he or she is in good hands, even if you haven't a clue of what to do.

The important thing to remember is to stay calm (Doctor Quiet) and let your youngster know that you will figure out the best course of action (Doctor Merryman). It also helps to have the phone number of your child's pediatrician right by every phone.

## MONITORING YOUR CHILD'S HEALTH ISSUES

Keep track of your children's allergies, medicines, and doctor's appointments while they're with you by recording all the pertinent information in a small loose leaf notebook. Have a separate section for each child.

The notebook is easy to bring to doctor's appointments and will help you remember which kid had what reaction to a particular medication. It's also the place to write down questions you want to ask the doctor when you're at the appointment. Dads who tried to keep these medical records on the computer acknowledged that they often forgot to add to them, whereas a small divided notebook seemed easier.

If your child gets a new medication, write down when you've given it, along with the dosage and the time you gave it. Don't expect your child to remember if you ask if he received his medicine. Always complete the full medication regimen and never stop giving an antibiotic just because your kid seems better.

Always share any information about your kids' health issues or changes that occur on your watch with their mom right away. Be sure to give your ex the medicine, instructions, and schedule for it when your child transfers to her care.

## EQUIPMENT YOU SHOULD HAVE ON HAND

You also need to have a few pieces of important equipment in your medical first-aid kit. The kit should be a container such as a plastic tackle box or other container with a handle that is easy to carry, holds a lot, and is easily available but can be locked or put away from kids' curious hands in a closet or kitchen cupboard. These items should include:

- A good first-aid manual, such as *The American Red Cross First Aid and Safety Handbook,* by the American Red Cross and Kathleen A. Handal, or *Handbook of First Aid and Emergency Care,* by the American Medical Association.
- An oral thermometer, unless your child is too young to keep it under his or her tongue. In that case, there are underarm, digital, and ear thermometers too. Ear thermometers are not accurate in infants younger than three months, and with improper technique you may be measuring the temperature of ear wax. Pacifier and forehead thermometers also are not reliable. When you report your kid's temperature to the doctor, be sure to say whether it was oral or in the ear. You can also use a rectal thermometer (the one with the bulb tip), but most dads prefer one of the other methods. Temporal thermometers are as accurate as rectal ones, but they are more expensive.

If you do use a rectal thermometer, dip it in petroleum jelly (at room temperature) first to make it easier to insert, and gently put the tip slightly into your toddler's rectum. Hold your child firmly over your lap, holding the thermometer between two fingers. Never push it. Leave the thermometer in the rectum for two minutes.

- A pair of tweezers, for removing splinters and ticks. Remove a tick by pulling straight up and out. Do not twist the tick as you will leave the head behind. Seek immediate medical care if difficulty breathing or swallowing occurs or if a rash develops because that may signify a potentially serious allergic reaction.
- An antihistamine, such as Benadryl liquid or capsule (dosage dependent on age and weight as approved by your pediatrician), for bee stings, hives, and other itches.
- Children's sunblock lotion to be applied frequently, even on cloudy days.
- Calamine lotion for poison ivy, poison oak, and poison sumac.
- A red towel or wash cloth (for nosebleeds and cuts around the face that bleed like crazy,) because if your child doesn't see the blood, he or she is less likely to panic, which also will keep you calm.
- An assortment of adhesive bandages in different sizes. If you have little kids, get bandages with their favorite cartoon characters on them. Younger kids almost universally love bandages and will ask for one for scratches that are invisible to the naked eye.
- An antibiotic ointment for small cuts, but wash well with soap and water first. Avoid Neosporin because of the potential for allergic reactions.
- A topical lotion recommended by your child's pediatrician for insect bites, such

as 1 percent hydrocortisone lotion or cream.

- Pain relievers such as Tylenol. Ask your pediatrician what pain reliever he or she suggests. Never use aspirin for children in any circumstance as a serious neurological disorder known as Reye's syndrome could develop. Instead, consult a physician if your child has flulike symptoms, chicken pox, fever, or a cold.
- A calibrated spoon or syringe for liquid medicines. Do not use a household teaspoon as they are not uniform in size and seldom measure exactly one teaspoon.

## HEALTH PROBLEMS AND WHAT TO DO ABOUT THEM

Following is a partial list of a few of the health problems you may run into with your kids. By necessity, it is incomplete and is not meant to substitute for your healthcare professional's advice. If you are ever in doubt about what to do (after consulting this or other sources of children's medical information) when your child appears sick, call your pediatrician or your health plan's nurse help line. However, if it seems like a medical emergency, don't drive your child to the hospital: call 911.

### Anaphylaxis

Anaphylaxis is a severe allergic reaction to a number of triggers, such as a bee or fire ant sting, an antibiotic, or food allergy such as to nuts, shellfish, or eggs. The child will show one or more of a number of signs, such as swelling of the skin, throat, tongue, or mouth; difficultly swallowing or breathing; and shock. Don't panic or frighten your child, but call 911 for immediate medical help. If this has happened before and you have Benadryl or an Epi pen, administer these while waiting for help to arrive.

If your child has a severe allergy to nuts, shellfish, bee stings, or fire ant bites, always have an up-to-date filled prescription of whatever antidote the physician has suggested in your home, in your ex's, and at school and daycare just in case it is needed.

Less severe allergic reactions include hives, vomiting, or gastrointestinal pain. Give an antihistamine, avoid the triggering agent, and let your child's mom and the pediatrician know what happened.

### Appendicitis

Appendicitis is an acute inflammation of the appendix, usually occurring in kids over two years of age. Its symptoms vary but include loss of appetite, vomiting, a low-grade fever, and a pain on the lower right of the child's stomach. If your youngster has these symptoms, contact your pediatrician immediately. A ruptured appendix can be serious.

### Asthma

Asthma is the most common chronic illness in children and adolescents, one that can be fatal if it isn't managed carefully. The symptoms may include wheezing, coughing, rapid or difficulty breathing, nasal flaring or retraction (sucking in of Adams apple, ribs, or stomach), and chest pain or tightness. It is a frightening feeling to the individual, and that sense of panic tends to make the symptoms quickly worsen.

There are many triggers for an asthmatic attack, some of which are smoke and other irritants, upper respiratory infection, allergies, cold air, pets, pollen, dust, mold, exercise, and even hard laughing in some cases.

If your child is struggling to breathe and has trouble talking or walking, or the fingertips or lips turn blue or gray, it's an emergency. Call 911 immediately. Don't wait to call. While waiting for help to arrive, give your child his or her inhaler or a nebulizer treatment of albuterol.

Once your child is stable, follow the doctor's instructions completely as far as medicine, the inhaler, monitoring breathing, removing dust and mold, and other preventive measures. If you or your ex smokes, stop; limit the contact of your child with anyone who smokes.

### Bites and Stings

Dogs, often the family (or grandparent's) dog, cause the majority of animal bites with cats coming in a distant second. Dog bites result in nearly 44,000 facial injuries in U.S. hospitals each year, with severe facial injuries occurring almost exclusively in children under the age of ten.

Although most dog bites are harmless, the site can become infected. If you don't know for sure that the animal is healthy or if the animal is wild, such as a fox, coyote, or feral cat, your child may require rabies and a tetanus shot, so contact your physician.

Bites from spiders, such as the black, red, or brown widow and the brown recluse, can cause severe reactions, as can bites from venomous snakes like rattlesnakes, cottonmouths, copperheads, and the coral snake. Keep your child calm if bitten. Call poison control or 911 and follow instructions. Wash the wound with soap and water and get medical help as quickly as possible.

If your child is stung by a bee or yellow jacket, rub the area with meat tenderizer, aluminum-based deodorant, or a paste made of baking soda and water. If your child develops hives, give an antihistamine, but if your child has trouble breathing or swallowing, call 911.

### Bladder Infection

A bladder infection is also known as a urinary tract infection (UTI). It is an infection in the bladder (also called cystitis) and sometimes the kidneys. The symptoms include frequent and painful urination (sometimes with blood), foul-smelling urine, possible fever, chills, nausea, and back pain. It is more common in girls than boys. Girls need to be reminded to wipe from front to back after a bowel movement to prevent bacteria from entering the opening of the urethra.

To prevent cystitis, encourage your daughter to drink enough water so her urine stays light in color rather than a dark yellow. Cotton underwear helps the area to breathe. Remind her to urinate every three or four hours during the day as she may forget or hold back when she's playing and her urine will become concentrated. (Some little girls are embarrassed to go to the toilet at school and will hold back until they get home.) Be sure no toilet paper is left behind when wiping and that she empties her bladder completely when she urinates. If symptoms continue, contact your pediatrician, who may prescribe an oral antibiotic. Don't ignore the problem because it may get worse and the infection could scar the kidneys.

## Dehydration

Kids get dehydrated very quickly. It can occur when they're playing and forget to stop for a drink of water or if they have diarrhea or vomiting.

Keep your kids well hydrated when they're playing outside, especially in hot weather, with frequent water breaks, even if they say they're not thirsty. The American Academy of Pediatrics recommends five ounces of water or sports drink for a child weighing eighty-eight pounds and nine ounces for a one hundred and thirty-two pound teen. (One ounce is about two gulps.)

Signs to look for include dry skin, sunken looking eyes, dry lips and mouth, lack of urine output, sleepiness, and fever. If your child refuses to drink or doesn't respond by just drinking water and the dehydration symptoms remain, call your pediatrician. He or she may suggest your getting an over-the-counter solution called Pedialyte, or Pedialyte freezer pops. As dehydration can be a medical emergency, call your physician immediately if your youngster seems weak, doesn't seem to recognize you, or is hard to rouse. You may need to take your child to the hospital for IV fluids.

## Depression

Children with depression almost sounds like a contradiction in terms as we often think of childhood as a magical time filled with laughter and the adolescent and teen years as a carefree time with endless text messaging, shopping, and partying with friends. But studies show that 15–20 percent of teens will be diagnosed with depression sometime during their adolescence, and another 30–35 percent experience mild to moderate symptoms. Even infants and toddlers have been diagnosed with depression. But with all the normal ups and downs of kids' emotions, how's a dad to know if his child is depressed? What's the difference between normal moodiness, sadness when the family pet has died or the child didn't make the team, and teenage fatigue and true depression that requires medical attention? It's difficult, but there are some specific signs to watch for. Note that some of these signs differ from warning signs in adults:

- A feeling of sadness. Your child may just look sad to you, with no expression on his or her face, and conversation, if there is any, is said in a monotone.
- Withdrawing from activities usually enjoyed. A depressed child tends to lose interest in those things that previously seemed important. This may be acted

out by quitting a sport team or drama group that once required great effort to join and gave the child much pleasure in belonging to. School work may be ignored or done to a degree to just get by. Former friends are slighted.

- Vague physical complaints like stomach aches or headaches. Complaining of vague distress is a safe way for some children to express depression. It brings comfort and attention. While you always need to check out the complaint to be sure you aren't ignoring a real appendicitis or migraine, be alert to other signs that your child may be using pretend hurts to hide the ache of real depression.

- Lack of energy. Kids are supposed to have endless energy. They can burn the candle at both ends and would in the middle, too, if they could find a way. But a depressed young person has no energy. He or she seems bored with the world. Everything is too much effort. "I'm tired" is a common complaint. Naturally you want to check with the pediatrician to make sure there isn't a physical cause, such as mono or the flu.

- Sleeping more than usual. Depressed children's sleep habits change. Rather than quickly falling asleep, some may toss and turn, or fall asleep but awaken early in the morning and be wide awake. Others, however, can't seem to get enough sleep. While normal teenagers sack out until noon on weekends and awake refreshed and ready to party, depressed kids sleep whenever possible, wake groggy, and are lethargic when awake.

- Mood swings. Depressed people quickly change moods from irritable to feeling hopeless to blue or down in the dumps.

- Low self-esteem. Pay attention to comments such as "I have no friends." "Why would anyone like me?" "I can't do any-

thing right." "My brother's the smart one." "My sister's the athletic one."

Most young people have trouble with self-esteem from time to time as they worry about not fitting in with their peer group, being too short or too fat, or that an unwanted pimple on their face spells disaster in their social world.

Depressed youngsters carry this shaky self-esteem a little further. They consider themselves to be so unworthy, so lacking, that they feel nothing they do or say is ever right. They put themselves down vocally and through their actions, causing their peers to withdraw, isolating the young person just at a time when social contact is so very important.

- Eats too much or too little. Depressed children may lose their formerly good appetite and just pick at their food at mealtime or say they've already eaten. The depression also may express itself through eating disorders such as anorexia, bulimia, or obesity (discussed in detail in Chapter 7).

- Difficulty in concentrating. Just like their adult counterparts, depressed children have difficulty in focusing. Their short attention span creates major difficulties for them at school because they only process bits of what's being said, miss instructions, and tend to drive their teachers into early retirement.

Some depressed young people tend to be accident prone. It may be explained away by parents and siblings as attention-getting behavior or just an overly active youngster, but often the accidents are caused because of the child's lack of ability to concentrate or by a self-hate that flirts with potentially self-destructive behavior, like cutting.

- Feelings of helplessness. This symptom of childhood depression is one you must observe subjectively. Your child seems . . .

well, lost, without direction or even caring. He or she may be frightened of many things, fearful to try the unknown, or a worrier. If you can imagine a stranger observing your child, that person might, without knowing anything about the child, sense depression from the body language and from the expression of hopelessness and of helplessness of the child's face.

- Thoughts of suicide. This is a scary word for any parent. Just as the word cancer used to be whispered for fear of catching it, suicide remains in the closet along with goblins and ghosts of our unconscious. If you don't let it out, you may reason, it can't get you or your kids. But it can and it does. It's estimated that more than 2,000 teenagers kill themselves each year, making suicide the third-leading cause of death (after motor vehicle accidents and homicide). This number is even larger because many motor vehicle accidents are said to actually be suicides. Suicides have been attempted and often succeeded by children as young as five. Like a hurricane, a successful suicide leaves untold destruction among family and friends in its wake. Although many young people who commit suicide give no warning, there are some warning signs of which you should be aware:
- Talks about committing suicide. Forget the myth that says people who talk about committing suicide never do. The truth is that most people who talk about suicide will try it. Take all suicide threats seriously. Be sure that if you have guns in your home they are under lock and key with the ammunition stored in another secure place. Do the same with medications you may have.
- Acting out self-destructive behavior. This includes darting in and out of traf-

fic, playing with guns, jumping from high places, mixing alcohol with drugs, cutting themselves, or engaging in promiscuous unprotected sex. Teenagers may race the car as fast as it can go, figuring if it flipped or missed a turn fate would have made the decision.

- Giving away favorite possessions. Your child may give away a favorite toy or a CD, DVD, or jewelry to a sibling or friend, saying, "Here, I won't be needing this anymore."
- Talking about death. If your child seems fixated on death and dying—listening to music with lyrics that speak about death, drawing pictures of dead people, romanticizing about Romeo and Juliet's suicide over love, or collecting newspaper or magazine articles about people who have committed suicide—watch carefully. He or she may be considering suicide.
- Changing behavior suddenly. A child who has been in a depression and suddenly seems upbeat and frantic with activity may not be better at all but rather may have decided to commit suicide and is relieved that the pain of the depression will soon be over.

### Suicide

What can you do if you think your child is thinking about suicide? Contact your pediatrician immediately for help. You also can call your area's crises hotline or 911. Consider it a medical emergency. You'll be put in touch with a psychiatrist (an M.D.), psychologist, or social worker, all of whom specialize in children's emotional problems. Don't ignore it because you think needing a therapist is a sign of weakness. Your child is in potential danger.

Fortunately, there are treatments that can help children with depression. In the book *Help Me, I'm Sad*, authors Lynne S. Dumas and child/adolescent psychiatrist

David G. Fassler wrote, "Effective treatment of children with depression depends on establishing a strong, three-way partnership among you, your child, and the therapist." (Of course, you'll always communicate any concerns about your child with your ex as soon as you have them.) For more information on the warning signs of depression and what to do if you think your child is depressed, check out *The Everything Parent's Guide to Children with Depression*.

### Earaches

Kids develop earaches quickly. They may run a high fever (fevers are more common in the one- to four-year-old age group) and cry or complain that their ear hurts. A cough is not uncommon. Toddlers may pull at their ear as they tend to be less able to verbalize just where it hurts. See your child's pediatrician for evaluation and therapy recommendations. As the cause is often viral, not bacterial, doctors today are less likely to immediately prescribe antibiotics. There are drops, however, that the doctor may prescribe that can help with the pain of the ear infection.

### Fevers and What to Do about Them

Fevers are not necessarily bad. They are the body's way of turning up the immune system to fight infection. Children run fevers for a number of reasons. Some children normally run hot, that is, have a normal oral temperature slightly over ninety-nine degrees. Others may suddenly spike a high fever because of an ear infection or strep throat. More important than actual temperature readings is how your child looks. If he or she seems ill to you or reports feeling sick, contact your pediatrician. For infants younger than three months, call your doctor if the temperature is higher than 100.4° F. For older children, ask your

child's pediatrician at what temperature you should call the office.

If the pediatrician approves, you can try children's Tylenol or another children's fever reducer (but never aspirin) to bring the fever down or put a cool washcloth on the forehead.

### Headaches

Some children frequently complain of headaches. They may be suffering from allergies or need corrective eye glasses. They also could be overly tired or coming down with the flu or an infection. A constant and severe headache could also be a symptom of a more serious problem, so have the pediatrician check your child if it persists for more than a day.

Children as young as three may suffer from migraine headaches. This is a severe headache that lasts for hours. Kids with migraines may have nausea, light sensitivity, see spots, and feel dizzy. Fortunately there are a number of medications that are prescribed for migraine headaches. For all types of headaches, it often helps temporarily to have the child lie down in a quiet, dark room, with a cold compress on his or her head.

### Head Lice

Don't think that head lice are only found on kids whose personal hygiene is suspect. Lice are found among privileged private-school kids, kids who play baseball (and swap headgear), and kids who go to the movies and lay their head on the back of their chair. You'll see your kid scratching his or her head, and if you look closer . . . ugh! You'll see the nasty crawling things as well as sticky little dabs of cottonlike white on the hair strands. Those are, sad to say, nits or eggs.

Ask your pharmacist for an over-the-counter medicated shampoo to wash your kids' hair, but never use it on children under the age of two. You may have to apply it again one week later. Comb your child's hair with a fine-toothed comb to remove the nits and wash your child's sheets, pillow cases, towels, infested clothing, combs and brushes, and sleep toys in very hot soapy water. Throw out any nonwashable baseball caps, hats, or head scarves they've been wearing, or seal them in a plastic bag for two weeks.

Check other members of the family for infestation as well. Unfortunately, close personal contact can spread head lice, and your child probably will not be allowed back in school until all signs are clear. While younger children may be more upset with the treatment than the fact that they have head lice, older kids may feel humiliated and dread going back to school once they are deemed clean. Let them know that lice, like roaches, have been around since the time of the caveman, and that adults get head lice too. Although you may be tempted to shave your son's head just to get rid of the lice, don't do it. Before it can grow back, he'll be back at school and really feel like a marked man.

## Head Trauma

Kids fall all the time and often develop a real goose egg on their head, or if there's a cut, it bleeds like the dickens and scares you half to death. Don't give them any pain medication. It's okay for them to rest or even go to sleep, but for the next forty-eight hours you need to wake them a couple times a night to check on their condition and be sure they're coherent when you wake them. The things to watch for with a head trauma are:

1. Loss of consciousness, even briefly

2. A headache so severe that they want pain medicine

3. You can't wake them up or they seem confused when you do

4. They vomit three or more times

5. Their breathing isn't normal

If these or anything that seems abnormal occurs, immediately call your pediatrician or take them to the emergency room for observation and/or treatment.

## Meningitis

Meningitis is a serious infection that causes an inflammation of the brain or spinal cord. A child may have nausea and vomiting, a stiff neck, severe headache, a fever, and a rash consisting of little red or purple dots called petechiae. Your child needs to be evaluated as soon as possible by your pediatrician or taken to the emergency room. While some meningitis is caused by a virus and is less serious, bacterial meningitis, which is spread through the air by coughing, sneezing, sharing drinking glasses, or kissing, can be potentially fatal and needs prompt attention. If you have a teen about to enter college, be aware that many states have passed laws requiring all freshmen college students living in a dorm to have a meningococcal vaccination.

## Night Terrors

Night terrors are more frightening for you than for your child (usually boys between ages of one and eight) because the youngster has no recollection of waking up from a deep sleep, screaming, babbling, and obviously terrified. You really can't wake him fully, and even if you could, he'll have no memory of your doing so. Just talk in a soothing voice and hopefully he'll drift back off to sleep.

Physicians think night terrors are triggered by kids becoming overly tired. Fortunately, they usually last between thirty seconds and five minutes, although some may last longer. Night terrors tend to run in families, so if you or your ex had them, your children may too. Luckily, kids usually outgrow night terrors when they're seven or so.

## Nosebleeds

Nosebleeds are common in children and most frequently are caused by nose picking and dry, cool weather. (Using normal saline or Vaseline to lubricate the nasal lining can keep the membranes moistened.) Other causes include nasal trauma (such as placing tissue in the nostrils), allergies, infections, injuries, and some more serious possibilities.

Chances are your young child will be frightened if he or she has a nosebleed. Apply direct pressure on the affected nostril for five to six minutes and have the child breathe through his or her mouth. Do not tilt the head back as that will cause blood to go down the child's throat. If you have a red towel, use that so the sight of blood won't be frightening.

If the nosebleed doesn't stop in fifteen to twenty minutes, go to the hospital emergency department. Keep track of the child's frequency of nosebleed by noting the date in your medical notebook, and be sure to tell your ex so she can keep track as well.

## Pinkeye

If your youngster wakes up with crust on the eyelashes, has gook coming out of an eye, or the eye itself looks red, itches, or is burning, chances are he or she has conjunctivitis, or as it's more commonly known, pinkeye. It's an infection of the mucous membranes of the eye, and if it's bacterial rather than viral it requires an antibiotic eye drop or ointment. Call your pediatrician for an appointment.

Pinkeye is extremely contagious, so wash your child's towels and washcloths in hot, soapy water, and wash your own hands thoroughly before and after touching the infected area. According to ophthalmologist Charles B. Slonim, clinical professor of ophthalmology at the University of South Florida, "If your child wears disposable soft contact lenses, toss them out and have him/her wear glasses. Don't let your youngster use new contacts until the infection has been totally gone for two days. If your child has gas permeable or 'hard' contact lenses, however, they do not need to be thrown out and can be worn again once the infection has cleared, providing they are properly cleaned and disinfected using the regular cleaning procedure for the particular lenses." Because pinkeye is so contagious, you may want to keep your youngster out of school until the eye stops oozing.

## Pinworms

Pinworms are white, quarter-inch little worms that invade the gastrointestinal track and are found in your child's anal and buttocks area. They affect approximately 20 percent of children, especially those between five and ten years of age. They're often caused by youngsters not washing their hands after using the toilet, after playing outside, and before eating. Children infected with pinworms can pass them along to other members of the family, so remind your other kids and yourself to wash hands with soap and water frequently, especially after playing outside, playing with a pet, or handling food. Wash bed linens and underwear in hot water to kill eggs and worms. While pinworms aren't serious, they itch like crazy and can disturb the individual's sleep. There are a number of medications available as well as ointment that can relieve the itching.

You can discover if your child has pinworms by turning a flashlight on the outer edge of the anus a few hours after he or she has gone to bed. Children need to know that you are going to do this beforehand so they aren't frightened if they wake up and see you shining a flashlight on their bottom. If you see a little moving white thread, it's a pinworm. Your child will need over-the-counter medication to clear up the infection. If your child continues to complain about itching but you don't see any signs of pinworms, it may be an infection or irritation from poor hygiene.

### Seizures

Some children suffer from seizures when they develop a fever. These are called *febrile* seizures and usually stop once a child is five or six years of age. Children with epilepsy have seizures that occur without fever and vary in expression. With some the child may lose muscle control and fall, while with others there may be muscle spasms or spasmodic jerking and shallow breathing. Regardless, if your child has seizures, it is frightening to both you and your youngster. When your child is having a seizure remember to:

1. Remain calm.

2. Place your child on his or her side or stomach to prevent choking.

3. Do not try to force anything in the mouth or hold the tongue.

4. Have the child evaluated immediately if it is the first seizure, especially if a fever or head injury is involved.

5. Call 911 immediately if the convulsion lasts more than five minutes, your child has been injured while falling, or if one seizure seems to follow the last.

### Sore Throat

Although many children have sore throats, always have them checked by a pediatrician as it could be a strep throat that may lead to rheumatic fever, a potentially serious heart ailment. Symptoms of strep throat include a sudden onset of a very sore throat with fever over 101 degrees, difficulty swallowing, tender lymph nodes in the neck, and often a headache or abdominal pain.

Your pediatrician can do a rapid strep test (about 90 to 95 percent accurate) in his or her office to determine whether your child has a strep infection, and if it's positive they will prescribe an antibiotic. If it's negative, they will do a throat culture test that takes forty-eight hours to give a definite result and will treat if it is positive.

Remember, your child is contagious for twenty-four hours after starting antibiotics. You should discard your child's toothbrush after being on antibiotics for twenty-four to forty-eight hours to avoid reinfection.

If your child's sore throat is caused by a viral infection, it usually will clear up on its own, but only your pediatrician can determine if your child has a more serious bacterial infection that may lead to rheumatic fever. Ask your pediatrician what you can give your child to ease the discomfort. Some pediatricians prefer fluids only, some suggest gargling with salt water (if the child is old enough to be able to comply), and others may suggest children's Tylenol. Over-the-counter cough medicine may contain ingredients not meant for your child's condition. Always ask your doctor for suggestions first.

# WHEN TO CALL THE DOCTOR

Whatever the medical concern, if you're in doubt after consulting this or other resources of children's medical information, call your pediatrician. If the office is closed, you can talk to the pediatrician on call. In addition, your insurance network may have a nurse on call service to help in decision-making after hours. Give the health-care professional your child's symptoms and age. Stay calm, even if you're told to call 911.

Many geographic areas now have pediatric walk-in clinics and urgent-care clinics where your child can be seen day or night if the problem is not serious enough for the emergency room.

Illness knows no schedule. If your kids are hurt or become ill while they're with you, be sure to contact their mother as soon as possible. It's the right thing to do, and if the situation were reversed you'd want to know as well.

# Chapter 15

# Picking Up on Cooking Clues

*Strange to see
how a good dinner and feasting
reconciles everybody.*
—SAMUEL PEPYS

You may have been a terrific backyard cook over the grill, but cooking well-balanced meals for your kids when you've been working all day is a different story. It may seem overwhelming at first, but there are ways to simplify your family's dining without resorting to fast food carryout.

Jack panicked the first weekend he had his girls and realized it was his responsibility to feed them. "I was fairly good at the grill," he said, "but they got tired of that very quickly. I found a meal plan at a couple of local restaurants like Ruby Tuesday and Beef O'Brady where kids could eat free. They'd do their homework until they got their dinner. But even that got expensive as I still had to pay for my dinner and I didn't have much money, so it was back to the grill. A good grill is very important for a single dad."

Nevertheless, at some point rather quickly, every single father is going to have to do some cooking. You may even find that you enjoy doing a little cooking once you get the hang of it.

## DO YOU KNOW WHERE YOUR KITCHEN IS?

Although you may be a gourmet chef, most men know where the kitchen is only because it's near where they eat breakfast or dinner and holds the refrigerator where the beer, cold cuts, and cheese hang out. This chapter is for those of you who find cooking actual complete meals for your kids confusing and overwhelming. Even if you already are a gourmet chef, this chapter can help you figure out if there are some much-needed kitchen tools that you took for granted when you lived in a house with a well-stocked kitchen.

Now that you're in your new digs, you'll suddenly realize that all those dishes and kitchen gadgets your ex received at one of her numerous bridal showers are absent. Unless you've had a divorced dad's kitchen shower, your cupboard is really bare, unless she's given you a few plates, spoons, and forks to tide you over. Not to worry. Those necessary items are still available and, for the most part, not too expensive.

## EQUIPPING YOUR KITCHEN

You don't need to create a Martha Stewart kitchen, but there are a few basic items you'll need as you begin to stock your kitchen:

- Ten-inch or twelve-inch fry pan (for pancakes and eggs)
- Wok or large fry pan (for stir-frying)
- Two-quart saucepan with cover (for pasta and soup)
- Strainer or colander (to drain pasta and vegetables)
- Cookie sheet (for fish sticks, roasting veggies, and cookies)
- Nine-by-eleven roaster pan (for roasts, chicken, or brownies)
- Set of measuring spoons
- Set of measuring cups for dry ingredients plus a liquid measuring cup
- Set of mixing bowls, assorted sizes (to mix stuff in)
- Toaster oven (more versatile than a simple toaster)
- Electric slow cooker
- Coffee pot (if you drink coffee)
- Oven mitts
- Set of quality knives (they're more expensive than cheap ones, but they are less likely to slip and cut you)
- One or more plastic carving boards that can go into the dishwasher (always wash your cutting board after using it for raw meat, poultry, or fish)
- Ice-cream scoop

• Spatulas, slotted spoons, and a cooking fork (oversize metal or plastic spoons are better than wooden spoons as the latter can't be cleaned and metal or plastic spoons can be put in the dishwasher or soaked in hot water before washing)

Also pick out a matching set of dishes, including cereal bowls, dinner plates, salad plates, and either mugs or cups and saucers. You can find inexpensive dishes at Target, Wal-Mart, or any department store, though you can go with more expensive bone china if you want (and can afford) it. Why a matching set? Because having a set of dishes that match, nice drinking glasses, and a matching set of cutlery improves everyone's self-image. It helps you all feel pride that you're a "real" family. If you just use odds and ends, it may seem to your kids that this is only a temporary situation or that they are really not that important, and that's not the message you want to send. Boost your children's self-esteem by serving well-balanced meals on nice dishes.

## LET KIDS HELP WITH THE PLANNING

Even if you're a gourmet cook, it makes no sense to plan epicurean meals if the kids won't eat them. You might try the Web site *www.childrensrecipes.com* for actual recipes sent in by kids, including ideas for breakfast, lunches, main dishes, and desserts. Most of them have just a few ingredients and are easy to fix. One of our favorites is "Crockpot Cheeseburger Sandwiches" submitted by Karen. You cook it in the slow cooker so it's ready when dinnertime comes. Let your kids experiment with making their favorite dishes and submitting them to the Web site.

> ✔ **Tip from the Trenches**
>
> Mike says, "Make meal planning an activity for both dad and the children. It offers fun and companionship while teaching the kids (and dad) about nutrition and healthy eating."

Helping to plan the meals also bolsters kid's self-confidence while encouraging them to try new foods such as artichokes, asparagus, and zucchini. Institute a one-bite rule so kids will begin to sample new foods. That means that everyone (you included) needs to take at least one bite of a new food. Otherwise, how can you and your kids know if you like it or not?

If your children are old enough, let each of them plan one night's meal, even if they make everything green but the chops. (We once had a meal where the kids added green food coloring to the mashed potatoes, served lime Jell-o and broccoli, and lime sherbet for dessert. It tasted all right, but we felt that although we had created a culinary masterpiece, it's better to have a little variety on the plate.) Either shop ahead so you don't have to take everyone to the grocery, or if they're old enough, take them with you so they have an idea of what things cost, learn how to pick out good melons, and know the difference between flank steak and sirloin. If you don't know, ask the staff in the fruit or meat department. They love to educate the public.

Although your kids may want candy and snack food when they're shopping with you, it's important to keep them on track by focusing on nutritious foods. It helps them learn that they shouldn't expect to get everything they want just because they see it.

# A SINGLE DAD'S FIRST GROCERY SHOPPING EXPERIENCE

Stan recalled his first foray into the grocery store to stock his larder for the first time. It may ring true for you.

"When I was still married, I had often run into the grocery store to pick up a carton of milk, some bread, and maybe a couple of other items. But I couldn't remember the last time I had done a complete shopping trip.

"I went to the grocery and grabbed an empty cart. Then I stopped cold. It was surreal. I didn't know what I needed—frozen foods, cleaning products, stock items, what? For the first time, I realized I was on my own again.

"I started grabbing things until my cart was chocked full. I had bought food for a family of three. I quickly realized that I needed just a quart of milk, not a gallon, half a dozen eggs, not a carton of twelve. Slowly, I put everything back and started over. I felt an extreme sadness and a failure, not of the marriage that hadn't worked out, but of not being with my son."

# MEAL PLANNING

Try to balance out a menu with a protein (meat, fish, chicken, or tofu), starch (potatoes, rice, barley, pasta, corn, bread), and one or two vegetables. Vary the vegetables so your kids get used to more than one kind. Researchers say there are just as many vitamins in frozen veggies as in fresh ones. If you use canned vegetables, however, rinse them off before serving to remove some of the salt.

Encourage your kids to eat fruit for dessert, saving ice cream and other sweets as special treats. Keep apples, canned mandarin orange slices, and grapes in the refrigerator for munching.

# THE ESSENTIAL SINGLE FATHER'S COOKBOOK

Most of these recipes are extremely kid friendly. They also are dad friendly since you will probably do the majority of the cooking and want things simple but good, unless your kids are old enough to want to play chef. Let the younger ones help out; that's how they develop an interest in cooking. Here are some recipe ideas:

### Macaroni and Cheese

1   cup pasta (elbow, small shells, penne, or wagon wheels)
1   tablespoon butter
¾   cup milk
6   ounces shredded cheese (American, although older kids might prefer sharp cheddar)

1. Cook pasta according to directions on box. Drain well.
2. Immediately return cooked pasta to saucepan and mix in butter, milk, and shredded cheese.
3. Mix well and cook over low heat, 3–5 minutes, until heated throughout, stirring frequently to mix sauce with pasta.

## Slow Cooker Ribs

Pork or beef ribs (ask the butcher how many you need for your size family)

One can of bouillon soup

2   cloves garlic (or more depending on the size of your family)

1   small onion, peeled and quartered (if you really like onions use a large one)

1–2   small potatoes per person, peeled

5   carrots, peeled and cut into chunks

1. Put ribs in the slow cooker.
2. Add a can of bouillon soup.
3. Add garlic cloves as desired.
4. Add onions, potatoes, and carrots.
5. Turn the slow cooker on low when you leave for work, and when you get home you'll have a delicious dinner. (Note: Although you can add prepackaged stew vegetables, they tend to become a little mushy in the slow cooker.)

**Note:** For a variation on this recipe, try using pot roast instead of ribs and adding some Italian seasoning.

## Matthew's Roast Chicken Soup

1   whole chicken

1   large Spanish onion, cut in half

2   cups chicken stock

1   quart water

3   carrots, finely chopped

1   celery stalk, chopped, including leaves

2   cloves garlic, if desired

1. Place the chicken and the onion in a roasting pan and bake at 400 degrees for 1 hour.
2. In a large pot with lid, add the chicken stock, water, and salt and pepper to taste. Add the roasted chicken and onion and simmer for 1½ hours.
3. While chicken is simmering, chop very finely the carrots, celery (including leaves), and garlic.
4. After simmering, pour liquid through a sieve (or strainer with small holes) into a large bowl and let chicken cool down.
5. When chicken is cool, remove skin and flesh by hand. Discard skin and bones.
6. Soften finely chopped vegetables by sautéing in olive oil in a large saucepan, then add salt and pepper.
7. After 5 minutes of softening, add liquid and chicken meat and simmer for 20 minutes. You can add water if necessary. Serve with baby new potatoes or pasta. This dish can be frozen as long as you bring to a boil when reheating.

## Taco Time in Turkey
(adapted from the tenth edition of *Betty Crocker's Cookbook*)

Takes 15 minutes to prepare and makes 8 tacos

½   cup chicken broth

½   cup finely chopped onion, if desired

½   cup whole-kernel corn (well drained if canned)

½   pound ground turkey breast (available in the meat department)

½   cup mild salsa

8   10-inch flour tortillas
Reduced-fat sour cream

1. Heat broth in a large, nonstick skillet.
2. Add onion and corn and cook on medium high for 2–3 minutes.
3. Reduce heat to medium and stir in ground turkey.
4. Cook 2 more minutes, stirring occasionally.
5. Add salsa and cook 5 minutes, stirring occasionally until turkey is no longer pink.
6. Spoon slightly less than ½ cup turkey mixture down center of each tortilla.
7. Roll and serve with a spoonful of sour cream, if desired.

## George's Slow Cooker Beef Tips

    Beef tips (ask butcher how much you need for your size family)
2–3 new potatoes per person
    Mushrooms (as many as your family likes, but remember they are 90 percent water and will significantly reduce while cooking)
1 can beef bouillon
3 cloves garlic

1. Put beef tips in the slow cooker, along with new potatoes (little ones), mushrooms, beef bouillon, and garlic.
2. Turn the slow cooker on low in the morning and dinner's done by dinnertime.

## Mince

    Ground round or ground turkey (ask butcher for amount needed for your size family)

    Potatoes, cut into chunks (three or more chunks per person depending on appetites)
5 carrots, peeled and cut into chunks
2–3 onions (or as many as desired), cut into chunks (adds flavor even if no one in your family likes onions)

1. Brown chopped meat in a big saucepan.
2. Add potatoes, carrots, and onions.
3. Add salt, if desired.
4. Cook over low heat until the potatoes are soft when you stick a fork in them, usually about 30–45 minutes.

## Easy Shrimp and Rice

2 teaspoons olive oil
1 yellow onion (if desired), sliced thin
1 large can of low-sodium chicken broth
1 cup instant rice
1 pound peeled shrimp, fresh or frozen
½ cup frozen peas

1. Heat oil in a large fry pan.
2. Cook the onion over medium heat until softened. (Omit this step if you don't like onions.)
3. Add chicken broth and rice.
4. Cover with aluminum foil or pan lid and simmer on low heat for 15 minutes.
5. Add shrimp, cover again, and cook for 5 minutes.
6. Season with salt, if desired.

## Easy Chicken Barbecue

1   cooked chicken from grocery or leftover cooked chicken
1   cup barbecue sauce

1. Shred chicken or cut into small cubes.
2. Toss with barbeque sauce.
3. Heat until warm in microwave or in a saucepan on the stove.
4. Serve over cooked rice or bread.

## Shrimp and Avocado Salad

1   teaspoon red wine vinegar
3   tablespoons olive oil
¼   cup orange juice
1–2 cans mandarin orange slices
1–2 ripe avocados (if your kids like them), sliced thin
1   pound peeled and cooked shrimp (fresh or frozen)
    Lettuce (romaine, iceberg, red leaf, or bib)

1. Mix together the vinegar, olive oil, and orange juice.
2. Add the shrimp, orange sections, and avocado slices.
3. Serve over lettuce.

## Dad's Chicken Salad with Apples

1   package frozen pre-cooked chicken breasts strips
    Juice of 2 or 3 limes
1   tablespoon white wine vinegar
2   tablespoons brown sugar (or Splenda brown sugar)
2   apples (Granny Smith or McIntosh), cored

1. Thaw the chicken out in the refrigerator (never on the counter).
2. In a bowl, mix together the lime juice, vinegar, and sugar.
3. Stir until the sugar granules are dissolved.
4. Chop the apples and toss into the mixture.
5. Cut the chicken in bite-size pieces and add to the mixture. Season with salt, if desired.
6. Serve on individual plates. Put over lettuce or in sandwiches if desired. Serves four.

## Sweet Potato Fries

3½  pounds sweet potatoes
3   tablespoons olive oil
1½  teaspoons low-sodium soy sauce

1. Preheat oven to 450 degrees.
2. Line cookie sheet with aluminum foil.
3. Scrub sweet potatoes and cut in half, then lengthwise.
4. Cut into four or six sticks.
5. Mix olive oil and soy sauce in a bowl and toss with potatoes so they're coated with the mixture.
6. Put potatoes, skin side down, on the cookie sheet.
7. Sprinkle with salt, if desired.
8. Cook 12 minutes, then turn the slices with tongs and cook for another 10 minutes.

## Mexican Eggs and Cheese

2  eggs for each family member
   Flour tortillas, at least one per
   each member of the family
   Shredded cheese (prepackaged
   available)
   Salsa, if desired

1. Scramble eggs.
2. Place them on flour tortillas.
3. Top with shredded cheese.
4. Roll them and wrap tightly in plastic
   wrap and refrigerate.
5. For dinner or in the morning, pop as
   many as you need in the microwave and
   cook for 2 minutes. (Note: Microwave
   times may differ from unit to unit.)
   What makes them Mexican? It's the
   salsa topping you add on top of yours.

## Dad's Smoothies

Frozen fruit, 1–2 cups per person
Low-fat vanilla or low-fat plain
   yogurt, 1 cup for each member
   of the family
Orange juice as desired

1. Divide frozen fruit, putting 1–2 cups
   each into small baggies.
2. Seal and put into freezer.
3. In the morning, put the contents of
   one baggie, 1 cup yogurt, and a couple
   of tablespoons of orange juice into a
   blender and blend.

## Jiffy French Toast

2  or more eggs, depending on
   number of people having French
   toast
3  tablespoons milk per serving
   (equivalent to ¾ cup for
   4 people)
8  slices slightly stale (not moldy)
   bread

1. In a pie plate or large bowl, beat the
   eggs and milk with a whisk or fork.
2. Soak the bread in the egg mixture,
   coating both sides.
3. Cook on a fry pan or griddle with a
   little butter, 1–2 minutes per side until
   golden brown.
4. Cool, then wrap each piece of toast in
   plastic wrap and freeze.
5. In the morning, unwrap the amount
   you need and heat in the toaster oven
   or microwave. Add syrup and enjoy!

## Blue Snow Parfait

1  container vanilla yogurt for each
   child
1  small box blueberries, washed

1. Put the yogurt in a small bowl.
2. Gently mix in blueberries that have
   been washed and carefully dried.
3. Spoon into sauce dishes or paper cups

## OTHER HELPFUL COOKBOOKS

There are thousands of cookbooks available to help the novice chef, as well as some
specifically for kids, quick meals, low fat, or

any other specialty. Most dads love cookbooks that have only a few ingredients that are easy to put together and have photos to give an idea what the finished product should look like.

One newcomer to the always expanding list is *Amazing 7 Minute Meals*, written by a graduate of the Art Institute of Philadelphia in Culinary Science, Yvonne Stephens. Stephens not only includes a shopping to-do list with each of her more than one hundred recipes, but she also includes the prep and cook time as well as a beautiful color illustration of each completed dish. Best of all, most of her recipes are cooked in a wok or large frying pan, so you only have one pan to clean.

Another new book is *Williams-Sonoma Fun Food*, containing twenty-five recipes by food writer Stephanie Rosenbaum that your kids ages eight and up can cook with a little guidance from you. This book also has color illustrations to show you and your kids what to do.

The *America's Test Kitchen Family Cook Book* has everything, including simple recipes, pictures, recommendations of kitchen products, and is all tabbed according to subject.

An old favorite, newly revised, is the *Better Homes and Gardens New Cookbook*. It not only has pictures of many of the recipes, but it also marks some of them "fast" so you know that they are quick to make.

These are just four of the myriad of cookbooks available, so check out the cookbook section of your favorite bookstore to find a few books that look interesting to you.

## TIPS FROM DADS

Here are some cooking tips directly from single dads who have been in your shoes. They are proof that, over time, it does get easier. Eventually you'll have your very own tips to pass along to other single dads. Our interviewees recommended:

- Cut meat, chicken, or fish into small pieces as they cook faster than big pieces.
- Soak pans overnight with dish detergent or dishwasher detergent and you won't have to scrub them as much.
- No time to cut up vegetables? Get your vegetables precut either frozen or at the grocery store's salad bar.
- To get kids to eat vegetables, serve them with low-fat ranch dressing and let them dunk the carrot sticks, zucchini slices, broccoli florets, or tiny tomatoes in the dressing.
- Many communities have businesses where you can assemble a variety of dinners for your freezer so all you have to do when you get home is to pop one in the oven. Everything is chopped, measured, and ready for you to assemble. You just put what you want into the provided containers, pack in your cooler, and take home. If you or your kids don't like olives, you just omit them. If they love brown sugar, add a little more than what the recipe calls for. It's great. Companies include Dinner Done, Dinners Ready, Dream Dinners, and Super Suppers. Some are even open evenings, which is great for single dads who work during the day.
- Take leftover cooked meat, shred it with two forks, and add it to spaghetti before adding sauce. It's a nice change from ground beef.

Cooking really isn't that complicated, and many men discover that they not only enjoy it, they want to keep experimenting with new recipes. Bon appetite.

# Chapter 16

# Fathers Afar

*. . . separation from those we love
shows us, by their loss,
their real value and dearness to us.*
—JEREMIAH BROWN HOWELL

Regardless how the saying goes, out of sight does not mean out of heart. As Brett McWhorter Sember writes in her book, *How to Parent with Your Ex*, "physical distance does not have to mean emotional distance."

## PERCEPTION

When dads don't live near their kids, they miss them terribly and know how much of their children's lives they're missing. But sometimes that is the reality. While according to Nancy Hutcheson Harris, a marital/family law lawyer, it's in the best interest of the children for their dad to live no more than a one to one and a half hours driving distance away, that's not always possible. Sometimes your business or, occasionally, severe problems with your ex causes you to physically move a distance from your children. The commute may make even weekend visits expensive and difficult to arrange.

Joel, a father of three, said, "I have the kids part time. My children used to live fifteen minutes away until their mother moved them forty-five minutes away, so activities are a struggle. Most take place near her and I have to kick and scream for her to agree on letting them participate in soccer and baseball near me. Last year my daughter took hip-hop dance class with her older brother. Anytime you can combine your kids into the same extracurricular activity, it cuts down on the driving and rushing around."

While you may have the kids one week or even most of the summer along with breaks from school and some holidays, you may sense that others often feel that you really aren't that into your children. It hurts and probably makes you both frustrated and angry. But don't waste time and energy trying to prove to others how important your kids are to you. Instead, show your kids by your actions that you love them and treasure the time you do have together.

## SHOW YOUR KIDS THAT DISTANCE DOESN'T DILUTE YOUR LOVE

Don't feel that you have no way to show your kids that you love and care about them when you're separated by miles, possibly even by time zones. Here are some effective ways to demonstrate your love for them, even when you are far away:

- Give them your full attention when you are together. Really listen.
- Be positive. Rather than telling them "I'm sorry we only have this long weekend together, but your mom won't let me have any more," say "I'm glad we're together. What would you like to do?" Then offer suggestions or listen to their ideas. Don't be surprised if they just want to hang out with you raking the leaves and jumping into the piles instead of going to a museum or movie.
- Don't expect everything to go perfectly as planned. Your kid may be whiney, say he's bored, complain about your old car, or actually feel ill and have to stay in bed when it's your turn with him.
- Give your kids a calendar that shows when they will be with you and stick to that schedule unless you are in the hospital or incapacitated in some other way.

## MAKING A HOME AWAY FROM HOME FOR YOUR KIDS

Just because you don't have the kids as often as you'd like, you still need to make them feel welcome when they are with you. Give them some space of their own, even if you're only in a one-bedroom apartment. Here are some ways of doing that:

- Partition off the back part of the living room with a screen or turn the dining area into a space for them.
- If there's no room for bunk beds, get some inflatable beds and make them up with new blankets or quilts.
- Have a dresser that is specifically for their things so they don't have to live out of a suitcase or backpack.
- Buy a disposable camera if you don't have one, and take lots of pictures of them while they're with you. Get the photos framed so the kids will see them on their next visit.

## WAYS TO STAY IN TOUCH

Kevin, the father of two sons, usually had them every other weekend. He said, "In order to stay connected with my sons, I chose to follow some advice I got in counseling while going through the divorce. I was told, basically, to 'date myself,' meaning to do the things I like to do in order to stave off boredom, loneliness, depression, etc. So early on, the boys went with me everywhere I did—playing league softball or basketball, ballgames, friends or family gatherings, whatever.

"This was made more difficult when I chose to move to a larger market for my career. But I made it a point to keep my weekend commitments. All that meant was thousands upon thousands of miles on the cars that I drove (along with hotel and food bills when I went to the town where they lived) and traveling halfway to their home to pick them up when they were to spend the weekend in the city with me. But, as a result, my boys and I have many, many mutual interests and it provides plenty of opportunities for engaging conversations, which keeps us connected."

He adds, "My advice for others is to be true to yourself. Make life decisions based on what's best for you. Stifling yourself professionally or personally, or playing any kind of martyr role (for the sake of the kids) will only lead to unhappiness for which you will ultimately resent your kids. If you are happy, the kids will know it and they'll be happy."

Often, however, the physical distance between you and your kids is far more than forty-five minutes. You may be in a different time zone, at the other end of the country, or in another country altogether. Nevertheless, you can still stay in touch with your kids in a number of ways:

### Telephone

Give them telephone cards so they can call you, but be sure they understand time differences so you don't get a call when you're sound asleep in the middle of the night. If you can receive calls at work, be sure they have your office number as well.

Have an answering machine so your kids can leave a message if you're not in, and be sure to check it daily. Get voice mail on your cell phone as well. If you can afford it, also add call waiting so you can click over to check to see if it's them on the line. What seems like an emergency to them may not seem that important to you, but if it's vital to them, you want to hear about it. It gives your kids an added sense of security to know that although dad is miles away, he is still available to them.

You also might want to get a special beeper number and give it only to your kids, so if they need to talk to you for whatever reason you'll know immediately. A beeper also acts as a fail-safe, second line of reception in case the other technological wonders get hit by lightning or just fail to work out of sheer meanness.

Paul's daughter lives with her mother less than two hours away from him. "I talk to her at least once every day. Sometimes I help her with her homework over the phone, while other times we just talk. I always tell her I love her and she tells me she loves me too."

## Mail

Send them cards and letters if you can count on your ex to properly deliver them to the recipients. Include jokes and cartoons, a description of a funny event that happened to you, a game you went to, or just a note that tells them how important a part they play in your life and how proud you are of them.

You also can send postcards that show special sights in your new community, such as the zoo, unique buildings, a football stadium, the beach, or mountains. Be careful what you write. Remember that your ex (and the postal worker) can read the postcard too.

If you have younger children, send them a bunch of self-addressed and stamped envelopes so they can send you pictures they've drawn.

## Blogs

If you know how, or have a buddy who does, set up a blog especially between you and your kids. You and older kids can keep a running commentary of what's going on in both your lives, so you know if they got the part in the play, how football practice is going, what parties they've gone to,

what their studies are, and whom they are dating.

Talk about movies you've seen, what's going on in your work, and what new restaurants you've gone to that you think they'll enjoy when they come.

## E-mail and Text Messaging

E-mail and text messaging are great if the kids are old enough to use them and if they have access to a computer or cell phone. If they don't have either, ask your ex if you can get one for them or, if expenses are tight, if she would share the cost of one with you. She might also need to contact you on occasion, so it could be an extra form of communication for you both.

## Photos

You can send your kids photos of your home, favorite spots, or activities you're enjoying either by snail mail or by e-mail. Send the kids a disposable camera so they can record their activities as well. They can send the camera to you (in a prestamped and self-addressed envelope) so you can develop the pictures.

## Audio or Videotape Recording

Give your kids a small audio or videotape recorder so they can use it and mail the finished product to you. You'll be surprised at the creativity of some of their productions that may include songs, skits, and interviews with friends. You can do the same for them by recording special messages, reading bedtime stories for little ones, or having someone videotape you at work, in front of your home, or cooking spaghetti. If you're particularly creative, write and sing a song telling them why you love them and think they are great.

## Videoconferencing

This method of staying in touch is beginning to be used more frequently as single dads learn about it. "Virtual visitation," as it is called, is a home computer or standalone video device system that allows you to enjoy a video call. While it's not the same as being there and can never take the place of spending time with your kids in person, virtual visitation does allow you and your kids to hear and see each other in real time. Children are visual in nature, and seeing you as they talk to you is a dramatic improvement over the telephone, especially for young children. It shows that you are there for them and can participate in many activities, including helping with homework and school projects, seeing their school work and art projects, and reinforcing parenting decisions.

This technology requires a computer with a broadband connection, Web cams in both locations, video call software, and a headset with a built-in microphone. For approximately $150 added to each existing computer, you can add a Web cam and headset.

Michael Gough, a computer security specialist, has written a guide to help you set up a virtual visitation in your and your former spouse's home so you can virtual visit your kids when in-person contact isn't possible. Contact Gough through *www. internetvisitation.org* for more information. His additional Web site, *www.videocalltips. com*, provides ratings on many of the solutions available and hardware and software to use.

According to a telephone interview with Gough, "Virtual visitation is nothing more than a tool, like the telephone, that is used as a more effective way to communicate between two or more people when in-person [visits] aren't possible." Virtual visitation is a tool to supplement or replace the

telephone, never to replace in-person visits. Seeing each other is a better form of contact than the telephone, and virtual visitation helps show your children that you're available when they need you.

### Gifts Specific to Their Interests

While you can't buy your kids love, it's okay to send inexpensive gifts that show you know their interests—a book about Ronde and Tiki Barber for your kid who's a football junkie, a video on the Canadian Rockies for a budding geologist, or a coloring book and large box of new crayons for the junior artist in the family.

These all are good ways to let the kids know you're thinking of them even though you're miles away. It makes them feel close to you and strengthens their sense of self-confidence. We all want our parents to be proud of us, and with conscious and continuous input from you they can brag about their dad, even though they don't see you as much as either of you would like.

### Art Projects

If your children are younger, ask them to send you some drawings. Frame their works of art and take photos of the framed drawings hanging in your bedroom, kitchen, or living room. Send them to your child with a note saying how the pictures make you smile every time you see them.

# RELUCTANT TRAVELERS

Sometimes your kids don't want to come for the weekend or summer stay that's scheduled. It's not that they don't want to see you. It's just that there's so much going on at home with their friends.

What happens when it's spring break and your teenage son would rather go to Florida with his buddies than come stay with you? Joseph Grenny, coauthor of *Crucial Conversations*, says "First he [the dad] must refuse to tell himself an ugly story about his son. Dads react poorly *not* because of what their kids do, but because of the stories they tell themselves about what their kids do. When your child seems disinterested in spending spring break with you, you've got two choices. You can tell yourself, 'Of course he's not looking forward to being with me—he has no friends here, and hanging out with an adult is not as fun at his age as it is to be with peers. This is normal. This is okay.' Or you can tell yourself, 'What a selfish jerk. I send money every month to pay for everything he needs, I buy him nice presents, I try to accommodate him—and this is the thanks I get!'

"Your response will be determined *not* by how your son behaves, but by the story you tell yourself about that behavior. Period. If you want to respond judiciously, kindly, and evenly to your son, you'd better first get a handle on your story. When you see him as a normal, decent, reasonable teenager (I know those words sound oxymoronic—but they're not), you're ready to talk."

When you do talk to your son about his visit, be sure to know what your goal is. It should be to have a conversation that serves both of your needs. It's normal for you to want time with your son, and on some level he probably wants that too. Try to devise ways for him to develop friendships where you live, but don't force it. Ask him if he'd occasionally like to bring a friend with him where possible. Do your best to accommodate his desires in a way that also satisfies yours.

Don't wait until a specific occasion arises to have this talk, because it can get emotional. Instead, talk about the long-term plan for his visits in general. Let him know why they're important to you, but also say that you'll understand he'll occasionally have conflicts with the times you get to be with him. Make it a two-way discussion, not a lecture. Get his suggestions on how you both can deal with schedule conflicts and competing desires. By talking to him about how you both will handle these things in advance, and develop some agreements, your son will feel much more responsible to keep those agreements when the schedule conflicts arise.

## ✔ Tip from the Trenches

Mike suggests, "Send little gifts from business trips or things you've found where you live, like a Tampa Bay Buc T-shirt or hat, some sea glass from Maine, or shells from the beach in California. Have someone take a picture of you standing by a giant sequoia, the Space Needle, or in Wrigley Field. The purpose is to give them a visual idea of where you are."

# WHEN KIDS CRISSCROSS THE COUNTRY

Getting the kids from their mom's home to yours may present a plethora of decisions. Do they fly, take a bus, or do you drive and meet their mom half way? What time of day should they travel? When are they old enough to travel alone? How can you make them safe during their journey? These and many other questions have to be answered, not only by you but also by their mom.

## Plane Travel

Fortunately, the question of unaccompanied minors (UMs, as they're known in the trade) has been answered by the airlines themselves. At the present time, airlines will not let any child younger than five years of age (even if only a day or two before that fifth birthday) fly unaccompanied. Most major airlines will only let a five-year-old UM fly if it's on a nonstop flight and require a child to be at least eight to be able to fly as a UM on connecting flights.

You or your ex will have to pay an adult fare, even for that five-year-old. Plus, on most airlines there will be an additional escort fee for the individual charged with the responsibility of getting your child on and settled before takeoff, off the plane, and, in the case of a nondirect flight, supervised and then put on the correct connecting flight. This person also hangs on to your child until you or your designated person picks him or her up at the destination. Here are a number of things you or your ex have to do before your child can fly as a UM:

- Make sure the airline knows (and remembers) that your child is flying as a UM.
- Book a morning or early afternoon flight, especially on nondirect flights, so your child won't have to sleep in a strange hotel with the escort he or she doesn't know if the flights are greatly delayed or canceled.
- Bring a birth certificate as proof of age and whatever other identification the airline requires. You'll have to put in writing the name of the designee, and be sure that it is that person and only that person who picks up your child. If you're the designee and your car breaks down

before getting to the airport, call the airlines as they will not release a child to anyone else.

- Get a special pass if you want to meet your child at the gate.
- Always explain to a child what to expect when flying alone (how to fasten the seat belt, where the bathroom is). Usually the flight attendant will show kids, but sometimes they get busy and forget.
- Remind your preteens that they are to obey the UM rules, one of the most important of which is to stay on the plane until the flight attendant takes them off. If they scoot off with the other deplaning passengers, it worries everyone. The airline has a system; don't let your kids mess it up.
- Be sure to pack some carry-on snacks, books, and other items to keep your child occupied during the flight, but no sharp objects or these will be confiscated just as they are with adults.
- Arrive at the airport early as you'll have forms to fill out.
- Airlines still serving meals may have kids' meals available, but you have to ask for them when you book the ticket.
- Every airline has its own requirements for children traveling alone. Ask your carrier for information.

## Bus Travel

Many of America's small towns are not served by rail or air, so kids traveling alone on buses are familiar sights. Here are some of the Greyhound requirements for unaccompanied children:

- The trip has to be no longer than five hours with no change of bus.
- The entire trip must be done in daylight hours.

- Children ages seven and younger must be accompanied by someone fifteen years old or older (such as a sibling).
- Children ages eight to fourteen may travel alone.
- Children are asked to sit near the driver.
- The parent is required to fill out a form that includes all pertinent information, including who will be meeting the child at the destination. That person must have a government issued photo ID
- There is a $5 additional charge for children who are traveling alone.

For more information about Greyhound, visit www.Greyhound.com. Various bus lines have their own regulations, so be sure to ask age restrictions and other details before you book a ticket. Bus travel is relatively safe as there is only one exit, and since there is a bathroom at the rear of the bus your child does not have to go into the terminal to use the toilet.

### Train Travel

Train travel offers more movement for an active child than a bus or plane and an opportunity to watch the local landscape as the train passes by, but unaccompanied children are relatively unsupervised. To make reservations for unaccompanied minors, you must call Amtrak at 1-800-872-7245. You may not book reservations for UMs on their Web site. Some of Amtrak's requirements include:

- Children fifteen and older may travel unaccompanied but do not qualify for any discounts available for children traveling with adults.
- Children fifteen and older may purchase tickets on their own from a ticket agent or conductor if they present a valid photo ID.

- Children seven years of age and younger may not travel alone. They must be accompanied by a person fifteen years old or older who has responsibility for the child.
- Children ages eight to fourteen may travel unaccompanied with the following restrictions, courtesy of www.Amtrak.com:
  - Travel is permitted only on Amtrak trains and is not permitted on Thruway motorcoach service or on any other connecting services.
  - The scheduled departure time may be no earlier than 6 A.M. and arrival time no later than 9 P.M.
  - No transfers of any kind are permitted.
  - Both boarding and arrival stations must be staffed. (Please note that even certain staffed stations don't allow for unaccompanied minors.)
  - An adult at least eighteen years of age must bring the child who will be traveling as a UM to the station. The adult and child must both be at the boarding station at least one hour prior to departure to allow for the required interview and to complete necessary forms. The adult must provide a valid current ID that meets Amtrak's ID policies.
  - Amtrak requires that the child be interviewed. On the day of travel, a station agent or other appropriate authority will directly interview the child to determine whether the child is capable of traveling alone.
  - For each unaccompanied minor, the adult bringing the child to the departure station must complete and sign a release form.
  - The child must wear an Amtrak-issued wristband for the duration of travel.

- The adult must remain at the station until the train has departed.
- Upon arrival, an adult (at least eighteen years old) must be present to pick up the child. The adult must display valid current identification meeting Amtrak's ID policies.
- Full adult fares are charged.
- The unaccompanied child may not have any life-threatening food allergies.
- Be sure your child knows at which stop to get off the train as the conductor may be in another car at each destination.

## Travel by Car

If your home isn't too far from your ex's home, perhaps you both could agree to drive halfway and meet at some designated spot. Be sure to identify that spot carefully so you aren't waiting at one McDonald's or Wendy's and she's at another with both of you getting angry.

# PART THREE

# GETTING YOUR LIFE BACK

# Chapter 17

# Handling Emotional Issues and Reaching Out for Therapy

*Time cools, time clarifies;*
*no mood can be maintained*
*quite unaltered*
*through the course of hours.*
—THOMAS MANN

It's unlikely that you'll get through your first few years of being a single father without some emotional turmoil, some on your own right, some triggered through dealing with your kids and their issues, and some arising from disagreements with your ex if you're single because of divorce. As with any loss, you are grieving and have the right to do so. You feel as though you have failed at something very important to you and it may be an emotion you haven't experienced very often.

Despite who or what triggered the final decision to divorce, there are bound to be some regrets that "'til death do us part" only meant the death of the marriage, and that the exciting, giddy, and long-range plans you both made when you got engaged died as well.

Your father may not have told you, but boys do cry. It's a human emotion. You may find your eyes filling with tears at the grocery store when you pass by the sugared cereals your kids clamor for or actually bursting into tears when you see kids playing baseball and you're not there to watch yours play. According to Barbara Montague, psychotherapist, "The emotional bond during the divorce process is the hardest bond to let go. Most men don't know what to feel. I tell my male clients, 'There are times when we cry. It's okay to cry.'"

## LONELINESS

It's only natural that you'll feel lonely at times, especially when it's nighttime or over a holiday and your kids aren't with you. You miss their constant clutter, their exhausting bickering and complaining, and, of course, their kisses and the way they look like perfect angels when you tuck them in at night. It would be unusual if you didn't feel some sense of loss due to the lack of companionship or not having another adult in the room to talk to.

## DEPRESSION

The months after a divorce are an adaptation period for you. You've suffered a loss and you need to give yourself some healing time. You may find that you're experiencing fatigue, a sense of sadness, some difficulty sleeping, and a loss of appetite. Perhaps you even wake up tired and have to drag yourself to work. Nothing seems like fun anymore, and it just seems like too much effort to get something to eat so you don't. Your underwear piles up on the bedroom floor and, rather than washing it (which would require your learning how to use a washing machine), you just buy more.

Some of our interviewees expressed the way they felt that everything was moving in slow motion. These experiences are called situational or reactive depression, and it's normal when you're grieving. Psychologist Ganz Ferrance suggests, "You need time to feel your feelings, but don't head for the nearest bar and spill your feelings out to the bartender. Instead, make an appointment with a qualified psychologist, psychiatrist, or social worker." See the latter part of this chapter for more advice about utilizing therapy.

### Drinking and Illegal Drugs

Depression can also cause you to lose interest in your work and to drink more alcohol than usual, a dangerous activity, especially if you drink and drive. Overindulging in alcohol and using illegal drugs can be extremely dangerous when your kids are with you (and also when they're not with you) and could cause you to lose whatever custody you enjoy with them. Usually this type of situational depression eases as time passes and you take on new interests. But if it lasts more than a few weeks and you feel your drinking or drug use is getting out of hand, make arrangements to see a mental health professional.

## ANGER

Anger is another normal and human emotion and its power may both surprise and frighten you. Perhaps the divorce was initiated by your ex-wife, not you. You feel as though you did everything to make your marriage work and resent that your efforts failed. But anger is a dangerous emotion. Uncontrolled anger hurts you and it hurts your children, who will sense your anger and be frightened of it. Often, they'll think it's directed at them, or as they get older they'll learn to mimic or to use the destructive expression of anger as power in their own relationships.

## BE PATIENT WITH YOURSELF

The bottom line is that you can't rush to end or suppress these emotions you're feeling. Like the grief a widower struggles with, dealing with this cornucopia of feelings that come about from divorce is a process that you'll have to let time work its magic on. Unfortunately, there's no timetable, and trying to ignore the emotions or burying them by working longer hours or using alcohol or drugs to make you forget only makes the pain worse. Try to get through one day at a time. Let yourself have some enjoyment without feeling guilty, even it's only an ice-cream treat or watching a DVD. Dr. Ferrance warns that you shouldn't "latch onto the first woman you see. You're in no condition to be a good partner until six

months to at least year-and-a-half after your divorce. And it can be longer, depending on the individual. If you rush it, you may repeat the same mistakes."

But don't be surprised or disappointed if just when you thought you were getting back to your old "normal" self that some of these overpowering, debilitating emotions return and in stronger form. Most importantly, if you find that you're having difficulty handling the emotional roller coaster that occurs when a marriage ends (and most people do), don't hesitate to get professional help from a qualified counselor.

## WHEN TO CONTACT A MENTAL HEALTH COUNSELOR

Despite what you may remember from your football coach's bark of "No pain, no gain," the manly thing to do is not to try to tough it out. You may need some help, especially if you have two or more of these symptoms:

- Feeling of sadness that just won't go away
- Trouble sleeping (or want to sleep all the time)
- Losing interest in your job and previously enjoyed activities
- Diminished appetite or wanting to eat everything in sight
- Just feeling stuck

If any two or more of the above symptoms sound like the way you're feeling, seek out a mental health counselor.

It doesn't mean you're a basket case, a nut, or are crazy; it means you're human. While your family or buddies may be supportive, you probably would do better finding a qualified mental health counselor. These professionals have been trained to help people in crises, people who are hurting. What's equally important is that whatever you share with your therapist, unlike with friends or relatives, is confidential, so you don't need to be concerned that he or she is inadvertently gossiping about you or what you've talked about.

## WHERE TO FIND A QUALIFIED MENTAL HEALTH EXPERT

Don't wait until you find yourself totally overwhelmed by your emotions or feel as though everyone, including your kids, would be better off without you. You can find a qualified therapist through the following means:

- Contact the American Psychologists Association at 1-800-964-2000; in Canada, contact the Canadian Psychologist Association at 1-888-424-0297.
- If you've lived in a community for a while, ask a friend who has recently been divorced or widowed for a recommendation of a psychologist, social worker, marriage counselor, or member of the clergy whom they have used and found helpful. In doing such a search, you'll be amazed at the number of people who have walked in your shoes. Actually, most of us from time to time have needed a helping hand or a shoulder to cry on.
- Check with your divorce attorney, if you had one, as many of them refer clients to qualified counselors.
- Contact the Catholic Social Services and the Jewish Social Services.
- Contact your local crisis center.
- Contact your minister, rabbi, priest, or physician and ask for recommendations.

- Check the Web site of your state or province's psychological association.

Some insurance policies cover the cost of a therapist, but often you will have to pay out of pocket for their services. Don't hesitate to get counseling just because you learn that your insurance won't pay for it. Many therapists are willing to work out some type of payment schedule for you or will help you find a social service agency where you can get counseling and pay on a sliding scale. When you're hurting, get help, just as you would if you had broken a bone or had pneumonia. It's important to help you gain your mental health.

Although your kids may require some grief counseling too, remember to put yourself first. If you're struggling with your own emotions, it will be more difficult for you to help the kids with theirs unless you all go in for family counseling, which in some cases may be helpful.

The most important point to remember is that it's always okay to ask for help. It's a sign of strength, not weakness.

## WHAT TO EXPECT IN THERAPY

Don't expect the stereotypical therapist you see on television and in the movies. You won't lie down on a couch and talk about your earliest memory or discuss why your mother loved your brother best. Instead, you'll probably sit in a comfortable chair with the therapist sitting opposite you. After a few minutes of general conversation, the therapist will probably say something like, "Well, what brings you here today?"

As the therapeutic hour is only fifty minutes, think about what your pressing concerns may be. Is it that you're lonely, feel depressed, are concerned that you can't be a good father to your kids on your own, or just that you can't make sense of what's happened to your life? It could be none of the above or all of it and more.

This is a time to be completely open and honest if you want help. Don't worry that the therapist may be shocked by what you're saying. Experienced mental health counselors have heard it all (and much worse) before.

You'll probably learn some techniques to change your thinking and your behavior, ways to handle problems in a new and more productive way, and get advice to specific questions. Unless your therapist is a psychiatrist (a physician specializing in psychiatry), he or she cannot prescribe antidepressants or other drugs and will contact a physician if necessary.

# Chapter 18

# Solving Custody Issues

*Let me tell you the secret
that has led me to my goal;
My strength lies solely
in my tenacity.*
—LOUIS PASTEUR

You might think that once the judge has approved your custody arrangements everything is set in stone. But it isn't. Custody decisions can be modified when there are substantial changes in circumstances that are material, involuntary, permanent, and unanticipated. The guiding principle is always what is in the best interest of the child. Issues keep popping up like sand flies on the beach and sometimes are just as irritating. But remember, TOYK (think of your kids). Agree to be as flexible as possible for their sake and hope that their mother will do the same.

## TYPES OF CUSTODY

After parents separate, they usually maintain shared parental responsibility of the children, meaning they share information about their children's welfare and make major decisions about the children jointly. Obviously, it works better if the parents can put their anger and differences aside and communicate frequently and responsibly.

### Sole Parental Responsibility

This restriction of one parent's right to continued involvement with his or her child is seldom used unless there is a history of abuse—sexual, physical, or very serious emotional or verbal abuse—or there is a substantial alcohol or drug abuse problem. In these cases, only the parent with sole custody makes decisions concerning the kids' welfare, and time-sharing with the other parent is typically limited in duration and is supervised at all times by an agreed upon adult or qualified agency.

### Primary Residential Custody

With this type of custody arrangement, the children are more often in one home, especially overnight, than in the other. One might describe the primary residence as the home in which the children keep their pillows. This is the more historically traditional form of sharing time between two parents and two households. This is usually a negotiated agreement between you and your ex. If you both can't agree, the judge will decide based on what's in the best interest of the child or children. The most typical schedule for the nonprimary parent is every other weekend and Wednesday evenings. A week or so in the summer may be given to the noncustodial parent.

### Rotating Custody

You may know this as *joint custody* or *shared physical custody*. This is the model that prevails as the more typical and accepted type of custody arrangement and is most successful when both parents can communicate effectively with each other. What it means is that the so-called primary custody shifts from parent to parent. One parent is not the primary residential provider, you and your ex both are.

"We prefer to use the term, 'time sharing,' rather than 'visitation,' which sounds so distant when referring to your own children," says Nancy Harris, a marital family law attorney. "In the Tampa Bay area, rotating custody is becoming more common especially in dual professional households, where divided responsibility is a practical necessity. This is often the type of custody with younger fathers who are used to being involved in the care and nurturing of their children. In most cases the father has the children at his home more than 40 percent of the overnights and receives the associated substantial reduction in child support provided by the Florida statutory child support guidelines."

There may be different schedules in rotating custody—every other week; three nights with the kids, four nights without, then four nights with; and so on. Be sure that whatever your time-sharing schedule may be, both parents are listed as emergency contacts at your kids' school, sports' team information sheet, and virtually any other place your kids could be and get hurt.

## ACT LIKE A GROWNUP, EVEN IF YOU DON'T WANT TO

There will be many times while working out custody arrangements when you'll need to think before you act or speak. Just remember you're a grownup and a role model for your kids. That means you'll do a lot of compromising for their sake. If possible, arrange holiday celebrations so both you and your ex can be with the children for either part of the day, the evening before, or, if you both can handle it, share the event.

Remember that the quality time everyone speaks so highly of doesn't just mean when you have your kids with you. Go back to Chapter 16 to get ideas on how you can still be involved in their lives when they're with their mother through the telephone, e-mail, and even virtual visitation. Attend their school and extracurricular activities. If you and their mom are comfortable with the idea, sit together. It will make your kids pleased because they'll know that, although you no longer want to be married to each other, you can be united when it comes to them. And that's a good feeling for kids. Also recognize that your children may feel lonely for their mother, even though they adore you and are in your custody. Be gracious and willing for them to call her when they need to.

## NOTHING IS CARVED IN STONE

What if you're not happy with the custody arrangements you previously had agreed upon? Maybe you were still in shock or perhaps you just had a lousy lawyer.

See if you and your ex can privately agree on your having the kids more often. She actually may be happy to have a little more free time of her own and compromise with you. If you can keep the changes between the two of you, that's great. Try not to have to go back to court to change custody unless there are overwhelming reasons, such as her boyfriend being abusive to your kids, alcoholism, or mental illness. When you bring lawyers in, it not only is expensive (to your wallet and to your continuing parenting relationship), it also creates tremendous tension for your kids to see you both arguing to that degree as they, despite everything, still love you both very much.

# Chapter 19

# Managing Money Matters and Insurance

*It's good to have money and the things that money can buy,
but it's good, too, to check up once in a while
and make sure that you haven't lost
the things that money can't buy.*

—GEORGE HORACE LORIMER

Which spouse were you? Were you the one who opened and paid the bills or the one who seldom, if ever, saw them? If you were the one who paid all the bills, the transition to being single and having to handle this chore should be relatively easy, other than that you'll have less money to pay them with and you'll have less time in which to do it. On the other hand, if you left the bill paying to your ex it may feel as though you are adding another full-time job to your already increasingly busy new life. The bills keep coming in and you have to check to see if you paid them last week and whether you already resubscribed when magazines send so many "subscription due" notices.

But as you'll soon discover, writing checks or paying your bills online is the easy part. There are other tasks—important finance-related tasks—that you must tackle right away.

Russ admitted, "I think the economics of the whole thing overwhelmed me at first. It was an amicable divorce, but the cost of two sets of everything caught me by surprise . . . clothes for the kids, bedding, dishes, furniture, TV, and so on. We're constantly negotiating on money matters and who pays what is often determined by our respective incomes. It takes communication and compromise. You're not going to get everything you want . . . but then neither is she."

Eric added, "Communication with my ex was originally strained. However, once the financial stuff was agreed upon, it has become much better and a degree of normalcy has returned/begun."

## HOW TO CLEAN UP OLD CREDIT PROBLEMS

Credit scores make the world go round. While maybe this was never the title of a hit song, once you enter the divorced world, you need to make sure that any credit problems from your ex don't follow you. According to the article "Why Divorce and Bankruptcy Often Go Hand in Hand" on *www .AllLaw.com* by Celeste Marchand, ". . . if your ex-spouse doesn't pay his or her share of the debts, the creditor can come after you for payment. If your ex files for bankruptcy after the divorce, the creditors will look to you to satisfy those debts." Ouch!

Most married couples open a number of accounts during their years of marriage—a Home Depot charge card to get twelve months free interest; the balance transfer from the credit card and myriad other credit cards piling up in the dresser, still active but unused and forgotten; the local department store card; the jewelry store; and so on. If you haven't already taken your ex off the authorization of those accounts (and telling her in advance so she can open new ones in her name only), do so immediately. You don't want to still be listed on your ex's charge card as a co-borrower in case she goes on a major shopping spree and can't or decides not to pay the bill.

As you move forward, knowing your credit score will be very important when you're buying a new house, a new car, or even opening your single-name charge cards. Monitoring that credit score for positive and negative changes is also vital for staying on top of any credit that might erroneously be opened in your name. All of the large credit agencies have monitoring services that will notify you anytime your credit is checked or any new accounts are opened in your name. For a cost of $10 a month, this is a service that is well worth it to any newly divorced person. Contact Experian (*www.Experian.com*), Equifax (*www.Equifax.com*), or Transunion (*www .Transunion.com*) through their Web sites for more information on their services. Most of the services e-mail you once a month with your updated credit score and will e-mail any changes to your credit profile.

Additionally, when you first sign up you get a listing of all current charge cards and liability accounts that are in your name or joint name with your ex-spouse. This is a great way to help you make sure that you have closed all of those joint accounts so that there are no unforeseen liabilities that rear their ugly heads. (Just make sure that you notify your ex before you close an account as she may be currently using the card without knowing that it is a joint account. You wouldn't want her to be at dinner with your kids or paying for a prescription for one of them when the credit card suddenly gets rejected.)

## UPDATE ESTATE DOCUMENTS

"What estate?" you may ask. Guess you've already figured out that two (plus kids) apart really can't live cheaper than two together. But you do have important legal documents that need to be changed and you need to handle that task immediately, even though you may not feel much like doing so. Estate planning is not just for multi-millionaires. While there is certainly a lot more for you to do in estate planning if you are wealthy, an estate merely defines all of your possessions, investments, and properties that are in your name. Every person has an estate of some type, and you want to make sure it is properly set up.

### A Will

When you have children, you need to have a will! This is mandatory for the protection of your children. Go to an attorney; it is a necessity. Your will, among other things, dictates what happens to your per-sonal belongings, house, and possessions at the time of your death. If you already have a will, you probably listed your ex as beneficiary of the majority of your belongings, which means if you don't change the beneficiary she still would inherit everything upon your death. Obviously it is very important to update your will as soon as your divorce is final. If you don't have a lawyer or your former lawyer was your ex's sister, brother, mother, or father, ask friends or colleagues to recommend attorneys they've used and have been happy with their services.

### Children's Guardianship

The guardianship of your children is also a planning area you need to address. Though the chances of you and your ex both dying at the same time is slim now that you're divorced, stranger things have happened. This is an item that you need to discuss with your ex because it obviously has large lasting consequences if it were ever to occur. You don't want your will to say the kids will be raised by Aunt Sally while your ex's will says they will be raised by her second cousin Jane. It would set up a nasty legal battle at a time that your kids certainly would need stability in their lives.

Keep in mind, however, that the "children of divorce subject to guardianship" issue is up to the courts discretion of what's in the best interest of the child. This means that if something happens to you and your ex-spouse and you both have different people listed as guardians in that situation, the court will decide which person or third party is best for the children to live with.

### Additional Changes in Beneficiary

Be sure to also change the beneficiary on your 401(k) and IRA accounts. We've heard many stories of men getting remarried and not replacing the first wife on the IRA beneficiary form with the second wife before they pass away. It doesn't create a happy situation.

### Living Will

Another estate document you need to update is your living will. This is the document that states what happens to you if you are incapacitated. You probably don't want your ex-wife to have the power to pull your plug!

In wealthier situations where trusts have been established, you need to meet with your attorney and really update things. Though you can't change any of the irrevocable trusts you may have established, you want to make sure your revocable trusts flow the direction that you really intend them to flow. Remember that if estate taxes are an issue for you, you now don't have your ex-wife's unified credit to use. You'll need to craft some other techniques with your attorney to make sure your kids don't have to pay a large estate tax.

### Life Insurance

Whether you are wealthy or not, life insurance is something that is mandatory for the sake of your kids. While no one really likes to think about death, do you like the thought of your kids struggling financially if something were to happen to you? Remember that the child support or alimony that you pay your ex is something that she relies on to support your kids. If something happens to you, how will she continue to pay her bills? Term life insurance is a very easy solution that costs very little money. At this writing, a healthy thirty-five-year-old male who doesn't smoke can get $250,000 in a twenty-year term policy for $200 per year. (If you smoke, this is a great time to stop.) Check the Internet or call an insurance agent, but put the protection in place for your kids' sake. If you are worried that

your ex will spend the money imprudently if something does happen to you, put someone else in charge of the money for the benefit of your kids or set up a trust that the money would go into and make someone you have faith in named as the trustee.

## HEALTH INSURANCE

Health insurance is another item that often sneaks up on people when they get divorced. If the family's health insurance was through your employer, then your wife will need to come off the policy and find her own coverage or COBRA (the 1986 Consolidated Omnibus Budget Reconciliation Act) that contains provisions giving workers and their families, under certain conditions including divorce, the right to temporary continuation of health coverage at group rates from your company for up to eighteen months at her expense.

As long as your kids were on your plan before the divorce, they will still be on your plan after. If the health coverage was set up through your ex-wife's employer, make sure you get coverage. You also would have the ability to pay for coverage through COBRA benefits for up to eighteen months, or if your employer offers coverage you can be added to your employer's plan. Keep in mind that even though most health plans only allow enrollment once a year, divorce and subsequent termination of an ex-spouses coverage is considered a "life event" that allows enrollment within ninety days of the qualifying event.

If neither you nor your wife has health insurance benefits where you work, you need to be sure your kids are covered. Call 1-877-kids-now for information about health insurance for low-income families with kids.

# REVIEW YOUR RETIREMENT SITUATION

Whether you become a single father at twenty-five or forty-five, the divorce and impending single life ahead will play havoc in your retirement analysis (especially if you got taken to the cleaners in the divorce). Retirement is something that everyone looks forward to, and you should already be contributing to a 401(k) or IRA account. After a divorce and the subsequent shakeup of your financial affairs, it's important for you to get a sense of how realistic your retirement assumptions are compared to the current savings level you have attained.

There are numerous ways to assess the current state of your retirement goals. The Internet offers many online calculators, plus you can purchase software that can give you projections and show you how much you need to start saving. If you have more sizable assets, you may want to consider securing the services of a certified financial planner to put a financial plan together for you. This plan helps assess all aspects of your financial life and gives you a great snapshot of where you are currently at. Their guidance can help you monitor your progress as you move forward. You can find a certified financial planner in your area at *www.cfpboard.org*.

### Do You Need to Increase Your Savings Substantially Now?

When you complete your retirement analysis, you'll probably find that you need a sizable amount in savings to meet your retirement projections. Don't get intimidated. Start small. Your expenses across the board have obviously gone up substantially, so the aspect of savings might be difficult. Start with twenty-five dollars a month automatically invested out of your check-ing account into a diversified mutual fund. (Don't figure you'll save whatever's leftover from your monthly budget, because there seldom is any.) Raise the amount every few months. What you'll find is that since it is being withdrawn automatically you don't even miss it. As you get more comfortable with your new expenses, you can begin to work on increasing the savings to get near those retirement calculations.

### Saving for Your Kids' College or Your Retirement: Which Is It?

How does your college planning look for your kids? If you're like most people, divorced or not, the answer to that question is not so good. College costs in this country are rising at an astronomical level, and the need for a parent to begin saving for college for their children at an early age is paramount in order to not affect the parents' retirement assumptions materially. Too often parents pull money from their retirement accounts to pay for the expense of their children's college. While this is extremely generous, it pushes the parents' ability to retire back many more years than if they would have planned accordingly when their children were younger.

There are some very effective and efficient ways for you to begin to build up the savings for the kids' college years that are very similar to the way you are slowly building up balances for your retirement in a 401(k), IRA, or other retirement savings vehicles. The most common tactic today to save for children's college expenses is the use of a section 529 plan. These are college savings plans in which you, grandparents, or other relatives can deposit as little a twenty-five dollars a month. The deposits in the 529 plans are invested in a basket of mutual funds, similar to your 401(k) at work. Any earnings in the investments grow on a tax-free basis as long as the money is withdrawn for qualified educational expenses. That means if you start a 529 plan when your child is one year old and it grows in value significantly until your child is eighteen and heading off to school, all gains in the investments are withdrawn and no tax is owed to Uncle Sam.

Keep in mind, though, that if the expenses are not used for qualified educational expenses, there is a 10 percent penalty on any distribution and you pay ordinary income taxes on the gains. There are many 529 plans offered by many different states. If you live in a state with a state income tax, there may be some tax benefits to using your own state's plan. The best resource for 529 plan information is logging onto *www.savingforcollege.com* and looking state by state for the 529 plan that best fits your needs.

There are some other savings plans in place for educational expenses, such as Coverdell education savings accounts and uniform gift to minors accounts. Each of these has its own benefits and limitations. Consult your financial or tax adviser for the plan that makes the most sense for your situation.

## WAYS TO REDUCE EXPENSES

It's probably fair to say that after the divorce you may find that money is a little tight as you begin to furnish a separate home, find child-care services, and do your own grocery shopping. Here are some tips to help you reduce your expenses:

- Budget, budget, budget. Use a computer program like Quicken or Microsoft Money to keep an accurate record of your spending.
- Pay your bills on time to prevent exorbitant late charges.

- Select two credit cards and destroy the others so you're not tempted to use them too.
- Check your bills carefully. Even banks have been known to make mistakes not in your favor. Keep your receipts.
- Be smart at the ATM machine. Don't take twenty dollars out five times a week when you're paying a one dollar and fifty cents surcharge every time. That's 7.5 percent surcharge. Instead, go once a week and take out what you need for the week. A $100 withdrawal with the same surcharge is only 1.5 percent. Just make sure you have willpower to not spend money just because you have it in your pocket.
- If you need dress shirts, buy a few of the kind that don't need pressing if you take them out of the dryer right away. You'll save a great deal in cleaning bills that will more than pay for the shirts.
- Buy perishable foods only in the amount you and your kids will eat before they spoil (the food, not the kids).
- Barter, borrow, or rent equipment that you seldom use, rather than buying.
- Service your car regularly to keep it in running order and to prevent large repair bills.
- Always make a list of what you need, especially when you're shopping at stores like Wal-Mart and Target. Otherwise, you'll find yourself just wandering up and down the aisles of these amazing superstores and end up buying things just because they look so appealing that you figure you can use them somewhere.

## THE UPS AND DOWNS OF CHILD SUPPORT

Child support is determined by the court according to a complex formula that differs from state to state. It is based on the number of children you have, their ages, both parents' incomes, and how long each of you have the kids with you. Chances are that if you make a great deal more than your ex, you'll end up paying more than what her actual expenses with the kids really are. If you and your ex can agree without the court getting involved, you may be happier with the result.

You can either pay the child support directly to your ex, or, as in many states, the amount is deducted from your paycheck and sent to a specific state agency, which in turn sends it to your ex.

Remember that you are legally obligated to pay child support for your kids. This holds true even if you move to a different state. In fact, the 1992 Child Support Recovery Act makes it a federal crime to try to avoid paying your child support by changing your state residency. And no, it won't do you any good to file for bankruptcy because you'll still be liable for your child support payments.

The amount that you pay, however, is not etched in stone. It can be changed by the court if your income is drastically reduced or if you suddenly win the Powerball lottery and are stuffing your mattress with thousands of bills with Ben Franklin's face on them. If in doubt, check with your attorney.

## SEPARATE YOUR EMOTIONS FROM CHILD SUPPORT

You may bridle with resentment every month as you write a check to your ex for child support, your kid's tuition, or music lessons. Hopefully you were able to negotiate that your ex would pay half or at least some of the latter two items. But if not, focus on how important they are to your child. Remember that mantra TOYK, and think of your kid.

Don't punish your youngster by sending the check late, "forgetting" to sign it, or waiting until your ex has to ask for it. Don't make her beg. It doesn't mean "you're the man." It means you're hurting your child, and that's not manly behavior.

### Expenditures to Avoid

Don't try to buy your kids love. They need you, your attention, and knowledge of your love and respect. Don't be tempted to buy them expensive gifts (that your ex may not be able to afford) to show that you love them more. Using money to try to buy affection will lead to bigger problems down the line.

## TEACHING YOUR KIDS ABOUT MONEY

Hopefully you and your ex share the same values about money and how to use it. Regretfully, that's not always the case. But now that you're a single parent, you have the opportunity to teach the kids your thoughts and values toward money, and if they're different from their mom's, you can gently remind them that people often feel differently about the same subject. This is just how you feel about it.

### Allowances: Who Pays, How Much, and Why They're Important

The best way to teach children about the value of money is to give them an allowance with which to experiment. It's best to start when they're about five or six, but better at any age than not at all.

Announce at a family meeting that each child will be receiving an allowance each week. Experts disagree on the amount to give and often offer complicated formulas to consider. Neale S. Godfrey, author of *Money Doesn't Grow on Trees*, suggests making their allowance the same number of dollars as their age. While four dollars may seem like a lot for a four-year-old, thirteen dollars doesn't go too far for a thirteen-year-old. The best and simplest way is to give less than they would like and enough so they can save a little, spend a little, and perhaps make a little mistake.

If your children are old enough, have them make out a budget, one that includes movies, magazines, makeup, some clothes, and charity. Some parents advise giving teenagers a large enough allowance so they can budget to buy clothes and still save up for the must haves in the ever-changing technological field.

Check out prices before you determine an amount. Be realistic as to the cost of things today. It makes no sense, for example, to give a teenager four dollars a week when movies, a snack, or a book cost far more than that.

Hopefully you and your ex can work out who pays for the allowance or split the cost. If she refuses, however, don't deprive your kids of this important experience of learning to handle money and the value of things.

### The Big Debate: Is Allowance Payment for Chores or Part of Being in a Family?

You'll find that experts also disagree as to whether an allowance is "work for pay," as Godfrey contends, or if it's money that's given to children because they're a valued member of the family. Whatever premise you ascribe to, if youngsters feel they need extra money for the latest electronic game or fad outfit, you should have a list of extra chores that can be carried out in return for payment.

What about being responsible for chores? Doing chores around the house is also part of being a valued member of a family, but it should be expected and not tied into children's allowance any more than you should expect payment for fixing their dinner, driving them to practice, or staying up to comfort them when they haven't made the team or have experienced an emotional breakup.

## THE EMOTIONAL ASPECT OF MONEY

Money is a fascinating subject for most, whether you've had too much or too little. It's the focus of plots for popular movies, books, and television shows and is often the motive for murder. It breaks up friendships when it's loaned, families when wills are read, and frequently becomes the pinch point in otherwise friendly divorces.

People on national television talk shows freely discuss their sexual problems, addictions, family issues, and mental health difficulties, but seldom, if ever, will many folks open up publicly to describe their finances, not even their salaries. Why? Because they say "it's too personal."

Most people agree that it's difficult to talk about money without emotions coming into play. One of the reasons for that reticence is the family attitude toward money that you were raised with. For some, going to bed with the pillow over their head to keep from hearing echoes of parents arguing over money was a familiar bedtime routine. For others, money was a mysterious subject (like sex) that was never discussed within the children's hearing. Still others recall their mother keeping a little of the grocery money as her rightful "mad money" and winking at the kids as she whispered, "Don't tell your father." (These moms were usually more creative in ways to juggle the checkbook than the most skilled bookkeepers around.) Some grew up with the mantra "If it costs more, it's got to be better" or "What are you saving it for?" while others heard "Do you think I'm made of money?" or "It's too expensive."

Toby recalled, "My father made good money, but he was a gambler. My junior year of college, he gambled away my tuition. I had to take a board job at one of the sororities. It wasn't that hard work, but it taught me to never depend on anyone else for money. It makes me want my kids to work for what they get, a policy my ex and I still fight about. It's not that I'm cheap; I just want them to know the value of their labor."

## BE FLEXIBLE

What if you learn that your child needs braces, speech therapy, or was selected to go to a summer theatre program or all-star baseball camp? If it isn't in your original agreement, are you going to say, "Hell, no. I'm not paying"?

Hopefully not. Instead, sit down with your ex if you can, or both of you meet with an objective financial adviser. Stick to the single objective issue at hand and don't get sidetracked by commenting on her new car or her other expensive recent purchases that you're aware of. Work out how much each of you can afford to pay for your child's unexpected expenses. If the youngster is old enough, encourage him or her to also earn some money to add to the pot. Chances are this won't be the last time some financial issue you hadn't counted on comes up, so you need to be flexible and consider all the possibilities.

It may be that you and your ex can't find the extra dollars, even if you both would like to. If you have to say no to your child, which is okay, try to come up with a plan to make it work in the future. But the reality is that kids need to understand that despite parents' love and desire to help, not every desire can be fulfilled. Nor should it be.

It's important for your kids to know that even though their parents are divorced, they're willing to work together to help their child. Neither of you should come off as the bad guy. Don't harp on the fact that you had to cancel your vacation or forgo moving into a bigger apartment or house in order to pay for this sudden expense. Never make your kids feel guilty; let them feel confident that their parents want to do as much for them as they can.

So much of dealing with money matters is like dealing with life itself: listening to the needs of the other person, being creative and willing to compromise, and keeping your priorities straight. TOYK.

# Deali
# Family (

Although you and your kids' mother have divorced, you haven't divorced your children nor, hopefully, their mother's parents. Kids need all the grandparents they can enjoy, as long as the grandparents are supportive of you.

Go out of your way to try to preserve healthy relations with your ex's extended family for the sake of your kids. They still need to experience the love and support from those grandparents, aunts and uncles, and cousins. Family is important, so stifle your pride, if necessary, and make the first move to smooth over any rough spots with your former in-laws. Set the ground rules that you won't talk about the circumstances of the divorce, even if a brother confesses to you privately that he never liked your ex either. Bite your tongue. TOYK.

## WHY GRANDPARENTS ARE IMPORTANT

All relatives, but especially grandparents, can become a stabilizing influence in their grandchildren's lives. Grandparents are, like your kids, a generation removed from you and your ex, and by being so, hopefully, they can remain somewhat above the fray. Grandparents on both sides can reassure your children that, despite the divorce, they are still loved by everyone who loved them before, that the divorce was not the kids' fault in any way, that nothing they did caused it, and that you and your ex both still love them deeply. Grandparents can emphasize that although the children's parents have divorced each other, they have not divorced their children and that the extended family remains as intact for them as it was before the divorce. You and your ex may have said the same things to your children, but it may get through to your kids when others repeat it.

## YOURS AND HERS

That being said, don't be surprised if things seem a little strained between you and your ex-wife's family at first. Even if the divorce was her idea, her family may have heard a different story from her or she may have embellished what actually took place, making you the bad guy.

If you were the one who wanted to leave the marriage, her family may harbor extreme ill feelings toward you and make you out to be a villain and vow that you'll never darken their door again. Nevertheless, these same people, who may have thought you were terrific before the divorce, are still your children's grandparents, aunts and uncles, and cousins. You need to be the adult and try to pass the peace pipe even if they are still smoking. Keep trying for your children's sake, and perhaps one day your ex-in-laws may quietly admit that you are still terrific, or at least not so bad.

It helps to remind yourself that members of her family are still part of your kids' family and will always be so. Reassure your ex's family, either face to face or in writing, that you'll encourage the children's continued relationship with them even when the kids are with you. Your kids have enough changes in their lives and need the positive support of their grandparents and other relatives on both sides of the family. Even if her family lives in a different part of the country, encourage them to call (even when the kids are with you), write, e-mail, and otherwise remain in the children's life as they were before.

Also be sure to let her family know when your kids are going to be in a school program, sporting events, award assemblies, or any other type of celebration when they're with you, even if your ex-relatives don't plan to attend. They're still your child's relatives.

Besides, that way they'll never be able to say, "He didn't even tell us that she was in a play at school."

## WHEN IT WORKS, IT'S WONDERFUL

But it need not always be adversarial. Russ, who is divorced with two kids, says he not only still calls his ex-mother-in-law "Mom," but he is also her lawyer and still does work for her. While that type of a relationship seems to be in the minority of those we've interviewed, it is certainly one that makes it easier for the kids who don't have to worry if they want to tell you something funny that happened at their mom's parents' house or need help to buy a special birthday card for a member of her side of the family.

Bert Kruger Smith, author of *Grandparenting in Today's World*, says this type of relationship works only if the grandparents "are determined that they will maintain loving relationships with the children of divorced parents [and] maintain a nonjudgmental attitude concerning the divorce. Taking sides with either parent or discussing either parent negatively with the grandchild can diminish chances that the grandparents will be able to reenter a familial relationship with the children."

Do everything in your power to maintain your children's relationship with both sets of their grandparents. It offers them continued security. The importance of grandparents in a child's life cannot be minimized. In his book *The 8th Habit*, Stephen R. Covey writes, "The most essential role of grandparents is to communicate, in as many ways as possible, the worth and potential of their children, grandchildren, and great grandchildren clearly that they believe it and act on that belief."

## WHEN YOUR FAMILY IS HOSTILE TO YOUR EX

You may find, on the other hand, that your family has hostile feelings toward your ex because of real or even imagined hurts you received at her hands. Perhaps you shared some bad experiences with them that you now regret telling. They'd like to erase any sign that she was once part of their family, even if she was most adored before the divorce. If so, you'll need to remind your parents and extended family that regardless how they may feel about your ex, they are not to speak badly of her in front of your children as she is still their mother (and hopefully she is telling her family the same about you).

Nancy Harris, an attorney specializing in marital family law, stresses, "I always tell my clients of the importance of celebrating the other parent, not only to the kids, but also to your relatives. Saying 'Their mom is a good mother' to your relatives encourages a most important relationship because your parents and other relatives know that despite the divorce and other differences, you and your ex can still respect one another as parents." Stan recalled that "While my family was sad for me that we were getting a divorce, they completely understood. After the separation, many members of my family (and my friends) came forward and wanted to know what took me so long to finally make the break, what did I see in her in the first place, and tell me how relieved they were that I would now be able to move on with my life."

While Stan's friends may have felt that these comments showed support for him, it also could have made him wonder why indeed it had taken him so long to make the break when it was so obvious to everyone else. But Stan admitted, "Of course, I also felt depressed. Not that my marriage had ended, because in my mind, it had ended years before—but depressed that I was now 'removed' from the daily life of my son. This, ultimately, has been the hardest part of the separation and divorce."

## WHEN YOUR FAMILY IS HOSTILE TO YOU

You may find, to your surprise, that while her family is reasonably civil to you, it is your family who gives you grief. Randy found that his sister called his soon-to-be ex-wife and told her, "It's about time you're dumping him." While his relationship with his ex remains somewhat cordial because of the kids, he admits that his relationship with his sister is still somewhat strained.

In his book *The Single Father*, author Armin A. Brott wrote, "Make sure your parents mail or deliver birthday and holiday gifts to your house. No matter who has the kids on those days, the presents—even if they get delivered a little late—should clearly be coming from your side of the family. If they're delivered to your ex's house, the kids may never know that the gifts are coming from your side of the family, and

they may take that as a sign that they aren't loved anymore."

## IF YOUR PARENTS DON'T ASK, YOU TELL

As you are fully aware, parents don't know everything and probably aren't mind readers. Your parents may be unsure how to best support you. They may want to help you in any way possible but don't know what you want and don't want to intrude. So they remain silent and frustrated because they want to be there for you and feel that they're not helping you.

Or, on the other hand, your parents may want to do too much to help, rather than not enough, and overwhelm you with constant phone calls, home-cooked meals, cash, furniture, and baby-sitting offers. The best way to handle this situation is to sit down and communicate your preferences. Thank them for their support and let them know exactly what you want and desire at this particular time. Remember that your needs may change in the future, so be sure to tell them if and when that occurs.

# Chapter 21

# Dating Dilemmas

*If a man does not make new acquaintances*
*as he advances through life,*
*he will soon find himself left alone.*

—SAMUEL JOHNSON

Eventually, although you sometimes may doubt it, you will want to start dating again for companionship. While you love your kids and enjoy their company, it's not the same as spending some time with another adult.

Mike says, "If you're like me, dating was never a whole lot of fun. Don't get me wrong, once you got a date, it was great. But going through the bar scene, blind date set ups, etc., was always a very humbling experience. However, unless the priesthood is your next step or you've sworn off women for any other reasons, at some point you will begin to want to date. It may seem very odd as you probably haven't dated someone other than your ex in a long time. Also, she may begin to date before you and that may make you angry, sad, or trigger a host of other feelings."

## WHEN TO BEGIN

The most important factor in determining when and how to re-enter the social scene depends on when you feel ready. Don't let well-meaning friends and family push you into a dating situation before that. It's not fair to you nor to your date, who, if you had waited until you were ready, might have turned into a nice relationship.

While you're getting ready to re-enter the dating scene, consider spending a little time with a therapist first. The sessions may help to clarify where things went wrong in your marriage, suggest ways to communicate better, prevent your repeating past errors of your ways (not listening, being sarcastic, hanging out with the guys too much), and help you to unload some of the emotional baggage you're probably carrying. A good professional mental health counselor can help you look within to see if there is a pattern in your dating and also keep you from mentally assuming that all women are the same. Refer back to Chapter 17 for tips on finding a therapist.

## DATING AS A SINGLE DAD

Michael offers this firsthand advice to dads just getting back into dating for the first time since they become a single father:

"It was the best of times, it was the worst of times." These famous words can pretty much sum up the time a guy decides to get back on the dating warpath. It is a brave new world out there whether you're back on the market in your twenties or your fifties. Things have clearly changed: Internet dating, blind dates, set-up dates, intro dates with your married friends, etc. The interesting thing about dating again is that we get back to that period when we first meet someone we really like and get those butterflies in our stomach, go through the decision process of when to call her and actually start thinking about how every conversation went. For most guys, these are things that we stopped thinking about once we got married.

The world has evolved into two areas where you can meet people outside of introductions or referrals from friends. (Although don't discount that cute single mom who drops off her kids at school.) These areas are:

---

✔ **Tip from the Trenches**

John wants to remind other guys that "It is the right of the previous spouse to be able to find happiness. So, as long as they shield the children from unhealthy dating practices, it is proper for both parties to want the best for their previous spouse."

- The social scene. Consider this the bar/restaurant scene, social/networking groups, or any setting that will have a large number of people of the opposite sex. This is definitely the hard one. Frankly, few like it or are comfortable in it, but most get out there and do it with the hopes of meeting someone who they may want to date. Find a group of other single guys you can do this with. Everything is easier with others and makes it much easier to meet women as well. It always is better to have a wing man.

- The Internet. The Internet has become an amazing tool to use in so many aspects of daily living, and it makes sense to use it to meet someone new as well. If you're in your twenties or thirties, you may want to check out sites such as Myspace.com or Facebook.com. In your thirties and up you may look at sites such as Match.com, eharmony.com, Christiansingles.com, Jdate.com, Americansingles.com, and many more. These online communities are like the world's biggest bar with no line for the bathroom.

If you've never used these Web sites, don't panic. It's easy. You just enter your search criteria and, presto!, up comes a feast (or famine) of female faces peering back at you, women who are looking for a guy, possibly just like you.

A word of warning about these sites: You must have tough skin because these online dating jungles are often an uninviting environment. Don't be surprised if you e-mail people who seem interesting to you but they don't e-mail back. It hurts your ego because you may have learned at an early age to fear rejection. Online rejection can be painful because you are essentially being judged on a few pictures your friend took of you and some descriptive information you typed in, perhaps too hastily.

As an old sales trainer once said, "you always have to remember that they're not rejecting you, they're just not interested in what you're selling." Don't take it too personally, because these people don't know you and they aren't making a decision based on knowing who you really are. If you are looking for younger girls to respond, (typically thirty-five and younger), they may be scared to death of that one line you marked in there that says you have kids.

Funny how people think, but it happens. Don't lie about having kids if you pursue online dating. You are asking for trouble and it doesn't start anything out on a good note.

Once you actually find someone to date, the important subject comes up of when to introduce that person to the kids. That is a very personal but important decision to make. You certainly don't want to parade girl after girl by your children. It isn't good for them to see a revolving door of women in your life, especially if the divorce has occurred recently. It's best to let the kids meet her when you feel that this person is going to become a significant person in your life. That doesn't necessarily mean that you have decided that this is the person you are going to marry, but rather that this is someone you want to incorporate into your daily life on a regular basis.

## FINDING RELIABLE BABY SITTERS

First, reread Chapter 12 on child care. Remember that it's just as important to check references with someone who's with your kids for only four hours as it is for all day.

- Ask other parents at your kids' school who they use, although sometimes parents are reluctant to share good sitters' names.

- Decide if you and your ex want to use the same sitters. The obvious advantage is that the sitters get used to your kids at both houses; the disadvantage is that the sitters may want to carry tales between homes unless you both squelch that possibility immediately, no matter how tempting it might be to hear some interesting gossip.
- Many communities have baby-sitting companies, but check out the organization first to be sure they verify their clients references, health status, and experience.
- If you're tempted to leave your preteens and teenagers home alone, contact your state's Department of Children's Services to learn at what age it is legal to leave youngsters alone in a home. A few states require that no child under fourteen can be left alone. But much depends on your child's maturity as some, even at age fourteen, will feel uncomfortable being alone. Also, use your own judgment if an older sibling will be in charge of younger ones. It's quite a responsibility, and younger siblings often don't listen to the older ones (and the older ones can become very bossy and dictatorial when given that much authority).
- Stay home the first time you have the sitter to see how he or she interacts with your kids. Obviously, both will be on their best behaviors with you around

Ask other parents what they pay for baby-sitting services as it varies widely depending on community standards, number and ages of your children, and what you expect them to do besides watch the kids (such as preparing a meal and cleaning up afterwards, bathing younger ones and putting them in bed, changing diapers). Charges usually range anywhere from seven dollars an hour to fifteen dollars per hour.

Be sure to leave the sitter a phone number of where you'll be as well as your cell phone number and the time you expect to return. Also leave your pediatrician's number in case of an emergency, along with your home address and phone number, so the sitter has that information if necessary to inform an emergency service. Many dads suggested leaving a reliable neighbor's number too.

Make it clear that your sitter is to have no friends over while you're out and to use the phone only briefly, although most teens and many older people have their own cell phones. Hopefully your sitters won't talk on their cell while your kids are getting into trouble. Have a snack available, and tell the sitter what it is and where so you don't come home and find that the food you planned for dinner the next night has been devoured.

## FINDING FRIENDSHIP FIRST IN A DATE

Although you may be tempted to run out and have sex with the first available and willing participant you can find, slow down. Take time to think about what you really want in a woman. If it helps you to think it out, create a list of the characteristics you want and don't want.

### What Are You Really Looking for?

Take your time and really think about it. Does she have to be blonde and have big boobs? Is it a deal breaker if she smokes? What if she has kids too? Drinks too much? If she's a successful executive and makes more money than you do? Do you want a twenty-first-century Ginger Rogers because you think you're a second Fred Astaire? Does she have to like dogs? Adore movies

> ### ✔ Tip from the Trenches
>
> Dan suggests, "If there's a particular trait you don't like, then avoid it. Don't be afraid to specify: no smoking, no heavy drinking, no drugs. On the other hand, it's also okay to say 'must like kids and have good sense of humor' if that's important to you."

and plays? Love hunting and fishing? Be Catholic or Jewish? Hate the Yankees? Love the Red Sox? Love to cook, or at least like to cook? While you don't need to look for the woman of your dreams just now, look for the positive aspects that are important to you and be very aware of any tendencies your ex may have had that you really didn't like.

### Where Is the Dating Scene?

Look for friendship first in a relationship, rather than just heading for the hottest babe you can find. As mentioned earlier, you'll find available women everywhere—doing volunteer work, at your church or synagogue, walking her dog, at Parents Without Partners (a national advocacy organization with local chapters providing social and educational activities for single parents, *www.parentswithoutpartners.org*), or through fix-up through friends or relatives. If you go the online dating route, and many people have found a good match that way, remember that what women write on the computer may not always be the truth. And she may not even be a woman, so be careful! Don't make your first date with someone a long one that includes dinner and theater. Instead, invite her for coffee or for lunch. That way both of you will be relieved if it's obvious you two have nothing in common.

Don't, however, look for a perfect person. They don't exist (no, not even you). By dropping someone after one date, you may be missing out on getting to know someone whose company you'd very much enjoy once you've both relaxed your defenses. Try to forget any preconceived ideas of what type of woman you do like. By doing so you may miss out on a great catch—someone who is not blonde but brunette, or who doesn't have a model's figure but is lots of fun—and may be a good match for what you need now in your new life as a single dad.

In his book *The Art of Loving*, psychoanalyst Erich Fromm wrote, "If there's a potential for intimacy, this is what happens:

"There is caring deeply about your partner's welfare and growth.

"There is respecting your partner's identity—for their right to be who they are, rather than who you'd like them to be.

"There is taking responsibility to care for the other person in an involved, active way.

"There is acknowledging the other person—his or her values, needs, desires, dreams, and foibles."

Isn't that worth waiting for? Take your time when you're dating and don't rush into anything. Many men admit that their second (or third) marriage took place because they were lonely or because they wanted a mother for their children. That may be why the divorce rates for a second (or third) marriage are higher than they are for a first one.

Slow down and keep things casual for a while. As the song "Love Is Better the Second Time Around" says, it can be better the second (or third) time around, but it's also worth waiting for.

### Déjà Vu

Another important thing to beware of when you start dating again is finding yourself dating someone who is basically your ex-wife in someone else's clothing. Whether you think you would do this or not, the human mind is a funny thing. When it gets comfortable with something, it looks to recreate what it remembers. In this case, you tend to remember the woman you originally fell in love with, not how you felt at the end of the relationship, and so you find yourself right back with another person with the same qualities, sort of a relationship version of the movie *Groundhog Day*. This may mean if your ex was very controlling and told you everything you could or could not do, so does your new girlfriend and slowly your relationship turns into the same controlling relationship, an identical twin of what you had before.

The same thing can happen the other way around. If your ex was under your control, you might find yourself dating someone who also does everything you say and doesn't have much of a mind of her own. Remember, there is a reason that your past relationship didn't work out. As the philosopher George Santayana said, "Those who cannot remember the past are condemned to repeat it."

Don't date the comfortable person; date the individual who makes you a better person. It is said that a successful business transaction is one in which the two entities together are better than they were apart. The same should be said for relationships. If you're dating someone who doesn't compliment who you are and make you a better person by being with her, then what are you hoping for? Make sure you are taking adequate time to really understand why you are attracted to that new person you've started dating, and be sure it isn't because of the comforts of what you are used to. Don't become another sad statistic.

## NEW RULES FOR YOUR EX WHEN YOU'RE DATING SOMEBODY ELSE

It is very important for you and your ex, regardless of how good your relationship is after your divorce, to agree upon the ground rules of dating. It is not appreciated by your new date or girlfriend if during an enjoyable dinner at a nice restaurant your ex calls on your cell to see what's going on or asks if you can help her with some computer problems.

Though you may have a friendship with your ex after your divorce (yes, it not only happens, but many of our interviewees said they actually were better friends divorced than they had been married), you have to respect the fact that a new date or girlfriend will see any communication from your ex to you that doesn't involve the children as a threat. Your new relationship will always see that ex-spouse as a possible bog of quicksand just waiting around the bend to suck you back in with her. Therefore, make sure you and your ex agree that phone calls at night are for kid-related matters only. If she needs something other than that, have her text-message or e-mail you. The same should apply to you respecting her new life.

## WHAT'S DIFFERENT ABOUT DATING THIS TIME?

If it's been a while since you last dated, you'll find that things have changed. You also have kids this time, and either an ex-wife or girlfriend, or if you are a widower, a late wife. Although you need to acknowledge her, don't wax poetic about how wonderful your late wife was and how you'll never love anyone as much again, and don't begin listing your ex's faults. Chances are your date will want to learn a little about you and a potential future with you rather than what's happened to you in the past.

Regardless if your date has kids or not, always mention that you have them on the first date. If not, she'll wonder what kind of dad you are or if you were trying to trick her by not disclosing that "small" fact. If she has kids as well, you can share a few stories and compare notes, but you should also try to learn a little about her in her nonmotherly role.

## WHEN TO INTRODUCE A DATE TO YOUR KIDS

Stan admitted, "I've never been much of a dating hound and tend to be serially monogamous in dating. Most of the women I dated I met through my work. I would typically not introduce my dating friends to my son until after it became apparent that we (she and I) would be together (monogamous) for the foreseeable future. I would never force the introduction. It would typically occur as a natural outgrowth of some event which my son, my 'girl friend,' and I would do together (such as a party, fair, concert, and so on)."

Matthew B, an unmarried teen father who has sole custody of his nineteen-month-old daughter, says, "I find that meeting women and getting a date is easy. Finding one that wants to be a mommy to another woman's daughter is totally different. Most twentysomething females do not want to commit and it is very frustrating to me."

If a woman dates a man with a young child, the youngster may begin calling the father's girlfriend "mommy." Obviously, this can become awkward and make an unexpected and unwanted impression of commitment.

Most experts agree that you shouldn't introduce your kids to your date until you've been dating for a while (three to four months at least) and think the relationship may be going somewhere. It's probably more difficult to put such a meeting off if she has kids too, despite the natural inclination to want to get the kids together. But this isn't the *Brady Bunch* yet, and you don't want your kids and hers to bond or for your kids to get fond of her and begin to think that she may be their stepmother only for you to break up with her.

Remember also that your kids may not want to think of your getting remarried, as that means you and their mom won't be getting back together again. It doesn't matter how many times you've told them that you won't get back together, they most likely still hold out hope. (Disney movies such as the *Parent Trap* don't help this either.) When you introduce them to your new woman, go easy. Make their visit with her and her kids, if she has any, informal and short, such as a picnic in the park, a trip to the beach, or a cookout in your backyard.

Although your ex should not quiz the kids any more than you should, never tell your kids to lie about your dating activities or whom you're dating. That puts them in the middle of their parents, both of whom they love, and regardless what they do they'll feel disloyal to one of you.

## POSTPONE DATE SLEEPOVERS WHEN YOUR KIDS ARE WITH YOU

Although there's nothing wrong with your having a physical relationship with someone you're dating, don't do it when your kids are with you. (If they're with you all the time, get a sitter and go to a hotel or to her house, unless she also has her kids full time.) It's confusing for the kids to see a revolving door of women at the breakfast table, and if you have preteens or teenagers, it's very difficult to say "I care for this woman and I am an adult" because they'll answer back "I care for my girlfriend too and I'm almost an adult."

## PUT PUBLIC DISPLAYS OF AFFECTION ON HOLD

It's hard for your kids to see you hugging, kissing, or fondling someone other than their mother, but it's also uncomfortable for other family members. Holding hands is one thing, but caressing or kissing in public is a real turnoff to many reluctant viewers, especially those in the "older" generation. Save your lovemaking for when you have privacy.

## WHAT TO DO WHEN YOUR DATE HAS KIDS TOO

When your date has kids too, it's tempting to do things together as sort of an ersatz family. But don't become too much a part of her kids' lives too soon unless you think you really may be getting serious. If you and your kids have picnics, dinner, or go to football games as a group, the kids will also begin to think of it as a family. They may either like the idea or fight it, but take it slow so they're not disappointed if things don't work out. How can you help the situation?

- By continuing to communicate openly with your kids and letting them know how much you love them and reassuring them that they are an important part of your life. By spending time alone with your kids and not making every outing one that includes the girlfriend.

- Although you don't need to keep your kids informed of the daily progress (or lack thereof) of this new relationship, you should tell them when you feel it's getting serious so they aren't surprised.

Don't expect your children to express undying love for this lady or for her kids. Youngsters can be very perceptive, and your kids may quickly have figured out that if you two got together they'd lose their position in the blended family with your oldest becoming the middle child and your "baby" losing out to her youngest.

## CHECK OLD BAGGAGE

If you have unsettled issues stemming from a former relationship, you might consider having therapy to help you deal with your past to prevent your bringing any old baggage into a new relationship. A qualified therapist can also help you cope with problems you may be having with your kids if they openly resent your having a new person in your life, or help you understand what's going on if you continue to resist any relationship from getting too intense.

If you're a single dad who has openly declared being gay, you might also find a therapist helpful in advising you the best way to deal with your kids' confusion, anger, and other emotions that may have arisen from your declaration.

If your wife is deceased, you might want to talk to the therapist about any unresolved issues, such as guilt you may be feeling by "betraying" her, even though you know realistically that she'd want you to go on with your life. For more information on where to find a therapist, see Chapter 17.

## SIMPLY SEX

While some of your friends may think that you're busy hopping in and out of hundreds of gorgeous chicks' beds, you may not be quite that active. It often is a little strange beginning a new sexual relationship (even if it's only a one-night stand) after a divorce. Like a football player traded from his old team, you suddenly have a new playbook and have to learn some different moves. The most important one, of course, is to always practice safe sex.

Remember that times have definitely changed with regard to the sexual activity and promiscuity of many women. If you meet her at a bar and she makes the decision to go home with you, it's pretty much a guarantee that you're not the first one she has done that with. No matter what, wear a condom to prevent both pregnancy and sexually transmitted diseases (STDs). She may tell you that she is on birth control, but do it anyway. By sleeping with her you are basically sleeping with anyone she has slept with, and if she is willing to have unprotected sex with you, she probably did with others as well. You owe it to your kids and your family not to contract anything during a one-night stand that can affect you the rest of your life. No sex is that good! Michael knows of several friends who have had those one-night stands only to get a call nine months later with notification of a blended family they really didn't want to deal with.

If you can remember what your first sexual experiences were, you may recall that they possibly weren't too successful. You either climaxed too soon or not at all. Don't panic if some of those old problems reoccur from time to time. You may subconsciously feel a little guilty about having sex with somebody new, especially if your wife is deceased. You may be worrying that your physique isn't quite what it used to be, even if you've started to work out. You also may be so exhausted from being a single dad that it's difficult to focus on being a successful lover.

Just relax and take it easy. Remember that most sexual dysfunction begins in your head. Don't worry about "being the best." That's too much pressure. Just enjoy the practice sessions. Don't be afraid to bring this up in your new relationship. It can make the sessions more relaxed and comfortable, and that will improve performance. However, don't bring up your old sexual relationships, especially those with your ex. Women are very visual thinkers. If you tell them a story about how your ex hated a certain position or act, they will tend to see you as thinking about sex with your ex. (A word of warning: It's rare for this conversation to go well.)

Although there are a variety of drugs that are advertised to cure erectile dysfunction, don't make that your first choice. Most likely your problem is temporary. Instead, focus on foreplay and enjoy the sensations of touch and taste. As you please your partner (and hopefully she returns the favor), you may find yourself rising to the occasion and all will be well.

# Chapter 22

# Who Gets the Friends?

*It is the friends that you can call*
*At 4 a.m. that matter.*

—MARLENE DIETRICH

Families are not the only people who hurt when a divorce takes place. Divorce also often becomes difficult for the friends you and your ex have shared. They often feel that they have to take sides rather than continuing to enjoy seeing both of you separately. Some may feel so uncomfortable with you or disloyal to your ex that they'll drift away. Others, who distanced themselves during the marriage as they sensed the strain between you and your ex, may flock to your side, happy to be able to be in your company again.

Eric, who is newly divorced and has a shared custody arrangement of his son, said, "I guess I'm just realizing what a big change divorce can have on your entire life. Along with the obvious changes of running a single household, I did not expect my friendships to change, but they did. To me, that has been very difficult and it is something you cannot control. So, once all these things have happened, you have to re-establish who you are again."

## MAKE THE FIRST MOVE

Frazier admits that after his divorce he discovered the caliber of some of the friendships he had shared before. "I lost some of the former friendships because I think they (i.e. the wives) were afraid of my single lifestyle."

Most of our interviewees suggested that you may have to make the first move with some of your friends, and although that may sound easy, it's actually hard. You may fear rejection, but what's the worst that could happen? It's unlikely they'd yell at you or hang up if you called, and if they did, you'd be better off without them.

### Open House
Begin by inviting a couple or two over for a cookout, out to dinner, or over to watch a game. It doesn't need to be fancy. Realize that at first things may seem a little awkward. Your ex's absence may fill the room. But hopefully, as you start talking and joking around, renewing the friendship, your friends will realize that you're the same person even though you're now a single father. It may be easier to break the ice when you have your kids and they bring theirs as well.

## DON'T DISCUSS YOUR DIVORCE

If, however, the conversation turns to the divorce, quickly cut it off. Just say "I'd rather not talk about it." Don't get caught up in explaining what went wrong or who did what to whom. You don't need to defend yourself. Chances are if they thought you were a wife beater or a druggie, they wouldn't have accepted your hospitality.

### Curiosity Kills More Than the Cat
Friends, being normal people, probably are curious as to what happened between you and your ex, especially if you two seemed happy together, but you don't need to be the one to give them ammunition for gossip. Your response to their curiosity can kill the friendship and hurt relations with your ex. Friends, even good ones, often can't help themselves when the opportunity arises to say, "Well, don't repeat this, but he said . . . ." Remember that childhood game of "telephone"? The odds of anything you say being repeated correctly are slim, and you don't want your ex to ever be able to complain that you were saying unkind things about her, regardless of how you may feel personally. Even worse, you don't want your kids to overhear that conversation, and the simplest way to prevent that is to say nothing.

## FORGOING THE FIX-UP

If your friends (usually female) ask if you'd like to be fixed up on a blind date, don't hesitate to tell them exactly what you feel. If you're not ready, say so.

If you'd like the opportunity to meet someone new, then say yes. Let your friends know if you'd prefer having them along too if a double date sounds more comfortable to you since you may be a little out of practice in the so-called art of dating.

Don't worry if you don't feel ready to begin dating just yet. (Chapter 21 offers information to help you when you do.) You have plenty of time, and it should happen when you're ready, not when your friends think you should. For some unknown reason, married couples (both male and female) seem to hate the thought of an available guy still out there, even if it's only for a few months. They must feel it's their duty to pair you off as quickly as possible, just in case there's another flood and only pairs can come on board Noah's ark.

# Chapter 23

# Keeping Busy When They're at Your Ex's House

*Determine never to be idle.*
*No person will have occasion to complain*
*of the want of time*
*who never loses any.*
*It is wonderful*
*how much may be done*
*if we are always doing.*
—THOMAS JEFFERSON

The hours right before you have to take your kids back to their mother's house are important ones, and it may be difficult for you as well as the kids. Give them a countdown so they'll be ready for the transition between homes. This begins to prepare you for the change as well. Help them gather up their homework, clothes, and anything else they may need at their other home. Be sure you've included any meeting information or other data from school that came home with them.

## TRANSITION TIME

You may experience loneliness after having your home filled with your kids' noise and laughter. You may feel at loose ends for a long time. Stan, one of our interviewees, remarked that he had "significant amounts of time where I was an individual. No requirements, no constraints, expectations, or priorities were placed upon me (other than those I placed upon myself). I found myself, on occasion, sitting in my one bedroom (empty, except for an air mattress, black and white TV, my clothes, and a telephone), wondering what I should (or could) be doing at that moment. In the very early days of the separation, life didn't 'flow,' it progressed in bursts of activities."

## ACTIVITIES FOR YOU

At first you may fill those transition times with no-brainer activities. You'll toss out the remainder of the pasta you fixed for the kids (or mindlessly eat it cold), wash their sheets, and put toys back in the toy box. You may be tempted to crack open a beer and sit in front of the TV night after night or head for the neighborhood bar where you'll essentially do the same thing. Unfortunately, before

too long you also may find your waistline expanding as your mind grows fuzzy. A better plan is to schedule activities, especially on the day or days right after the kids leave your home for their mom's home.

## APPEAL TO YOUR SENSES

Give yourself something to look at rather than the four bare walls in your house, condo, or apartment. If you're handy, paint a room or wall hanging, or hang a picture or two. The pictures don't have to be great works of art, though you might find some fairly good ones at neighborhood garage sales or secondhand stores. Otherwise, wander through art galleries and art museums. You'll be with other people rather than alone. What's more, museum gift shops always have prints of the artwork you've enjoyed in case you want to buy one and learn to frame it yourself

Listen to music either on the radio or CD, go to an open-air free concert, or join a church or synagogue choir. Learn to play the piano, guitar, or harmonica. Watch the cooking channel in your area and try some of the recipes yourself.

## VOLUNTEER POSSIBILITIES

Indian spiritual and political leader Mahatma Gandhi said, "The best way to find yourself is to lose yourself in the service of others." That's great advice. There's nothing like reaching out to help others to help you forget your own troubles. You'll meet other people who share your interests. Regardless of where you live, there are hundreds of volunteer opportunities depending on what you enjoy doing. Try something new; you may like it. Here are a few options:

- Habitat for Humanity is extremely worthwhile, and you really don't need to know anything about construction work because they have people who do. They are extremely patient, even if you put the siding on upside down.
- Meals on Wheels always needs drivers to help carry prepared meals to shut-ins and the elderly. If your area doesn't have this organization, put a notice in the paper and see if you and others can organize one.
- Hospitals are always looking for volunteers in their gift shops, to plan fundraising events like golf tournaments, or to help out at the information desk.
- Become a coach for Little League, softball, or other children's sports.
- Your church or synagogue can always use a volunteer, either in the office, teaching religious school, singing in the choir, or making phone calls.

## CLASSES AND HOBBIES

Rather than sitting in front of the television, mindlessly watching whatever happens to be on, stimulate your brain by signing up for classes at your local YMCA, community college or university, or church or synagogue. Think about a hobby you'd enjoy in your free time, one that you could even share with your kids if they were interested.

### Take a Class

You may have always wanted to learn a foreign language, learn to ballroom dance, fix a carburetor, learn woodworking, cook Chinese or Indian meals, or improve your skills to help you in your job. Now's the time. Check with your community college, YMCA, JCC, or the local university to see what they offer. Most noncredit classes are reasonably priced, but if money's tight, perhaps you can offer to teach a course in return for taking one. Stores like Home Depot and Lowe's often hold classes in painting rooms, applying wallpaper, simple carpentry, and other handy skills.

### Start a New Hobby

Treat yourself to a new hobby that has always piqued your interest. It could be tennis, golf, fly-fishing, painting miniature soldiers, magic tricks, or stamp collecting. If you often said, "Someday I'd like to . . . ," today may be someday. What's more, your kids may become interested in your new hobby when they are living with you.

## STAYING IN TOUCH WITH YOUR KIDS

You also should agree, if possible, with your ex that whenever the kids are at their other home, the parent without the kids can call them at specific times to hear what they're doing. With older children you can send e-mail or a text message in order to stay in touch. It's important for both you and your ex to keep communicating and staying aware of what's going on in your children's lives, but it's as important that the kids know that you care and are thinking of them even when they're not living with you. Remember: TOYK.

Your time without your kids also is a good opportunity to get in touch with friends and relatives both in town and out of town. With e-mail, IM, the phone, and even snail mail, you need not be lonely long.

## STOP FEELING SORRY FOR YOURSELF

"Most folks are about as happy as they make up their minds to be." This quote from Abraham Lincoln rings true. Rather than feeling sorry for yourself when your kids aren't with you, set out to make your life a happy one. It will not only make you feel better, but it will make you more fun to be around and a better parent because your kids see that we all need to learn how to find joy within ourselves.

This quote from Joseph Conrad sums it up: "Happiness, happiness . . . the flavor is with you—with you alone, and you can make it as intoxicating as you please." So drink up! To your health.

# Chapter 24
# Reducing Stress

*Stress: the confusion created when one's mind overrides the body's basic desire to choke the living daylights out of some jerk who desperately deserves it.*

—ANONYMOUS

S tress. You can almost hear the hissing of those double s's, like a snake about to attack. But you can learn to tame it and have it work for you. There are numerous techniques to reduce harmful stress, but what is most beneficial tends to vary from person to person. Hopefully you'll discover that a few of the following methods work for you.

## IS STRESS HARMFUL?

Stress, in itself, isn't bad. Dr. Hans Selye, the late researcher and expert in stress, said "Complete freedom from stress is death." Nevertheless, you probably wish you could have just a little more freedom from stress in your day-to-day life. But like the (polluted) air around you, stress is everywhere.

In 1967, two psychiatrists at the University of Washington Medical School, Dr. Thomas H. Holmes and Dr. Richard H. Rahe, devised a way to measure stressful events, both good and bad ones. This scale, known as the Social Readjustment Rating Scale, is still applicable forty years later, though some of the financial levels have elevated considerably.

## SINGLE FATHERHOOD IS STRESSFUL

According to this rating system, the most stressful event is the death of a spouse. Coming in second is divorce. So it's no surprise that single fathers are under a great deal of stress. But add to that the "normal" stress factors in your life—always being available because of the curse of your cell phone or the computer's instant messaging program, the neighbor's barking dog or late-night television blaring, disliking most aspects of your job, juggling your responsibilities with

your kids, and financial concerns—and you say, "What? Me worry?" And the obvious answer is, "Heck, yes."

## FINDING THE RIGHT STRESS REDUCTION TECHNIQUES

There are many ways to reduce stress in your life, but unfortunately there's not one best way nor one that works for everyone. You're going to have to try them all until you find those that work for you. It's really a combination of methods—exercise, meditation and prayer, visualization, progressive relaxation, massage, proper sleep and eating habits, improved communication techniques, and using your sense of humor. Although you may think you don't have time to add relaxation to your to-do list, you really can't afford not to.

Stress is like rainfall: A little may not be harmful. Indeed, it may be good. But too many drops soon erode even the hardest granite. Stress—even "good" stress—piling up too long and too fast can wear down the sturdiest of souls.

## MEDITATION AND PRAYER

Meditation is a relaxation technique that has been used successfully for centuries by followers of most religions. It often is referred

---

✔ **Tip from the Trenches**

Eric says, "It's just a stressful time, dealing with a lot of changes—some foreseeable and some not. You cannot let it overwhelm you. Eventually, everything will work its way out."

to as prayer or self-hypnosis, but the procedure is basically the same regardless what it is called. Follow these easy steps:

- Retreat to a quiet spot and get comfortable. Loosen your belt, kick off your shoes, and relax.
- Take two or three deep breaths. Focus on slowing your breathing.
- Repeat a specific word or phrase. It could be peace, Jesus, love, God, or anything else. The actual word you use really isn't important. It serves to clear your mind and keep other thoughts from entering.
- If other thoughts do intrude, let them float by and refocus on your word or phrase.
- Practice meditation twice a day. You'll soon achieve a state of peacefulness and may find that it can slow your heart rate and reduce your blood pressure. For many, meditation also increases a sense of their spiritual side.

In an article in *Reform Judaism*, "Overcoming Our Pain: The Life Lessons of Dr. Bernie S. Siegel," the doctor is quoted as saying, "True peace of mind comes when you have a divine source to help, support, and accompany you, to get you through difficulties and to show you the strength you really have. A relationship with God can help you overcome things that defeat other people."

According to Dr. Herbert Benson, associate professor of medicine at Harvard Medical School and director of the Benson-Henry Institute for Mind Body Medicine, meditation and prayer along with visualization, yoga, progressive relaxation, and music therapy evoke what he calls "the relaxation response." He adds that prayer may lower harmful stress hormones such as adrenaline.

The beauty of meditation is that it requires no equipment and no set amount of time. You can do it while you're waiting for an appointment, at your office, or before you go to sleep at night. You might not want to meditate while you're caught in a traffic jam, but meditation does make you feel more peaceful and focused.

Practice meditation before you meet with your ex or have to call her on the phone. Stress floats away without the use of any harmful and expensive drugs.

What's more, you can teach your kids to meditate so they're more relaxed before tests, sports competition, recitals, and so on. Meditation also can be helpful if your youngster has trouble sleeping, especially the first few nights he or she is at your home.

## VISUALIZATION

Visualization is similar to meditation in that you need to get comfortable first, then close your eyes and clear your mind of troublesome thoughts. But instead of focusing on a word or phrase, visualize some scene that is particularly peaceful to you, evoking all your senses. It could be on a bench by a harbor filled with sailboats, in a swing high on a hill with the gentle breeze in your face, or on a rowboat watching the bobber on your line float in the water. Open your other senses to your visualization so you can smell the salt air by the sea, hear the rustling of the leaves on the trees in the forest in fall, or feel the warm sun on your face.

Inhale and exhale slowly as you focus on your visualized peaceful scene. Don't worry if your mind wanders at first. Just bring it back to your private scene. You'll be surprised how refreshed you can feel after one of these sessions, even if you only visualize for just five or ten minutes. If you can find a picture in a magazine that conjures up a peaceful scene for you, use that to get started.

Your children, from toddlers to teens, also may benefit from learning visualization as they picture themselves successfully walking into preschool, taking a test, trying out for a play, or shooting free throws. Present it as a calming game and be patient. You'll be teaching your kids a beneficial skill they'll be able to use the rest of their lives.

## PROGRESSIVE RELAXATION

You've used progressive relaxation before—when you were a baby. When you were tired, you just relaxed and zonked out on the floor, over your parent's shoulder, or wherever you were. It's a simple formula: If you're relaxed, you cannot be tense.

The pioneering physiologist Edmund Jacobson, author of *Progressive Relaxation* and *You Must Relax*, stated that once someone became aware of tension in a specific muscle group, he or she could learn to dispel that tension by relaxing the muscles involved.

There are two forms of progressive relaxation—passive and active. Both achieve the same result in that you reduce tension in your body and relax your mind.

With passive relaxation, you lie down and close your eyes. Concentrate on each muscle group, relaxing them as you move up your body. Say to yourself, "My toes are relaxed and warm. So relaxed they float." Then do the same with your ankles, calves, and knees until you get to your forehead. Then just think, *calm, love, peace,* or any other word that makes you feel relaxed. By focusing on your relaxed word, you can't think about problems at the office, how to keep your kids from fighting, or what you're going to say when you see your ex. You can't have two thoughts at once. If other thoughts pop into your mind, as they will, just let them float by.

Visualize those problems or extraneous thoughts actually moving away from you as though you were a magnet and had reversed the magnetic field, repelling all stressful thoughts and forming a safe protective barrier around yourself. Float, breathe in and out, and relax.

For active relaxation you also need to lie down and get comfortable. Close your eyes. Slowly tense the muscles in your forehead, then relax the muscles and be aware of how that feels. Do the same with your cheek muscles, your jaw, lips, and neck, then work down your body. The idea behind active progressive relaxation is that when you feel a muscle tightening, you'll remember the sensation of relaxing that muscle and will be able to release the tension at will.

Experts suggest that you practice progressive relaxation at least once a day for ten to twenty minutes. You can add a second session if you desire, but no more than that. "The idea," said a psychologist, "is not to withdraw from the world, but to be equipped to handle stressful situations by being able to relax and release the tension you feel."

Obviously, it's difficult to try to relax while you're holding this book in your hand. You might want to make a tape of the instructions or use one of the many instructional tapes or DVDs available. For more information about meditation, visualization, and progressive relaxation, read Dr. Herbert Benson's book *The Relaxation Response*.

## HUMOR IN, STRESS OUT

There's nothing like laughter to make stress disappear. Focus on the funny side of situations rather than thinking of the awful. Surround yourself with people who have a good sense of humor, and bring home some comedies when you're getting DVDs to watch.

Have a comedy night when you have the kids, with everyone telling jokes. Give a prize to the funniest joke. Be silly, even when you may not feel that way. Teach your kids to laugh their stress away and you'll give them a wonderful gift they'll use the rest of their life.

## FIND YOUR OWN STRESS REDUCER

Everyone is different, and what may reduce stress for your friend may cause even more for you if you were to try it. Here are a few stress reducers some of our interviewees recommended:

- Gardening. The young man who mentioned this to us said, "Planting and watching things grow is a good lesson in life. There are no 'quick fixes.' You have to invest time and energy into things you want to develop and give them time to bloom." (A lot like kids.)
- Fishing. Fishing is almost self-hypnotic whether you sit on a pier or float in a rowboat. Catching an actual fish is great, but just the peace and quiet of sitting there, letting your mind wander, and enjoying nature is a wonderful way to relax.
- Hobbies. Stamp collectors, artists, knitters, needlepointers, and model train devotees all suggest that you cannot be

stressed while you're intently focused on your particular hobby. If you don't have a hobby, consider working with your kids at theirs.
- Music. In 1697, William Congreve said, "Music has charms to soothe a savage breast." And, indeed, it does. You may have seen or heard about music hypnotizing a cobra. Music can also actually reduce stress. Parents sing lullabies to their kids to help them sleep, people sing prayers in churches and synagogues, and many symphonygoers rest their eyes when attending symphonic concerts. Music has the ability to calm, whether it's played in the milking shed so the cows will let down their milk, in restaurants so customers order more, or in operating rooms where surgeons ask their patients what type of music they want to hear, even though the patients will be under a general anesthetic at the time of the surgery.

Try playing classical music as background during the dinner hour or just when you're all trying to wind down. Just as a John Philip Sousa march can get the heart beating, a concerto, especially one with a tempo that matches the human heart beat, can be calming.

A groundbreaking study reported in the February 2005 issue of the international research journal, *Medical Science Monitor*, reported for the first time that "playing a musical instrument can reverse multiple components of the human stress response on the genomic level." So get out your old guitar or ukulele, and start picking away your stress.

# Chapter 25

# Caring for Your Health

*Look to your health; and if you have it, praise God,*
*and value it next to a good conscience; for health is*
*the second blessing that we mortals are capable of—a*
*blessing that money cannot buy.*

—IZAAK WALTON

Guys are not known for going to doctors. Married men have wives who nag them to see their physician when it's suspected that something is wrong, but as your wife is now your ex, you need to become your own health advocate. You don't have to become a hypochondriac or perform an organ recital every morning to be sure everything's shipshape, just be smart. If you're having any kind of chest pains, blood in your stool, dizzy spells, a mole that changes color or shape, or something else that's different, make an appointment to see a doctor. Take care of your health; your kids are counting on you.

## HOW TO EAT BALANCED MEALS ON YOUR OWN

You may not feel much like eating regularly, especially on days when you don't have the kids and you come home to an empty house. One way to avoid this is not to eat alone. Either meet friends for dinner or invite them over for a cookout. Hopefully they'll offer to bring something, and you can encourage them to bring salad or vegetables. Chances are you're not eating enough of either of these.

When you eat alone the temptation is ripe for junk food. But to stay healthy and to keep your immune system strong, you need to eat a fairly regular proper diet, one that includes a lot of vegetables and fruits, whole grains, and protein that includes fish, chicken, lean meats, and dairy.

How can you tell if you're eating the right foods? Use the jeans test. If your jeans are baggy, you're losing weight because you're eating a balanced diet; if they're too tight, you're eating too much of the wrong foods. If you really haven't a clue what constitutes a balanced diet, call your local hospital and set up an appointment with a dietitian or nutritionist.

## EXERCISE IS NOT A FOUR-LETTER WORD

For many guys, the word exercise conjures up visions of a physically fit male jogging on a beach along side a gorgeous woman in a tiny bikini. Although that's not a bad vision to keep you motivated, it shouldn't be one to make you throw in the towel and get discouraged as you get yourself another beer and settle back on your couch.

You don't have to be in shape to begin to exercise, although you do need to check with your physician before beginning any exercise program. Don't figure that you'll go from couch potato to a triathlon champ over one weekend. Take it slow to build up your endurance, muscles, and knowledge of what you are attempting. Keep a written chart to track your progress and give you encouragement. It takes time to develop the habit of exercising. Believe it or not, at some point you actually will look forward to working out.

## WHEN IT COMES TO EXERCISE, ONE KIND DOES NOT FIT ALL

You need to discover what type of exercise you enjoy, and it may take a bit of trial and error before you zero in on one or two types of exercise you really like enough to keep doing them. Don't give up too soon. There's a wide variety—aerobics, baseball, basketball, cycling, climbing, dancing, fencing, golf, gymnastics, hiking, handball, ice hockey, judo, jogging, karate, rowing, racquetball, soccer, swimming, softball, tennis, volleyball, walking, and weight lifting—and . . . well, you get the idea.

Ask yourself if you really like team sports or if you prefer to work out in solitude. Can you pace yourself or are you ultracompetitive? Walking briskly still holds its own as a safe, beneficial, and lifelong form of exercise. While you may be a closet walker, clocking your miles in privacy on the treadmill in your bedroom as the kids sleep, most walkers seems to prefer the outdoors so they can see people, enjoy the changing seasons, and breath the fresh air.

Remember that the purpose of exercise is to enjoy moving your body as you firm up and improve your sense of well-being. It isn't to make you feel more stressed, but rather to reduce stress. If exercise is making you too competitive and creating more stress in your life, find something else or find partners who play tennis or racquetball, run, or lift weights for the joy of it, not to see if they can wipe you out. Good-natured kidding is one thing; gnashing your teeth and arguing over points until your face grows red is another. If you or your partners toss golf clubs or smash tennis racquets after bad shots, it doesn't take a genius to figure out that that particular form of exercise probably isn't a very good idea for you if it creates more stress in your life.

## FIND SPORTS OR EXERCISE PLANS TO FIT YOUR BUDGET

Don't run out and buy skis and ski clothes, golf clubs, boxing gloves, or a racing shell until you know you really enjoy those activities and have the available time to pursue them. You can always rent sports equipment. In fact, in many communities there are stores, such as Play It Again Sports, that sell treadmills, skis, free weights, and golf clubs that are used but still in good condition.

The simplest solution is often the best. There's nothing wrong with just speed walking or jogging for exercise, and all you really need is a good pair of proper shoes. You can quickly work up a sweat while you just as quickly reduce stress.

### Dance

Don't forget that dance provides a good physical workout while offering the comfort of touching when you have a partner in your arms, something you may be missing right now. Never underestimate the importance of touch, even nonsexual touches. As Sherry Suib Cohen, coauthor of *The Magic of Touch*, says, "You can't give a touch without getting one right back. You can talk, listen, smell, see, and taste alone, but touch is a reciprocal act." So whether it's fox trot, tango, tap, or ballroom, give dance a chance.

### Yoga

Yoga, an ancient form of exercise from India, is great for stress reduction and relaxation. If you think that yoga isn't manly, then read *Yoga for Regular Guys* by three-time world champion wrestler Diamond Dallas Page and you'll quickly change your mind. Yoga moves provide a hard workout, and you'll quickly work up a sweat.

Yoga not only firms up muscles, but it also improves lung capacity, balance, your cardiovascular system, and promotes flexibility. Contact your local YMCA, JCC, gym, or community center to check on availability of classes.

Your kids will enjoy learning yoga, and many of the poses, like the cat, three-legged dog, dead bug, and the lion, are fun and let them stretch their imagination as they exercise. As there also is a meditation component to yoga, your kids will learn to calm themselves when they're feeling stressed, an ability that will serve them well throughout their lives.

## HAVING THE KIDS IS NO EXCUSE TO NOT EXERCISE

Sorry, but having the kids is not an acceptable excuse to skip your workout if you have your kids on a frequent basis. If you only have them every other weekend, it's okay to forgo the workout to spend more time with your kids. When you have the kids often, you may need a plan B workout schedule. For example, you may enjoy swimming laps, but you can't do it when you have the little guys in tow. But you can still take them to the pool and bounce around in the water with them. If they're old enough, you could challenge them to swim laps with you, but don't be surprised if you tire out first. Your kids also need exercise to reduce their stress.

While you may not be able to work out at the gym when you have your kids, you can take them for a walk or a jog before dinner. Give each of them a pedometer to keep track of steps taken and record them in a personal journal. See who can reach 10,000 steps a day first. If you can afford a treadmill or free weights, you also can work out when they're in bed or before they get up in the morning.

Take your kids biking, hiking, skating, cross-country skiing, or just walking with you. Play catch, toss a football, play badminton, or run relays. Play softball or badminton on the weekend instead of spending money going to an amusement park or movie. You'll communicate more and have more laughs, and by getting the kids active they'll enjoy exercising too, though they may just think of it as playing. Whatever it's called, it's a good stress reducer for all of you.

Two caveats concerning exercise:

- Always check with your physician before starting an exercise program.
- Don't try to get all your exercise done over the weekend. Space it out so you don't pull a muscle.

## LIMIT ALCOHOL USAGE AND AVOID ILLEGAL DRUGS

Although it may seem tempting to mellow out with a drink or two or three, limit your alcohol intake. It impairs your judgment, contains empty calories, and could be a deciding factor in your losing custody, shared custody, or even your weekend time shared with your kids. Judges today are more concerned about drug and alcohol usage by either parent in deciding custody agreements. Don't give your ex any ammunition that could be used against you.

Don't be tempted to use any type of illegal drugs, and be cautious about over-the-counter sleep aids as they can affect both your driving and judgment. What's more, if you are caught by the police for any type of drug offence, you could lose your kids. Is it worth it?

## MASSAGE THERAPY

No, this isn't the kinky massage image that may have just popped into your mind. Massage therapy is the manipulation of the superficial tissues of the body, used for therapeutic purposes and stress reduction. Massage was used by the ancient Greeks and Romans and has been used by the Chinese, Japanese, and other Eastern cultures for centuries.

Although there are different types of massage—Swedish, sports, shiatsu, hot stone, reflexology, deep tissue—they all work out tension and help you to relax. Some go deeper into the muscles to improve circulation.

Most health clubs and spas offer the services of a massage therapist. If one comes to your home, check out references and be sure he or she is licensed by your state. Be sure to tell your massage therapist what type of a massage you prefer—light touch or deeper pressure. If you don't want music in the background, say so, and if you are allergic to any kind of scent in the oil, be sure to mention that as well.

## THE IMPORTANCE OF SLEEP

You may not think sleep is important. Perhaps you've bragged that you can get along with only four or five hours a night. But the truth is too little sleep can increase your risk of heart disease, diabetes, and weight gain. What's more, your brain needs more than four or five hours of down time. In a December 20, 2004, article in *Time,* author Christine Gorman wrote, "After about 18 hours without sleep, your reaction time begins to slow from a quarter of a second to half a second and then longer." She states that two hours later, "Your reaction time, studies show, is roughly the same as someone who has a blood-alcohol level of 0.08— high enough to get you arrested for driving under the influence in forty-nine states."

No wonder that when you're sleep deprived you feel foggy, can't focus on your work, and even have trouble answering the simplest question your child might pose you. It makes you cranky, abrupt with your kids when you don't want to be, and causes you to function at less than your personal best.

Your judgment would be clouded in case of an emergency.

## CREATE A WELCOMING SLEEP ENVIRONMENT

In order to get a good night's sleep you need to:

- Maintain regular bedtime hours and routines, even on the weekend.
- Have a cool, dark bedroom. If you can't make the room dark enough with curtains, shutters, or blackout shades, wear eye shades.
- Get comfortable. Your bed should have a good mattress. Don't skimp on quality if you're buying a new mattress. Tell the salesperson whether you like a firm mattress or a medium one. If you're not sure, take off your shoes and lie down on a few. Buy the best sheets you can; the higher the thread count, the softer the sheets. (If you're a stomach sleeper and the buttons on your pajamas bother you, buy some with a slipover top, sleep in a T-shirt and shorts, or go nude unless you have a young child who likes to climb into bed with you.)
- Avoid coffee, tea, chocolate, and soft drinks with caffeine after 5 p.m. Even decaffeinated coffee and tea products contain some caffeine, and if you're sensitive to it your sleep can be affected.
- Avoid alcohol before going to bed.
- Stop exercising three to four hours before bedtime. Try to finish working out before dinner.
- Avoid large meals close to bedtime.
- If your clock has glow-in-the-dark numbers, turn it away from your bed so you're not disturbed by the light or keep opening your eyes to watch the time change.

- Practice visualization or progressive relaxation to help you relax and clear your mind. If you find yourself thinking about your problems or your kids, focus instead on your special safe place and relax those tense muscles. Sleep, you'll find, does make problems lessen. This is not a new concept. Aeschylus, who lived 525–456 B.C., wrote in *Agamemnon*, ". . . and even in our sleep pain that cannot forget falls drop by drop upon the heart, and in our own despair, against our will, comes wisdom to us by the awful grace of God."

If despite all these suggestions you're still having trouble sleeping after twenty or thirty minutes, don't lie in bed fighting it. Get up, go to another room, and read. Don't watch TV.

If your insomnia continues, see your doctor or check to see if your local hospital has a sleep center. For more information, check out the National Sleep Foundation at *www.sleepfoundation.org* or the American Insomnia Association at *www.american insomniaassociation.org*.

# Chapter 26

# Coping When You're a Widower

*Though lover be lost love shall not;*
*And death shall have no dominion.*
—DYLAN THOMAS

Despite what others may think or even subtly suggest to you, there are no rules or time limits when it comes to grieving. You must do it in your own way, and there's no doubt that it's extra difficult when you have children you need to comfort as well. Don't try to ignore your own needs as you attend to those of your children. Grieving is a process that needs to run its course, no matter how long it takes. If you try to dam it up and deny your emotions, you will eventually have a major emotional or physical flood on your hands.

## THERE'S NO TIME LIMIT ON GRIEVING

Unfortunately, time alone seldom moves you out of grief. If it were that easy, you'd just mark the calendar and at the end of your "official" grieving period go on with your life. But it doesn't work that way.

There is a great deal of pain, sadness, regret, and even guilt that has to be acknowledged before you can put your life back together again. You have lost your helpmate, your lover, and, in many cases, your best friend.

In their book *Getting to the Other Side of Grief*, authors Susan J. Zonnebelt-Smeenge and Robert C. DeVries said they "believed our futures had been ripped from us when our spouses died. We needed to grieve the death of hopes and dreams before we could begin to build again." And that grieving takes time, mourning not only the loss of the partner in marriage but also, as the authors wrote, for the loss of their "hopes and dreams."

Unfortunately, for the most part, our culture doesn't have specific rituals for handling grief so it's basically every man for himself so to speak. Of course, there is the funeral or memorial service, the burial or cremation service, and the obligatory meal (with more cakes, cookies, and pies than substantial food) that follows. Then everyone goes home and you are left—with your kids—to grieve alone.

In the Jewish culture there is a tradition to sit shiva, which is a seven-day period of mourning where friends and relatives come to console and to pray with the bereaved family. And at the end of a year (the official mourning period), a headstone is laid on the gravesite. But a person's mourning doesn't usually follow such a perfect schedule. That ache in your heart and sense of loneliness can last years, even a lifetime, even though you will eventually go on to live an active and fulfilled life.

## EVERYONE GRIEVES DIFFERENTLY

Forget the myth that says men don't grieve. Men do, but often they grieve alone because they don't think it's manly to show emotions to friends and family, and because they lack any specific grief rituals to help them.

In his book *Swallowed by a Snake: The Gift of the Masculine Side of Healing*, author Thomas R. Golden describes grief rituals as "behavior that consciously and intentionally move us out of our ordinary awareness and into the experience of the pain of grief." He describes examples of such grief rituals as "simple as leafing through a photo album or as complex as writing a symphony."

Most men perform their unique grief rituals, whatever they may be, in private, leaving friends, relatives, and, most importantly, their kids to wonder if the widower is over his grief when chances are he is still struggling with it. If you and your wife were each other's best friend, then you have lost the one person in the world who could have comforted you. If, on the other hand, your marriage was a somewhat contentious one, then you may be dealing with a sense of guilt as well. Don't hesitate to reach out for counseling from a therapist, your religious leader, or a social worker if you feel you need guidance.

When Walter's wife died after a long battle with breast cancer, his friends agreed with one another that he seemed to be coping well. Privately, however, he kept the audio tape recording from the answering machine because it had his late wife's voice on it, and he played it over and over again as he sobbed, alone in his bedroom.

Other widowers quietly admit to creating "action" grief rituals, running until they literally dropped from exhaustion or working out in the weight room until their muscles cried uncle. Only by wearing themselves out physically could they momentarily burn off the emotional grief of their loss.

## LET YOUR KIDS KNOW YOU'RE HURTING TOO

Because these men mourned in secret and did not or could not verbalize their grief, their kids also often suffered in silence, hesitating to tell dad how much they missed their mom and wondering what they could do to relieve the hurt they felt inside. If they didn't see their dad crying, they figured maybe they shouldn't cry either. So the kids wept alone and in silence.

That's why it's so important to take time to share with your kids your feelings of pain, anger, loneliness, and emptiness, so they can open up and express their feelings to you as well. Remember that while kids must grieve in their own way, you give them permission to mourn when you communicate that you are also grieving and share with them what has helped you.

Don't be shocked if at times your kids act as though nothing's changed. They laugh, joke around with their friends, and talk incessantly on the phone. It may be that they just need some respite from the sadness or fear they are feeling. Encourage them to be with friends if they want to, talk with you, or just have some quiet time looking at photos of their mom. Suggest that they read some of the age-appropriate books about death (see the suggested readings in Appendix B), play music, shoot hoops, write in a journal, draw pictures, or do whatever works for them.

Regardless if your wife died suddenly in an accident or had her death anticipated due to a lingering illness, you are never ready to lose a loved one. There's always the hope that a miracle could be right around the corner to wake you from this nightmare you are all living. But the problems basically remain the same. Your helpmate is gone and you now have the sole responsibility of raising your children while at the same time grieving your loss and fighting a bewildering array of emotions, such as anger, guilt, despair, fear, and overwhelming loneliness. These are normal reactions, and it's also possible that your kids are experiencing similar ups and downs. They may be angry at their mother for leaving them and scream that they hate her for doing so, then break down, sobbing, because they miss her. You need to let them know that it's okay to experience these feelings and that you're having similar thoughts.

You and your kids may wonder why God let this happen and what will become of you. You shudder to consider how you will cope with all this responsibility now on your shoulders alone. If both of you needed to work for financial reasons, the growing pile of unpaid bills may seem overwhelming. And suddenly you think of a zillion questions you wish you had asked your wife before this vast emptiness filled your life.

# FOCUS ON YOURSELF FIRST

In their book *When a Man Faces Grief*, Thomas R. Golden and James E. Miller state that "grief has an important purpose. It helps you heal." If you try to deny your grief or rush the process, it's like hurrying back to the tennis court before your knee is healed from surgery; you may very well fall and become hurt permanently.

A great deal of the advice in Chapter 24 on reducing stress and caring for your health can be applied to the grieving process. Your kids depend on you right now for physical, emotional, as well as financial support. This is no time for heavy drinking or using drugs in order to try to help you forget your loss or to start eating junk food because you really don't care anymore and it's too much effort to cook. If you haven't exercised before or stopped in order to take care of your ill wife, you need to take it up again. You may not feel like exercising, and even walking seems like too much of an effort, but once you get moving you'll find that exercise helps to ease the depression and the heaviness in your heart. Get the kids moving as well, even it's only to join you in an afterdinner walk or a game of kickball.

### Get Adequate Sleep

You may find it difficult to get to sleep, or, if you do, you wake up often during the night and reach out your hand, hoping that it was all a bad dream and that she's really there right next to you. When there's only emptiness, it leaves you feeling hollow.

Don't lie there with your memories. Get up, go into another room, and read until you feel sleepy. Some men prefer to watch television, but if you do, stay away from the gun battles and other violent films that will stir you up, not lull you back to sleep. If you feel like crying, go ahead. You're crying for what you've lost as much as for whom you've lost. That's okay. It's a normal reaction.

# THE THREE A'S OF GRIEF: ANGER, ABANDONMENT, AND ABSENTMINDEDNESS

You may see the need for other words, such as awful, agony, or adrift, but the bottom line is that you feel alone, even though you have kids. Your wedding vows may have included "'Till death do us part," but you didn't think that would come so soon.

### Anger

You can't very well be mad at your spouse for dying and leaving you alone with the kids. It wasn't her fault; she would have wanted to help you parent and see her kids grown. Nevertheless, it's human nature to be angry and want to strike out at the fates that took her away from you. It may help if you try to remember that your anger is at your loss, not at your wife.

Try to keep your temper under control and don't snap at your kids, peers at work, or others trying to help you even though they don't know how or what you want.

Be especially on guard for signs of road rage—screaming at other drivers who cut you off, take your parking spot, or drive too slowly. If you feel that anger is controlling you (or others mention it to you), get counseling, chop wood, punch a punching bag, or run until you're tired. Try meditation and prayer. Forgive her for leaving you and perhaps the anger will dissipate.

### Abandonment

When you're grieving there's also a terrible sense of being abandoned. While you must recognize that in your kids as well and assure them that you're there for them, you also have to accept that terrible loneliness in your own life. You were supposed to be a pair, a table for two, bookends. You may feel a loss of part of you. She was the one who kept track of family birthdays, knew where the Thanksgiving decorations were stored, and maintained the social calendar. You feel as though you're in a strange, new world where you're not totally fluent. Fortunately, that sense of being in a foreign land will eventually fade away, but the passport may be slow in coming.

### Absentmindedness

Be aware too that grief can cause a type of absentmindedness. It's as though your mind has shut down. You may not hear your kids when they ask you a question and they'll have to repeat it a few times until you tune them in, you'll burn the dinner because you forgot to set the timer, or you'll hit the delete button on the computer when you meant to save the file. Be especially careful when you're driving as you may drive through a red light without really seeing it or end up in front of your house without remembering the drive home. Treat yourself gently.

## YOUR KIDS MAY GRIEVE DIFFERENTLY THAN YOU

People may tell you that kids snap back fast, or because they're so young they'll get over it, but don't listen. While kids do grieve differently than grownups, they still grieve. You may not always recognize the signs, especially while you're grieving too.

### Death Is Not a Stranger

Thanks to television news and violent entertainment programs, magazines, and movies, your kids have seen or read about a lot of people dying. Every day they see footage of children starving to death in Africa, masked terrorists shooting civilians, kids shooting other kids in school, bombs exploding over houses, trains, and subways, or people dying in floods, tornados, and hurricanes. They may have had a beloved pet die or witnessed a grandparent's illness and eventual death.

But regardless how many deaths kids may have seen or read about, it's different when their mother dies. They may be angry at her for leaving them, experience great sadness, feel sorry for themselves, and take their bewildering and fluctuating assortment of emotions out on the only person around—you.

### Expect the Unexpected When Kids Grieve

Don't expect your child or children to mourn the same way you do, but listen carefully to what they say or don't say. Depending on their ages, they may demonstrate a variety of physical and psychological problems (including bed wetting, nightmares, crying, loss of appetite). They may lose interest in school or extracurricular activities and disregard personal hygiene. You may find your daughter, who previously took hours primping in front of the bathroom mirror and deciding what outfit to wear to school, not bothering to comb her hair and wearing yesterday's wrinkled shirt—or she may dress provocatively. A teenage son may skip classes, quit a sports team, or pick fights with others at school. Some kids don't want to mention their mother because they're angry she left them and feel abandoned, while others may write notes to her, frame photos of her for display in their room, and talk about her constantly, as in "Mom always liked pink roses, didn't she, Dad?" or "Mom cooked it this way," or "Mom let me."

## Talking about It

Allow your children to talk about their fears and feelings, if they will. Don't try to protect them from the reality of death and never use euphemisms such as "Mommy is sleeping," "Mommy passed away," or "Mommy has gone away." Younger kids may worry what will happen to them if they go to sleep or if you need to "go away" on a business trip. The reality is that Mommy died and she isn't coming back. Stewart told his three-year-old that "Mommy is in heaven." They may wonder and worry what happens if they die. Is it like when the TV dies and the repair man comes to fix it?

## Kids Wonder "What about Me?"

As children tend to feel that the world revolves around them, reassure them often that nothing they did caused their mom to die and that it isn't punishment for anything. They may feel guilty because once, when angry, they shouted, "I hate you. I wish you were dead!" and now she is.

Chances are one of the first questions they'll ask is, "Are you going to die too, and what will happen to me?"

Your answer needs to reassure them that you're in good health and will continue to care for them the way you and their mom always did. If you have a close family, mention that those relatives also will be on hand to help. If you and your wife made arrangements for your children's guardianship if anything happened to you both, you can share that information with your kids. It reassures them that someone will always be there to take care of them and offers them a sense of security. (If you haven't selected a guardian in case of your death, put that on your to-do list.)

While intellectually you know that you need to reach out to your kids to soothe their pain, remember the message given by airline attendants that states in case of an emergency you should reach for and put on your own oxygen mask first before helping others. It's important because your kids will take a cue from you during this troubled time. If you can show confidence (even though you may not feel it just now), your kids will reflect that confidence that life will go on because "Dad's in charge."

This doesn't mean that you shouldn't let the kids know that you're grieving, but at the same time you have to convince them that you know that you all will get through this troubled time together. Mention how much you miss her at Christmas when you're all decorating the tree, and don't be surprised if some of your kids offer their remembrances of a past Christmas when she was still with you all. Be comfortable telling them their mom would have been so proud of them in the play, at the game, or getting into the honor society. Show them that even though her presence is absent, the memories of her remain alive.

If your kids mention that they sometimes mentally talk to their mom even though she's no longer around, admit that you do too and how it comforts you. Elaine wears one of her mother's rings at special events and feels her mother's spirit with her. Your kids may want to similarly wear a ring, necklace, or favorite sweater that their mother enjoyed to help them keep her memory strong.

Expect that Mother's Day and your wife's birthday (and your anniversary) may be difficult days for everyone. Acknowledge the fact and allow the kids to put flowers on her grave if they want, write a letter to her, or say a special prayer in her memory.

If one of your kids seems to have difficulty coping with the loss of his or her mother and won't talk to you about it, ask your rabbi, minister, or priest for the name of a grief counselor. Remember that it takes time, and every person copes at his or her own time table.

While you're trying to handle the loss of your wife, make sure you stay physically and emotionally strong for the sake of your kids. In their book *When a Man Faces Grief*, authors Golden and Miller reaffirm this message by saying, "Take good care of yourself. . . . Care for your physical needs . . . your emotional needs . . . your social needs . . . your spiritual needs." Then, and only then, can you reach out to others.

Stewart says that to celebrate his late wife's birthday, he takes his son, a few of the boy's friends, and a chocolate cake to the cemetery where "we pay our respects. Then we walk around looking at all the other tombstones trying to do the subtraction between birth and death to figure out how old the people were when they died. Then we eat the cake and remember the good times as I try to forget the bad."

## KEEP COMMUNICATION WITH YOUR KIDS FLOWING

Keep communication flowing so everyone feels comfortable expressing his or her feelings. It's okay to grieve, but do so in a healthy way, without withdrawing. Like it or not, you're a role model for your kids. They need to see how you express loss in order for them to learn how to express theirs. Let them know that you loved their mom and miss her, but emphasize that you're still a family unit and that their mom would want you to continue as such.

Encourage younger kids to draw pictures to express their feelings about their loss, while older ones may want to write poems or even essays about their relationship with their mom. Tell them you need their help around the house to do some of the chores she used to do, but don't let them, especially

your daughters, try to take over her place and attempt to be the lady of the house. Try to make her favorite Thanksgiving dish, or dig out her favorite recipes for apple pie and give it a try. Mention her often, even if it makes you and them a little teary, and tell the kids often how much she loved them and how proud she'd be of them. Keep their mom's memory alive while you all go on with living.

## REMAIN WATCHFUL FOR SIGNS OF DEPRESSION IN YOUR KIDS

It was not until 1980, when the American Psychiatric Association published the third edition of the *Diagnostic and Statistical Manual of Mental Disorders*, that depression in children was finally officially recognized. But now it's accepted that all children, even infants and toddlers, can be depressed.

### Adolescents Struggle with Loss of a Parent

It can be extremely traumatic if a parent dies when an adolescent is beginning to separate and develop a little independence from his or her parents. The youngster often is overwhelmed with guilt because he or she has been at odds with the parent and regrets things said with no time to take them back.

In their book *Getting to the Other Side of Grief*, authors Susan J. Zonnebelt-Smeenge, R.N., Ed.D., and Robert C. DeVries, D. Min., Ph.D., remind that because adolescents may have the most difficult time dealing with the loss of their parent, such a trauma can trigger a suicide attempt in some susceptible youngsters. "Most adolescents do not allow themselves to go through the grieving process at the time of their parent's death," they write. The warning signs and symptoms of depression were covered in Chapter 14 (also see *The Everything Parent's Guide to Children with Depression*), but you should watch for changes in behavior, especially:

- Continued withdrawal and isolation
- Discontinuing normal activities such as sports
- Avoiding friends
- A disinterest or drop in academic performance
- Change in sleep habits, either inability to sleep or sleeping a great deal
- Loss of energy
- Loss of appetite or voracious eating

If you see the above signs of depression in any of your kids, but particularly in those who are adolescents, contact a professional mental health counselor; your minister, priest, or rabbi; or your community's crisis center help line immediately. Don't hesitate, especially if your youngster talks about suicide, starts giving away possessions, or says life isn't worth living. Don't believe the myth that says people who talk about suicide never do it. That's false and wishful thinking. Take all suicide threats seriously, even in a young child. Many kids under twelve don't realize that death is permanent. Be alert for unexplained:

### Bruises

Some children who are depressed will hit themselves or take part in risk behavior to punish themselves for whatever guilt they may be feeling because of their mother's death.

### Burns

Children from toddlers to teens have been known to play with matches and watch things burn as a way to feel in control of some part of their lives.

### Cuts

Some seriously depressed kids are cutters; they cut themselves with scissors, knives, or razors to distract themselves from the emotional pain they're feeling. They may cut their arms and wear long sleeves, even in hot weather, to keep adults from seeing the results of their pain. Others will cut their legs or face, a silent but obvious cry for help.

## Help for Grieving Kids and Dads

There are many good books dealing with grieving, although just a few specifically written for men. Check out the ones mentioned in the suggested reading list in Appendix B. Your bookstore or local library may have others. Your community's hospice organization also can help with loss and bereavement issues and may have support groups for children whose parent has died. Many communities have specific peer support groups for grieving children.

Be patient with yourself and your kids, but don't put off getting help for the family. If you have family or close friends, encourage their support, but beware of people who think that their advice is as good as a trained therapist's.

## WHEN TO REMOVE HER THINGS

You may have kept your wife's closet just as it was when she died. Don't let well-meaning friends and relatives clean it out before you're ready. Be firm now so you're not sorry later. Many widowers spoke of frequently opening the closet door, just to get a whiff of their wife's perfume on her clothes. It wasn't until the scent was gone that they were able to give her clothes away to Goodwill, Salvation Army, or their church or synagogue thrift shop. The operative word here is when you are ready, not when her mom, sister, or anyone else thinks it's time to toss everything out. A caveat: if the kids want something of their mom's—a sweater, skis, tennis racquet, stuffed animal, scarf, whatever—even if you think it's a strange request, let them have it. It will help them feel closer to her.

What about your wedding band? When should you take it off? There's really no rule. It is up to you. Wearing it may let you feel closer to your wife. Taking it off may be a wrench, a sense of finality, and confirmation that she's really gone and you're alone. The obvious answer is to wear your wedding band for as long as you want to, even if that is for the rest of your life. The choice is yours.

## What Possessions to Keep

Keep the things you feel your children may want when they're older, such as pieces of jewelry, furniture, dishes, silver, scrapbooks, and photos, or that they might want now. You'll probably keep using the dishes and good silver, but if you aren't, pack them away carefully for the kids when they're grown and have places of their own. Daughters especially often like to use things their moms and grandmothers used.

# THE GHOST THAT LURKS

People often tend to remember only the good things about a person after he or she dies, and year after year the pedestal grows taller. Be careful that you don't raise your kids' mother to such a height that they feel she was a saint and that they can't possibly be good enough to be worthy of being her children. You want to promote their self-esteem by helping them to foster doing good deeds, being honest, and caring, along with other virtues. Let them know that they have these qualities within themselves and they don't need to compete with anyone (deceased or alive). Praise them for their abilities and love them for themselves.

## Ghosts Can Be Frightening

Don't minimize your children's successes by the reflection of a ghost with whom they can't possibly compete. Telling your daughter that she should take art and music because her mother was so talented in those fields can be frustrating and humiliating to a young woman who can't draw a straight line with a ruler and is tone deaf. Let her instead discover her own special qualities so she can find success on her own and not try to be a copy of her deceased mother.

Telling your son his mom always wanted him to become a doctor or some other similar message can cause great anxiety and conflicts in a young person who wants to honor his late mother's desires for him but who really has no interest in going into medicine.

## Competing with Ghosts

Be mindful when you begin to date again that you don't measure every woman to your late wife's standard. The new woman may have other outstanding traits that your late wife didn't. While it's obvious that you have been married before (and have the kids to prove it), be careful not to share story after story showing how fantastic your late wife was or you may find your present date fading away into your past. It's hard to compete with a ghost.

# ASK FOR HELP

Don't try to be both mom and dad to your kids. Just focus on being a loving father to them and listen to what they say and don't say. When you find yourself overwhelmed with housework that never seems to be done or when your daughter needs a motherly hand in redecorating her room, buying a prom dress, or learning to use makeup, reach out and ask for help. Ask relatives, friends, or find a professional who can step in. It doesn't mean you're lacking or that you don't try. It just means that you can't do it all and that you're human. Besides, a professional house cleaner or painter needs the work (so you're doing a good deed), and an aunt, grandmother, or good female friend would be delighted to offer advice to your daughter.

## ACCEPT YOUR NEW ROLE AS A SINGLE FATHER

If you're like most men, you're probably amazed at the number of tasks your late wife carried out that you never knew or thought about. Some of them probably don't have to be done, like keeping scrapbooks on each child or putting summer slipcovers on the couch and living room chairs. You can put all the photos in shoe boxes, one for each child, after dating the back of each picture. If you feel a need to use summer slipcovers, get your kids to help.

But there are many chores that do need to be done, such as cleaning out the freezer, cleaning the vents over the stove, and removing stains in clothes before washing them. If you don't know how to carry these out, ask for help.

Is your seven-year-old son still wearing size five pants and complaining that they're too tight? Does your twelve-year-old daughter want to do away with the Disney character prints on her comforter and get

something more adult? What should you do about your three-year-old who keeps climbing out of the crib?

If you're just keeping your head afloat with your job and the weekend isn't long enough to get all the household tasks and shopping done, ask a friend to give you a hand, shop through catalogs, or take advantage of shopping on the Internet. You can buy new pants for your son, help your daughter pick out a new comforter, and even order a new big boy bed for your three-year-old online. These days it is also possible to order groceries online and have them delivered to your door in many communities. Check out *www.peapod.com* or contact your local grocery store for more information.

In some cities there are concierge services that you can call and they'll pick up and deliver your dry cleaning, buy birthday presents, decorate your house for the holidays, and even do your grocery shopping. (They don't car-pool kids, however.) These services are expensive, but if you can afford them, they're wonderful time savers. Look in your phone book to see if there's such a service near you.

### You're the Decision Maker
You may feel uncomfortable making all the decisions about the kids now that asking mom isn't an option. If you don't know what age your daughter can wear makeup or go out on a date, or when your son can play contact sports, ask a friend or relative who has kids near your child's age but take the answer only as a guide, not something written in stone. You still have to decide what's right for your own kids. If you've gotten friendly with other single dads, you can ask them or check with the mother of your kids' friends to see how they handle those and other situations. The buck still

stops with you, but at least you'll have some guidelines.

## WHEN TO START DATING AGAIN

Most of the dating suggestions in Chapter 21 also pertain to the widower. It's more difficult re-entering the dating scene as a widower because the kids may feel that your dating means you've forgotten their mother. Preteens and even teens may resent the fact that you have expressed a need for adult female company. Try bringing up the discussion when you have the kids in the car so they can't slip away. Assure them that you'll always love the memory of their mother but that you're lonely. Listen to their reactions and never minimize their feelings. These may range anywhere from "But you shouldn't be lonely. You have us!" to "Thank goodness. You're driving us all crazy." Some may express anger at the idea of your seeing another woman who could try to take their mother's place while others may say nothing, leaving you to wonder what's on their mind.

Give your children time to get used to your dating. Tell your teenagers when you're meeting a female friend from work or a woman you met at your creative writing seminar. Just say that she seems nice and you wanted to have coffee or dinner with her. Usually, if they feel you're being honest with them, most kids won't give you any arguments. Younger children may ask if she's going to be their new mommy. If they do, just laugh or smile and say that for now she's just a friend.

Be careful, however, about letting yourself be dragged into the dating scene before you feel ready. While you may feel lonely and miss the companionship of your late wife, you don't want to feel guilty when you do go out, as though you're cheating on her somehow. Give yourself permission to re-enter the world when it feels right to you, and know that you would have her blessing for doing so.

## KEEP REMINDERS OF YOUR DECEASED WIFE EVEN IF YOU REMARRY

Although it's understandable that a new woman in your life would like to make your home reflect her tastes too, don't wipe out all traces of your children's mother. Seymour's children were of college age when he remarried, but when one daughter came home during vacation, she said to her dad, "How come there aren't any pictures around of mom anymore?"

While she understood that her father needed to get on with his life, she didn't want her mother to be forgotten. Fortunately, he understood where his daughter was coming from, and together they went through the scrapbooks and found a few pictures of his original family to frame and leave out. Later, his daughter was content to have new photos of her dad, stepmother, herself, and her sisters lined up on the bookcase next to the other pictures.

You may want to keep some memories of your deceased wife around as well. Mention to the kids that you're using mom's favorite dishes for Easter or have a pair of her gold earrings made into cuff links for your French cuff shirts. While it's fine to keep favorite pictures of her in your bedroom, you need to put them away if and when you remarry.

Hopefully you'll still stay in touch with your wife's family so they can enjoy their grandchildren, nieces, and nephews. Encourage your kids to see them often so they can grow up hearing stories of their mom when she was little, stories with which you may not be familiar. If they all live in a different town, encourage your kids to visit if possible, or send pictures and letters telling what they're doing if visiting is not an option. Also, be sure that they always write thank-you notes for gifts.

# PART FOUR

# EX-MATTERS: DIPLOMACY WITH THEIR MOTHER

# Chapter 27

# Respecting Different Parenting Styles

*Now we've made the revolutionary discovery*
*that children have two parents.*
*A decade ago, even the kindly Dr. Spock*
*held mothers solely responsible for children.*
—GLORIA STEINEM

Although Gloria Steinem said the preceeding statement in 1983, it still holds true in the minds of many. Dads we interviewed said some people look amazed when they say their kids live with them full time, part time, or even on weekends, as though this was some kind of an amazing feat.

It may be tempting, but don't consciously parent differently from your ex-wife just to get even. It's easier for your kids if the house rules are somewhat the same in both homes. However, if you do have major differences, try to communicate and compromise as best you can for the sake of your children.

## CONSIDER YOUR OWN PARENTING STYLE

Take time to think about your own parenting style before you criticize that of your ex. It may be similar to that of your own parents or, if you didn't like the way your parents raised you, it may be almost the direct opposite. Are you laid-back and do you pretty much let the kids do what they want until they step over your vague line in the sand? Are you a perfectionist, remaking their beds and reloading the dishwasher in order to fit in one more plate? Are you fairly strict, like your military father, who expected his kids to toe the line? Are you a worrier, always fantasizing the worst that can happen, constantly feeling your kids' foreheads to see if they're feverish and always feeling anxious

---

✔ **Tip from the Trenches**

Mark reminds that "You don't owe anyone an explanation of why it is that you, the dad, have full custody. Just smile and say, 'It works for us.'"

---

that your kids are going to get hurt when they're outside playing?

What type of parenting makes you comfortable? Respect your ex's parenting enough that if she is a stickler for something at her house, try to get the kids to do it at your house as well. This shows that you're willing to make an effort at meeting in the middle and will go a long way toward goodwill with her and with keeping parenting styles consistent in both households. Hopefully she will return the favor to you. If neither you nor your ex care if the kids make their beds, give them comforters, duvets, or quilts so they can just toss them over the bed so it looks made or just shut their bedroom doors. It's okay to occasionally let them skip a bath one night as a special treat, even though you know their mom insists on a bath or shower every night before they go to bed, or allow one TV dinner night where everyone gets to eat off the coffee table in front of the television and watch a favorite program. But don't allow these times to occur just because it differs from your ex's preferences, and never tell the kids to keep these indiscretions from their mom.

Be sure to let your ex know that although you do have specific rules at your house, they occasionally may be different from hers and that it's okay with you if she has different ones at her home as well. Acknowledge and stress to your kids that although you and your ex may have a few different rules, it doesn't necessarily mean that one way is right and the other wrong. They're just different.

## ACCEPT DIFFERENCES

Just as you need or would like your ex to accept, or at least acknowledge, your differences in parenting styles, don't anticipate

> ### ✔ Tip from the Trenches
>
> Mike says, "You can't anticipate every situation that may come up with your kids. Fortunately, my ex and I are on relatively good speaking terms in regards to our children. If there's an issue, I'll call and tell her how I think I'm going to handle it and listen if she has a different suggestion. We try to stay united, if possible."

or expect that she'll necessarily agree or approve. Do, however, make every attempt to compromise on major issues such as discipline, bedtimes, curfews, and school work. Try to meet with her in person or contact by phone and discuss how you feel about major concerns, and listen carefully to why she may feel differently. If she thinks grounding a teenager for a first offence is acceptable and you prefer a warning first, talk it out. See if you can win her over to your way of thinking, but don't be surprised if she convinces you that she's right. Do the same with bedtimes, curfews, and other house rules. If, however, your ex refuses to consider hearing your side or even meeting with you, then let her know what the rules are at your house and tell her that you accept that hers are different.

## PARENTING CLASSES CAN HELP

You may have taken a parenting class when you and your then-wife were expecting your first child, but you'll probably need a different kind of instruction now. In fact, eight states—Arizona, Florida, Hawaii, Iowa, New Mexico, Tennessee, Utah, and Virginia—consider parenting after divorce when there are kids involved to be so important that they require couples about to be divorced to attend a class in parenting before the divorce can be finalized. In eleven additional states, a judge may mandate educational classes for divorcing couples with kids.

Even if your state does not require such a class, you might look into taking one. Everyone we interviewed who had taken such a course felt that it was a real eye opener and helpful in becoming better parents even after a divorce. You not only learn specifics from the instructor of such a class, but you'll have a chance to chat informally with other single parents with kids and discover how they handle similar situations.

The truth is you as a parent are always playing catch-up when it comes to your kids in that your response to a specific incident may differ greatly depending on your mood and fatigue factor, the age of your kids, and the act itself. Has any parent ever thought to tell his or her child "Don't put peas up your nose" or "Don't cut your sister's hair"? But despite your best intentions, kids do these things and more!

> ### ✔ Tip from the Trenches
>
> Bob says, "In the beginning, after my separation, I was so angered that I didn't even want to talk to my ex and would send messages through the kids. It was only from going to a state mandated class that I realized the damage I was really doing."

Chapter 28

# Communicating with Your Ex

*I like to listen.*
*I have learned a great deal*
*from listening carefully.*
*Most people never listen.*
—ERNEST HEMMINGWAY

Communication is a vital skill, especially when you're a single dad. There's a saying that a tree falling in a forest miles away from human earshot makes no sound because there's no one there to hear it. Though this theory has been hotly debated, it's plain that effective communication can't take place unless someone hears and understands the message you, the speaker, intended. How you communicate greatly affects what you communicate and often negates or totally changes the meaning of what you intended.

According to communication experts, effective communication must be a two-way exchange. That is, you speak and your ex hears, and then, most importantly, she reflects back what she has heard and what she thinks you meant. This takes constant practice and cooperation. It takes listening more than speaking.

There are communication experts who are trained to deal with communication issues between parent and parent, parent and child, friends, and parent and school personnel. These professionals include members of the clergy, psychologists, psychiatrists, child development specialists, social workers, and school counselors. They may suggest family counseling, individual counseling, or a combination of both. Your pediatrician or internist can often furnish names and credentials for you. If there is a university nearby, contact their psychology or child development department for referrals.

## REMEMBER THE I-C IN COMMUNICATION

Those two letters are the most important part of communication, because if the other person can't say "I see" and truly understand what you're trying to say, effective communication hasn't taken place. Note that this is very different than saying "You're right." Communication is not about winning a conversation, it is about making sure both sides are heard and all sides of an argument have been made in a respectful way. This is vital because effective communication is the glue that holds successful parenting together, even after divorce. Although you may rather have a root canal than communicate with your ex, you must keep talking (and listening) because not communicating creates a devastating vacuum between your children's parents. Divorce can't erase the fact that although you and your ex no longer are husband and wife, you are still and will always be father and mother to your kids.

In his 1924 novel *The Magic Mountain*, author Thomas Mann summed up the importance of communication by writing, "Speech is civilization itself. The word, even the most contradictory word, preserves contact—it is silence which isolates." As you can't jointly raise your children in isolation, you must find a way to do what's best for your kids.

## CREATE A COMFORTABLE ENVIRONMENT

For some couples it is still painful and difficult to communicate face to face without

---

✔ **Tip from the Trenches**

Tom recalled, "When we first separated, we made sure that we made appointments to meet by ourselves. Now we talk regularly on the telephone, share information by e-mail, and see each other when our daughter goes back and forth."

getting into an argument. If this is you and your ex, don't ever try to have a conversation in front of your kids. It frightens kids, regardless of their age, to see their parents yelling at one another. According to psychotherapist Barbara Montague, "Children around the ages of eight to twelve would be scared, take the anger personally by feeling they'd better be perfect or Dad or Mom will hate or distrust them." That puts a tremendous burden on your kids.

Also understand that criticizing the parenting techniques of your ex is like criticizing 50 percent of your kids. You are basically telling your children that you hate, distrust, or can't stand (or whatever adjective you want to use) 50 percent of them. Is that the message you want to convey to your children?

Instead, agree to meet your ex without the kids to discuss important issues in a public place like a coffee shop, park, or mall where neither of you wants to make a scene. Don't head for a noisy restaurant where you have to scream just to be heard. Turn off your Trio or Blackberry, and obviously, no text messaging. Both of you need to give your children's other parent the courtesy of listening.

But if one or both of you won't even agree to a public meeting spot, then use snail mail, e-mail, voice mail, or the telephone when you need to discuss things. All of these devices are far wiser and cheaper than requiring your lawyers or your kids to pass along messages. You can make the child exchange from one home to the other without having to face each other by one person dropping the kids off at school and the other picking them up.

But before you give up meeting in person, ask yourself why you feel unable to face your children's mother to discuss their welfare. Joseph Grenny, coauthor of *Crucial Conversations*, told us, "The greatest challenge is being vigilant at examining and choosing our motives. The natural order of things when we're in pain is to lash out, or seek revenge. And while taking a pot shot here or there can provide some immediate gratification, it comes at an incredible cost—the cost of finding peace for ourselves and creating a psychologically safe world for our children. Those who transition to a healthy new reality are those who are the clearest about what they *really* want. They create a picture in their mind of the new reality they want to form—one where civility and mutual respect grow over time between themselves and their ex-spouse, one where their children feel peace, security and support from a larger group of adults rather than be prisoners to an eternal popularity contest where their every action is a vote for one parent or guardian or the other. The most important thing a single dad can do for himself and his children is to focus on what he *really wants* when what would feel good right now serves lower motives."

So don't come out swinging. Most likely what you really want, if you're honest with yourself, is to reduce any pain your kids may be feeling because of your divorce. As their role model, you need to cooperate and communicate for the greater good, which in this case is the welfare of your children. Teenagers especially don't see this happening too often in today's political arena or on the playing field; let them observe it with their parents.

---

### ✔ Tip from the Trenches

George says: "Try your hardest to communicate face to face with your ex. It's too easy for things to be misunderstood when you use e-mail."

Communication about your kids is so important that you must find a way. There are too many parenting issues that arise and will arise over the years to ignore one another. Regardless of how you feel about the other person or what hurts you still nurse, your divorce is between each other; you're still your children's parents. TOYK (think of your kids).

## ALL COMMUNICATION ISN'T VERBAL

You may think that you and your ex are communicating when you are speaking to one another, but you may be conveying a totally different message than the words would suggest. According to psychologist O. Rex Damron, in *An Introduction to Interpersonal and Public Communication*, "A further obstacle to the accurate communication of feelings is that your perception of what another is feeling is based on so many different kinds of information. When somebody speaks, you notice more than just the words being said; you note the gesture, voice, tone, posture, facial expression, etc. . . . Beyond all this you also have expectations based on your past experiences with the other individual."

With the above in mind, is it any wonder that you and your ex often misunderstand what the other is trying to say? People often react even more to the nonverbal message than they do the actual words spoken. You may be letting your anger at her speak louder than what you're saying by your expression, use of sarcasm, or even your tone of voice. She, in return, may be doing the same.

## DESCRIBE WHAT YOU'RE HEARING

How can you head off this type of problem? By calming down, trying to control yourself, and describing what you think you're hearing. You can say to her, "I feel that you're upset when I said I'd like to have the kids Tuesday night rather than Wednesday night. Is there a problem?" or "Am I right that you're disappointed that I can't switch weeks with you?"

You also can paraphrase what she said, such as "You want me to keep the dog the week I have the kids because you're going out of town. Is that correct?" At first this repeating what you think you heard might feel awkward and strange to you, but if you give it a chance you'll find that checking out the verbal intent of a statement makes it easier to be certain that you understand. It also gives your ex (or any other speaker) the opportunity to explain the body language that discounted what was actually said. An example of this is if your ex says "Of course you can bring the kids back early," and she makes a face and sighs. You can then say to her, "Although I hear that you're saying it's okay, I get the impression that it's not what you feel." Hopefully she'll fess up that she's frustrated that she can't plan her day because you keep changing the return time.

## WHAT TO AVOID SAYING

In addition to becoming aware of your body language, there are other aspects of communication that you need to keep in check.

### Overgeneralization
This is when you exaggerate or give an understatement of reality in terms of the importance or frequency of an event.

You'll know you're overgeneralizing when you catch yourself saying to your ex, "You always . . ." or "You never. . . ." The problem with overgeneralizations is that the other person gets so preoccupied in proving that she doesn't "always" do something (but only did it a few times) or that you're wrong in saying that she "never" does something (because she can show you times that she did) that you both forget what the original discussion was about. You totally get off track and fail to communicate about what really was important.

### Mind Reading

Don't try to second-guess what your ex is thinking. It's too time consuming, and chances are you'll be wrong unless you're skilled in ESP. Experts claim that up to 90 percent of communication between two people is nonverbal, with only 10 percent coming through the choice of words. So when in doubt as to what's been said, ask. It may be that your ex's frustration is not with you at all but that she feels stressed out at her job or with her parents' dependency on her. She may be screaming at you because she's worried about one of your kids and thinks you're oblivious to the problem. Chances are if she feels you are concerned, or at least interested, in her feelings, she may become less emotional. If not, rise above your instinct to yell back and remain courteous to your children's mother.

Never assume you know what your ex is feeling when she says something.

For example, your ex may say, "This shared custody isn't working," and you immediately begin to sweat and think, "Oh, my God. She's going back to court to take the kids away from me."

She, on the other hand, may mean that she'd like to rework the days you each have the kids, wants more notice when you want to change dates, or doesn't think either of you are communicating effectively with each other.

Rather than jumping to conclusions and telling her that she can forget about any increase in child support if she's going to fight you on custody, take a deep breath and tell her that you're confused by her statement. What does she mean? Then shut up and listen.

### Ditch Fake Facts

Try to keep fake facts out of your conversation as you try to build up your argument. You may say, "It's a well known fact that . . ." and "Everyone knows that . . ." or make up false statistics. It puts your ex on the defensive, which may have been your subconscious intent, but it does not make for effective communication. Talk face to face, if at all possible, and stick to the facts.

## THE POWER OF GOOD COMMUNICATION

There is real power in effective communication. It not only helps you find solutions to problems, it impacts your kids in a very positive way. In her workbook *Parents, Children, and Divorce*, Nancy Porter-Thal, M.S., LMHC, CDM, states "Research shows that the better parents communicate, the better their children adjust to divorce." It just makes good sense. Your kids feel safer when they know their parents talk to each other. Hopefully you'll be able to communicate face to face, but if not, find a way to talk to one another on a regular basis. Make notes of points you want to discuss so you don't forget or get so focused on some other issue that you realize you omitted some things that you feel are important.

Remember too that if you and your ex rely strictly on e-mail, writing, voice mail, or phone calls to communicate, you only receive 10 percent of the communication and miss out on seeing and translating each other's body language. While you may feel that you can't bear to talk in your ex's physical presence, at least give it a try. Your kids will feel the anger and tension between you and your ex when communication is strained. They benefit, on the other hand, when they know that even though their parents are divorced, they can still meet and discuss their kids' welfare. Remember: TOYK.

There is a definite advantage in letting your kids know that you communicate frequently with their mother. First of all, it makes them feel more secure and loved. Secondly, and equally important, when your kids know you and your ex-wife are on the same page as far as they are concerned, there is far less opportunity for them to play one parent against the other (though they will still try from time to time as all kids do).

# Chapter 29

# Avoiding the Blame Game

*There is so much good in the worst of us,*
*and so much bad in the best of us,*
*that it hardly behooves any of us*
*to talk about the rest of us.*
—EDWARD WALLIS HOCH

You promised to love, honor, and cherish in your wedding vows, so when it doesn't last, it's human nature to want to point the finger at someone—your ex, her mother, the economy, or the fates—as the villain. But remember the old cliché: when you point your finger at someone else, three other fingers are pointing back at you.

It's so easy to blame your kids' mother when things go wrong because she's no longer around to defend herself, because you're still angry or bitter, or because you feel you may have screwed up somehow and you want to shift the guilt. But don't do it. Button your lip every time you want to blame your children's mother, especially in front of your kids, for faults ranging from being a lousy cook and housekeeper to being late when she picks the kids up or being the cause of their problems in school. When you blame her it puts your kids in the middle because they love and want to protect both of you.

According to divorce attorney Nancy Harris, "Regardless of your custody arrangement, celebrate the other parent to your kids. Fostering your child's relationship with your ex makes a child feel safe with you." Don't ever add that Mommy is a lush, she kicked you out because she was having an affair with the pool boy, or that she was a shopping addict and you were going broke paying all her bills. Just remind your kids what a good mom she is. If they know better, agree that everyone has faults but that she did her best. As Ms. Harris reminds, "Try to remember that your child is half you and half your ex. If you demean your ex, you are, in essence, demeaning half your child. Never say, 'You're just like your mother.'" This advice has been repeated elsewhere in this book, but it is important enough to stress it again.

## DON'T ASK THE KIDS ABOUT THEIR MOM'S LIFE

It's tempting to learn what's going on at your ex's house, to know if she bought that giant flat-screen television after pleading near-poverty to you or if the house is still as cluttered as when you left. If you ask your kids, chances are they'll tell you the inside scoop and then feel disloyal to their mom as well as resentful of you that you made them talk. It really puts your kids between a rock and a hard place as they want to please both of you. Don't ask, even if the question is about to burst out of your mouth.

You may wonder if she's dating yet, or worse, if she's still dating the ex-con with tattoos of Hitler all over his body. The first issue is strictly curiosity. If you really have a burning need to know, ask her directly and in a positive and friendly way so she'll give you an answer. If not, you'll have to wonder unless you bump into her at a restaurant where she's having a cozy, candlelit dinner and is holding hands with a gentleman who resembles (wouldn't you know it?) a young Robert Redford. But whatever you do, don't turn your kids into junior James Bonds.

The second issue is a more legitimate one. You do have a right to know that your children are safe in their mother's home. If you can frame the question in a nonthreatening way with your ex, you may find that "Tattoo Man" was only in jail for not paying his traffic tickets and that he had the tattoos done in high school when he was young and foolish and had a crush on his German teacher. That information may not give you much comfort, but at least you'll know the truth of the situation directly from the ex-wife. However, if you two aren't talking directly and you really are concerned that your children may be in harm's way, contact your attorney and ask what your options are. They differ from state to state.

## ✔ Tip from the Trenches

Dave says, "Sometimes my kids will drop a hint of what's going on at their mom's house. Obviously, I'm curious to know more, but I don't ask, unless I think there's a problem that they want me to know about."

Obviously, if you worry about her drinking or drug use, that she's leaving the kids alone in the house for hours while she goes shopping or heads to the local bar for a drink, or is dating a violent man, you need to talk to your attorney to ask how best to handle the situation. Never try to handle this type of situation on your own.

## BLAMING PROBLEMS ON THE DIVORCE MAY MASK ISSUES

It's very easy to blame all problems with your kids—everything from not making their beds to failing algebra to quitting the softball team or using drugs—on the divorce and, indirectly, on your ex-spouse. But don't be too quick to assign blame. Kids from intact families have those issues too, so before you blame the divorce on your ex and accept guilt yourself, consider other underlying causes, such as their growing up and rebelling, which is normal. If their behavior is a serious problem, work together with your ex, the school, and a counselor to try to solve it.

Depending on the ages of your children, there could be a number of factors other than the divorce causing behavioral changes. Ask yourself these questions:

- Have you or your ex had your child's eyesight and hearing checked lately?
- What is the school situation? Has your child mentioned bullies at school or on the playing field? It's a common problem in many schools today.
- What about difficulties with a particular teacher? Ask some of the parents of your child's friends if their youngster has mentioned a teacher who embarrasses or harasses particular students. Unfortunately there are teachers who seem to enjoy humiliating kids who are having academic trouble in a particular subject or who may have developmental delays. While these teachers are in the minority, your child may have been unlucky enough to be assigned to one.
- Might it be a peer problem? Kids are very loyal to their friends and may not want to tell on them, even if they are afraid their friends are taking them down the wrong path by getting them involved in drugs, alcohol, or risk-taking behavior. In acting out a behavior problem, your child may be crying out for help.
- Have you sat down, one on one, with your child and asked what's going on? Don't begin when there are others around or your time is limited. Instead, take the youngster for a walk, a ride in the car, or go fishing. It's hard to get away from dad when you're alone in a boat, and waiting for a fish to bite is often conducive to conversation. But be patient. Give your kid time to get the words out as he or she might feel embarrassed or not exactly sure what the trouble is or how to explain it.

If problems continue, you and your ex should let a professional step in to help. Ask your pediatrician for the name of a child therapist or social worker who is trained to help kids with their problems.

## DON'T AIR DIRTY LINEN TO OTHERS

It's tempting to tell your friends what really happened. It takes the pressure off you when you can list your ex's faults, transgressions, and personality defects. That way you don't have to mention your own possible contribution to the cause of the divorce. But it really isn't anyone's business why the two of you decided to end your marriage. Gossip, which this is, can get back to your kids (or your ex) and hurt them.

You might be furious that she's still letting the kids stay up until midnight on school nights or that, in your opinion, she still drinks too much, but unless you feel that your kids are in danger, don't tell your friends and family. Tell her.

Do you really want your kids to know that your ex was having an affair (or that you were), that she drank too much (or you did), or that you just grew apart? No? Then just smile and tell curious people that it just didn't work out and change the subject. In the blame game, no one wins.

## LITTLE PITCHERS DO HAVE BIG EARS

You may think you're alone when you're complaining about your ex on your cell phone, but the kids could be in the next room hearing everything you say. They may be in the back seat of the car where you assume they're busy with their iPods or computer games. But they probably are listening to your every word. It's amazing how these kids, who don't hear when you call them for dinner or tell them it's bedtime, perk their ears up when you think you're speaking quietly having a confidential conversation with someone else. If you feel you really must talk about how she did you wrong or what she's doing now that you really don't approve of, confide in your therapist. That way you can do no harm.

# Chapter 30

# Agreeing to Disagree: No Kids Allowed

*Most quarrels amplify a misunderstanding.*
—ANDRE GIDE

You are bound to disagree at times with your ex, sometimes with reason and sometimes just arbitrarily. Healthily married couples have fights and disagreements at times, and it only makes sense that you and your ex will have fights and disagreements as well. But life isn't all black and white. There's an awful lot of gray in there, and if you can't agree on either ends of the spectrum, perhaps you can agree to a place somewhere in the middle. It's called compromise. You can also think of it as agreeing to disagree on some issues.

## FOLLOW THE RULES FOR RESPECTFUL ARGUING

Remember that you are an adult (and perhaps your ex will remember as well). Whether you call it "discussing" or "arguing," agree to specific rules to argue by. After all, you both are your children's parents and you need to demonstrate to them by your behavior that people can disagree without name calling, can argue without changing the other's position, and can still maintain cordiality, if not civility. But keep the kids out of it.

After interviewing more than fifty single dads, numerous couples in blended families, and talking to many single moms and asking for their suggestions, we've come up with ten guidelines for respectful arguing. Try them out and see if they turn more of your arguments into discussions and successful compromises.

- Have a definite time period and a convenient neutral place to meet, such as a restaurant or park, to discuss issues concerning your children.
- Agree ahead of time what issues you'll be discussing.

- Be on time and don't cancel unless absolutely necessary.
- Turn off your cell phone or beeper; give your full attention to the discussion at hand.
- Stick to the specific issues you agreed to discuss and don't add to the agenda.
- Do not bring up past history.
- Agree to and maintain fair fighting rules, including no shouting or name calling.
- Avoid expecting your ex to read your mind.
- Practice active listening skills (see Chapter 2), even if you can't stand the sound of your ex's voice.
- Verbalize the action that will be taken and by whom. Put it in writing and date it so there's no question of the decision at a later time.

That may sound too formal to you, but the very fact that it is formal should take some of the emotion away. You are two intelligent adults who, though no longer married, have created these children and are responsible for them. They aren't a project that you can toss because it didn't work out; they are a part of you, the best part, so treat them as the precious gift they are.

## USE CODE WORDS TO DIFFUSE HOSTILITIES

In the heat of a verbal battle, you may not realize when things are getting out of hand. Before one of you blurts out something you'll be sorry for later, agree on a code word that will stop you both in your tracks and give you a few seconds to cool off. It can be "Stop!" or "Red alert" or even something silly like "Pillow fight." What you actually say isn't important. It's merely a tool to warn both of you that your arguing has taken a potentially dangerous turn. Act respectful toward one another; you're talking to your kid's other parent.

## FIRING THE MIDDLE MAN (YOUR KIDS)

There's an old Spanish saying: "To whom you tell your secrets, to him you resign your liberty." It means don't ever give your kids control over you. Kids get that control when you make them the power person between you and your ex. So fire them as the go-between between you and your former wife. As parents, you can't afford them.

Too often divorced parents use their children as the messenger between them. "Tell your dad that he's late with the child support," or "Tell your mom that she's to bring you to my house no later than five." It's not fair to the kids to put them in the middle. It's stressful and makes them feel guilty. It also gives them a sense of power over you both, which may make them feel important but also frightened.

You may feel that your ex isn't following the house rules you both agreed on, such as those dealing with homework, bedtime, and chores. But don't roll your eyes when the kids say, "We don't have to do that at Mom's." Just bite your tongue. If it really bothers you, communicate directly with your ex by phone, e-mail, or the way that works best between you both. (Don't ignore the possibility that she is doing just what she said she'd do, and your kids—those little rascals—are trying to see if they can get out of something at your house. Yes, kids do that, even when the parents are still married.)

> ### ✔ Tip from the Trenches
>
> John adds that, "It's important to elevate their other parent. The children never asked for the divorce so the parents need to resolve their differences privately and publicly support the previous spouse. At night, we say prayers for their mom and her family, and conversely, she prays for me and my family. Speak in high regard for the other parent to your kids and demonstrate a healthy distant love for the other parent. You should be able to do this because you courted and married each other and had children with them. Remember, it's not about you or your ex."

## KEEP THE KIDS NEUTRAL

Please don't ask them to tattle on their mom either, even though you're dying to know if she's still dating "that creepy guy" or if she's finally cooking dinner for a change. If they offer juicy information, just nod or say, "Oh," and leave it at that. Never throw in your two cents as it just gives them the opportunity to tell her, "Well, Dad said . . ." and then you've got trouble, which you really don't need.

Even though you may think your ex is making a fool of herself, dressing like a teenager and going out with her boy toy, or overdoing the Botox and plastic surgery, keep your thoughts to yourself (or share them with your therapist, but never your kids, friends, or relatives).

Don't tell your children a secret and then make them promise that they won't tell their mom. They'll feel terribly conflicted, feeling they've betrayed your trust if they do tell (or it slips out) or they don't tell and thus are keeping a secret from their mom whom they also love. The ensuing anxiety can create tremendous stress on your kids.

## LISTEN TO THEIR COMPLAINTS; THEY COULD BE VALID

Although kids do a lot of complaining about the other parent, just to see what you'll do, you need to tell them that they have to take their grievance up with their mom. You don't need to get in the middle of that battle or get quoted or misquoted to your ex. But you do need to listen carefully to your kids complaints in order to sort out what is just your kids trash talking (because they're miffed or don't want to do something) and what may be valid evidence of potential real trouble at their other home.

If they say that they're tired of making their school lunches, for example, it may be that their mom figured they were old enough to take the responsibility for what they eat. And that's good. But if they're making it because she's so hungover she can't get up in the morning, that's bad news, so you need to follow up their comments with a few noncommittal questions to ascertain what the real situation is.

The same options are yours if your daughter says, "I hate mom's new boyfriend." Don't jump to conclusions by mentally telling yourself a story and thinking the worst. And don't ask "Is he making moves on you?" or spout off about why you don't like him either. If you listen carefully to her gripes, you may learn simply that he insists on watching football on television when her favorite show is on, so don't open a can of worms or give her any ammunition she shouldn't have.

How can you discern between truth and fiction? Listen carefully, ask unemotional questions such as "Why?" or "How is that a problem?" If your kids are of preschool age, ask them to draw a picture of what's bothering them.

If you don't rush in to give your opinion or, worse, are critical of their mother, your kids may open up and give you additional information that will help you make a decision as to the innocence or seriousness of the problem. Obviously, if it is serious, you need to speak directly to their mom.

# Chapter 31

# Avoiding Being Manipulated by Your Kids

*A clean glove often hides a dirty hand.*
—English proverb

Kids of all ages, even in families where the parents are not divorced, will try to play one parent against the other. Looking you right in the eye, they'll say "Mom lets me do (blank)" even when you and they know without question that their mom would never let them. They'll often tell you other tall tales if they think they can get by with it.

## KIDS ARE KIDS

It's no better when you're divorced, so never jump to conclusions by believing everything your kids say. They may tell you that they don't have the money for flag football or cheerleading because their mom spent the extra money you gave her on a new chair for the TV room. Rather than picking up the phone and yelling at your ex, hurrying to the computer to type a scathing e-mail, or leaving a voice mail saying that you're going to contact your lawyer, take a deep breath and get control of your emotions.

The advantage of keeping your communication open with your ex is that you can ask her firsthand what the truth really is. Don't accuse her, though. Instead, make your opening nonthreatening by saying, "You know how the kids often try to manipulate us? Well, they came up with something that I wanted to check out with you." This should make her feel less defensive and perhaps even admit that, yes, the kids do try to play you both against each other. Hopefully she'll even tell you the truth of the matter, explaining that she did indeed use your check to buy the chair.

But before you blow your top, she may also add that she bought the chair because it was on sale that weekend and because she knew signup for flag football and cheerleading was a week later, when she could

use her parent's birthday check to pay for the kids' activities. Wouldn't you have felt stupid for accusing her based on the kids' gossip alone?

On the other hand, your ex may admit that she spent the money on a chair, and if you want the kids to have their activities you need to give her another check. Instead of yelling at her or punishing your kids by not signing them up, take them with you and pay for the flag football and cheerleading as you personally sign them up, even if financial constraints mean you have to make arrangements to pay their fees on a weekly basis rather in one payment. Does that mean your ex wins? No, it means your kids don't lose.

If you really can't afford to pay a second time for your kids' activities, level with them without blaming their mother. (They know what happened.) Promise them that next time you'll go with them and sign them up so you know the money's going where you meant it to go.

If, however, these situations continue and your ex ignores your complaints that she's misusing the money you give her for the kids, you may need to talk to your attorney, knowing that if you do you also will have to *pay* your attorney.

### But Dad, Everyone Is Doing It

One of the manipulating tricks kids seem to know instinctively is to play on your sense of guilt. If your teenager tells you that everyone is going to the Smith's house for a party, you need to call the Smiths to make sure they are home (and in town) and that they are aware of the party. Younger kids will tell you that they are the only kids in middle school without their own cell phone, and on it goes. Discuss it with your ex and see how she feels about kids and cell phones. Who will pay for it? What rules can you agree on? Should it not be used during school hours and that the user will not go over the allotted minutes?

## ANTICIPATE YOUR VULNERABILITIES

You know your weaknesses and should be able to recognize when your kids are attempting to manipulate them. If you feel guilty that you only have them every other week, tell them when you feel they are playing on that sense of guilt. You can make a joke of it to let them off easy, so they can say, "Well, you can't blame a kid for trying."

Or if it happens frequently, you can have a more serious conversation with them. Again, start off by making them feel safe by saying something like, "You know I love and miss you kids. I'd love to have you more often and maybe in the future I can. But until then, it makes me sad to feel that I need to give in to you more often just because I miss you. That's not fair to me and really isn't fair to you." They may not have thought of things that way, and perhaps your leveling with them about how you feel will give them the opening to tell you how they feel. Then you can have an honest relationship with your kids without their feeling that they need to trick or manipulate you.

## DON'T LEAD WITH YOUR CHIN

It's possible to feel a little paranoid when you're a single dad. You may wonder if everyone is trying to get whatever they can, at least financially, from you. It's probably because you're paying child support, pos-sibly alimony, and paying for part or all of the kids' school expenses, maybe some of the ex's mortgage, and your new housing and furnishings. You wonder where it will all end, especially if you were agreeable at the time of the divorce and gave more than your attorney said you needed to.

### Thought Stopping

But before you lash out at your kids when they ask for something, do what's called *thought stopping*. Experts say that 75 percent of what you think is negative. Since your body tends to react as your mind thinks, you can change your overt reactions by transforming negative thoughts into positive ones. Rather than thinking "Do these kids think I'm made of money?" tell yourself to stop and change that thought to the more positive one of "I wonder why they feel they need this bike, dress, or toy." Then ask them. You may be surprised at the answer.

The answer may be "Everyone has one." Or, "I know I'd be more popular if I had a mountain bike," or "I feel ugly, and if I had more expensive clothes I'd feel better about myself." Once you know the reasoning behind the question, you're not going to want to yell at your kid but rather sit down and have a special one-on-one conversation. Your child will know that you care and are interested in what's important to him or her. And you will know something about your child that you wouldn't have known if you hadn't stopped the negative thought and opted for a more positive one instead.

Yes, your kids will continue to manipulate you from time to time because all kids do, but by taking the time to change your immediate negative thoughts to more positive ones, you'll develop a closer relationship with your children than you ever thought possible.

# Chapter 32

# Conclusion

Our parting words are the same as our beginning premise—TOYK: think of your kids. Most parents want their kids to be happy. The second you're divorced, it's not about you or your ex anymore. You should never regret the marriage you had with your ex because without it you wouldn't have your kids. Unfortunately, sometimes marriages end and now it's about the kids. In order for that to occur, you need to work through your anger and bitterness. You need to forgive, and that's often a difficult task as it's human nature to want to get even. Yet, as Dr. Dean Ornish said in a September 27, 2006 issue of *Newsweek*, "In a way, the most selfish thing you can do for yourself is to forgive other people." That's because holding grudges and hanging onto anger and bitterness is bad for your health. When you learn to forgive, says Edward M. Hallowell, M.D., author of *Dare to Forgive*, ". . . your blood pressure may go down, your resting heart rate may decrease, your immune system may get stronger, your susceptibility to a heart attack or stroke may decrease, headaches and backaches and neck pain may abate, your need for medications may diminish, and even your sexual self may gain strength." Doesn't all that alone make it worthwhile to give forgiveness a try? And those are just some of the physical benefits. There are numerous emotional benefits as well, including making you smile rather than snarl, and feeling happy, not harried.

## LEARN TO FORGIVE

Learning to forgive is a process, one that doesn't happen overnight. But it can be done and will make you a healthier and happier man. Carrying a grudge or anger and bitterness against your ex is a heavy burden. To help ease your load, ask yourself

these questions: How does continuing to feel anger and bitterness against my ex help me? How does my continuing to feel anger and bitterness against their mother help my kids? Should I focus on the good things in my life that bring me pleasure rather than continue to wiggle the tooth of anger and bitterness that brings me pain?

Once you forgive your ex, it will help to cut the emotional bond between you and her. As Brette McWhorter Sember writes in her book, *How to Parent with Your Ex*, "You and the other parent are no longer emotional partners, and you need to separate yourself from him or her emotionally, while continuing to parent together."

So doesn't it make sense to allow yourself to forgive whatever wrongs you associate with your ex? You don't have to excuse what happened, but you can forgive and move on.

Perhaps your arguments with her are triggered by lingering hurts and resentments. Ask yourself just what you achieve from arguing. Do you really feel better when you win? Are you just arguing for the sake of arguing, to show that you're a better debater? George Bernard Shaw said, "The test of a man or woman's breeding is how they behave in a quarrel." Are you proud of your behavior? Think about your responses to your ex. Are they on the child level ("Am not," "Am too.") or do you respond as the responsible adult and parent you really are? Unfortunately, too many arguments never evolve past the seven-year-old (or even younger) level.

While it's never healthy to bottle up emotions because they have a way of sneaking out and grabbing you, you need to learn how to get a grip on your anger. If that's a problem and you're having difficulty in forgiving, get help from a qualified mental health therapist or your rabbi, priest, or minister.

If you're a widower and are having difficulty forgiving either the powers that be or what you perceive to be your own lack of ability to save your late wife, you may still be grieving and may need the support of a grief counselor to help you learn to accept her death, even though you miss her. Ask yourself: Am I still grieving for my late wife and yet somehow blaming her for leaving me? Is my anger really at my lack of control that despite my prayers and love for her she still died?

You need to forgive yourself for being unable to control her dying. In his book *Dare to Forgive*, author Edward M. Hallowell writes, "If we can accept that we lack control, if we look at death and accept it without rage, then the chains that keep us unforgiving and angry can begin to break and disappear. We can then rise above what holds us down, namely anger, resentment and hatred. We become free."

## FORGIVE YOURSELF

While you're learning to be forgiving, remember to be forgiving of yourself as well. No one is perfect. Everyone makes mistakes and wishes they had a do over. Hopefully you learn from your mistakes. To paraphrase Alexander Pope in his 1711 writing "An Essay on Criticism," "To err is human; to forgive, favored by the father of your children." But also realize that this forgiving business isn't an overnight miraculous conversion. It takes time and a lot of work to learn to be forgiving. Dr. Edward M. Hallowell says, "It's a process, not a moment."

## WHAT DO YOU WANT FOR YOUR KIDS?

Focus on what you really want. For the majority of the dads we interviewed, it was to raise their kids in such a way that the fact that their parents had divorced created as little negative effect on their lives as possible. To achieve that, you and your ex must learn to communicate in a civil and productive way. Numerous studies have shown that when parents are able to communicate effectively with each other their children are better able to adjust to the divorce.

You must always show your children that you respect their mother because she is their mother, regardless how you may feel about her as a human being. If you openly criticize her, it is as though you are criticizing half of your child, as each child is partly you and partly the mom. But if you and your ex can get to an effective working relationship, your children will be vastly healthier and you'll be happier. And isn't that what you desire?

## SACRIFICES

There's no doubt that as a single dad you'll have some challenges in your working environment (the same obstacles your ex has if she works outside the home).

- You'll have to leave early or promptly at quitting time to pick the kids up, leaving your somewhat resentful peers still working.
- Days that you drop them off at school or daycare you may have to come in late.
- You'll take sick days off when your kids are ill or have to see the doctor.

- You may not be able to advance in your career if to do so means moving to a different location and your divorce decree requires your staying in the same town as your ex.

Eric said, "The most difficult part? Again, the social changes, but also just learning the day to day stuff [such as] making arrangements at work to pick him up from school when it's one of my nights during the week we share him fifty-fifty. It took a lot of effort to get my employer to allow me a flex schedule to accommodate this."

It doesn't matter whether you're a doctor, lawyer, teacher, plumber, or salesman, being a single father will affect your working hours. The more custody you have, the greater the affect. Children have all sorts of activities they are involved in, whether it's sports, music classes, or tutoring, and when there isn't that second person around to pick the kids up and take them places, the job falls to you.

If you worked a sixteen-hour day before your divorce, you may find this very difficult, if not impossible, to juggle. You may find that it interferes with your desire and effort to move up the corporate ladder. The truth is you may be right.

However, some serious soul searching needs to take place so you can come to a decision on how you are going to manage your time crunch. Many may decide, if they can afford it, to hire a part-time or full-time nanny to help with the kids so that you can still work those hours you used to and keep working up that corporate ladder. Others may feel that their priorities are now spending time with their children, even if it means not getting the promotion they hoped for.

Fortunately, corporate America has become a lot more easygoing and understanding on this issue than it used to be. It is very important to bring your boss into this conversation. Explain your current situation and reinforce that it doesn't affect your desire to work as hard as possible for the company. Ask if there is another alternative, like working from home in the later afternoon. In many situations, you may find that your supervisor is in the same situation as you.

The key is to have the conversation. If you don't tell anyone and you try to work as you did before but keep having to leave early for this or that, you run the risk that your boss may misconceive your actions as lackluster performance or lack of interest in your position.

## THE GOOD NEWS

The good news, Michael says, is:

When I was married, I was like a lot of dads and let my ex take care of many of the "kids things." I never really knew my kids back then, I didn't know those little things like their favorite foods, what type of Band-aids they liked best, or even their best friends at school. These were all things that seemed unimportant in my busy world that my ex could take care of. These are all conversations I now look forward to every day. Even though I have more parenting responsibilities than before, I look back and say, "It wasn't the fairy tale the way it was written, but I still got the happy ending. I know my kids."

# Appendix A

# The Single Dad's Move-In Checklist

Y ou open the door to your new digs and stare at the blank walls. Although you know your furniture—the little you took from your former home because you didn't want to change it too much for your kids—is on its way, you also know that there's going to be quite an echo here. You know you'll need to have a bed, dresser, table and chairs, couch, bookcase, TV, and maybe a little more, but what about the other things, those miscellaneous items that just seemed to appear before?

To get you started in your new home, the following lists contain those things you probably should have to make life a little more comfortable.

## Your Bedroom
❒ Bed
❒ Nightstand
❒ Bedside lamp
❒ Clock radio
❒ Sheets and blankets
❒ Pillow
❒ Dresser
❒ Hangers (lots of them)
❒ Wastepaper basket
❒ Tissue
❒ Telephone
❒ Laundry basket or bag
❒ Flashlight

## Bathroom
❒ Toilet paper
❒ Tissues
❒ Toothbrush cup or holder
❒ Toothpaste
❒ Kids' toothpaste if they're under six years of age
❒ Waste basket
❒ Towels and washcloths
❒ Shampoo
❒ Conditioner
❒ Bar soap
❒ Night light

## Kids' Bedroom
❒ Beds (bunks, inflatable, trundle)
❒ Dresser
❒ Hangers
❒ Sheets and pillowcases
❒ Blanket, duvet, or quilt
❒ Clock
❒ Night light

## Cleaning Supplies
❒ Vacuum cleaner
❒ Broom and dustpan
❒ Trash bags
❒ Paper towels
❒ Dust rags (old T-shirts are good)
❒ All-purpose cleaner like Mr. Clean, Formula 409, or Lysol
❒ Laundry detergent
❒ Laundry stain remover

## Kitchen
❒ Ten-inch or twelve-inch fry pan
❒ Wok or large fry pan
❒ Two-quart sauce pan with cover
❒ Strainer or colander
❒ Cookie sheet
❒ Nine-by-eleven roaster pan
❒ Set of measuring spoons
❒ Set of measuring cups for dry ingredients plus a liquid measuring cup
❒ Set of mixing bowls, assorted sizes
❒ Toaster oven
❒ Electric slow cooker
❒ Coffee pot if you drink coffee
❒ Oven mitts
❒ Set of quality knives
❒ One or more plastic carving boards that can go into the dishwasher
❒ Spatulas, slotted spoons, and a cooking fork
❒ Ice-cream scoop
❒ Matching set of dishes, including cereal bowls, dinner plates, salad plates, and either mugs or cups and saucers
❒ Extra light bulbs

❏ Dish soap
❏ Dishwasher soap
❏ Manual can opener (in case power goes out)
❏ Calendar with spaces to mark appointments for you and the kids

## Tools

❏ Claw hammer
❏ Scissors
❏ Screwdrivers, both Phillips head and flat head
❏ Pliers
❏ Tape measure
❏ Variety of screws and nails

# Appendix B
# Selected Reading

Baumbich, Charlene Ann. *365 Ways to Connect with Your Kids.* Franklin Lakes, NJ: Career Press, 2001.

Beck, Carol. *Nourishing Your Daughter.* New York: Penguin Putnam, Inc., 2001.

Berkenkamp, Lauri, and Steven C. Atkins, Ph.D. *Talking to Your Kids about Sex from Toddlers to Preteens.* Chicago: Nomad Press, 2002.

Brott, Armin A. *The New Father: The Single Father.* New York: Abbeville Press, 1999.

Brown, Laurie Krasny, Ed.D., and Marc Brown. *What's the Big Secret? Talking about Sex with Girls and Boys.* New York: Little, Brown and Company, 1997.

Condrell, Kenneth N., Ph.D., with Linda Lee Small. *Be a Great Divorced Dad.* New York: St. Martin's Press, 1998.

Covey, Stephen R. *The 8th Habit: From Effectiveness to Greatness.* New York: Free Press, 2004.

Erwin, Cheryl L. *The Everything® Parent's Guide to Raising Boys.* Avon, MA: Adams Media, 2006.

Fromm, Erich. *The Art of Loving.* New York: Continuum, 2000.

Gipson, C.F. *The Black Man's Guide to Parenting: 50 Ways to Be an Effective Father.* Santa Barbara, CA: Blue Point Books, 2006.

Godfrey, Neale S. *Money Doesn't Grow on Trees.* New York: Fireside, 2006.

Golden, Thomas R. *Swallowed by a Snake: The Gift of the Masculine Side of Healing.* Gaithersburg, MD: Golden Healing Publishing LLC, 2000.

Golden, Thomas R., and James E. Miller. *When a Man Faces Grief.* Fort Wayne, IN: Willowgreen Publishing, 1998.

Grollman, Earl A., E.D. *Bereaved Children and Teens: A Support Guide for Parents and Professionals.* Boston: Beacon Press, 2005.

Gurian, Michael. *A Fine Young Man: What Parents, Mentors, and Educators Can Do to Shape Adolescent Boys into Exceptional Men.* New York: Tarcher/Putnam, 1997.

Harris, Robie. *Goodbye Mousie.* New York: Harriet K. McElderry Books, 2001.

Hallowell, Edward M., M.D. *Dare to Forgive.* Deerfield Beach, FL: Deerfield Communications, Inc., 2004.

Ireland, Karin. *Boost Your Child's Self-Esteem.* New York: The Berkley Publishing Group, 2000.

Lansky, Vicki. *Vicki Lansky's Divorce Book for Parents.* Minnetonka, MN: Book Peddler,1996.

Lermitte, Paul W., with Jennifer Merritt. *Making Allowances.* New York: McGraw-Hill, 2002.

Long, Nicholas, Ph.D., and Rex Forehand, Ph.D. *Making Divorce Easier on Your Child.* Chicago: Contemporary Books, 2002.

Mayle, Peter. *"Where Did I Come From?"* New York: Kensington Publishing Corp, 1987.

Neuman, M. Gary, L.M.H.C. *Helping Your Kids Cope with Divorce the Sandcastles Way.* New York: Random House,1998.

Page, Diamond Dallas, with Dr. Craig Aaron. *Yoga for Regular Guys.* Philadelphia: Quirk Books, 2005.

Pardes, Bronwen. *Doing It Right: Making Smart, Safe, and Satisfying Choices About Sex.* New York: Simon Pulse, 2007.

Pardini, Jane Crowley. *The Babysitter Book: Everything You and Your Babysitter Need to Know Before You Leave the House*. Chicago: Contemporary Books, 1996.

Patterson, Kerry, Joseph Grenny, Ron McMillan, and Al Switzer. *Crucial Conversations*. New York: McGraw-Hill, 2002.

Peel, Kathy. *The Family Manager's Guide to Summer Survival*. Beverly, MA: Fair Winds Press, 2006.

Pollack, William S. *Real Boys: Rescuing Our Sons from the Myths of Boyhood*. New York: Random House, 1998.

Pruitt, David B., M.D., ed. *Your Child: What Every Parent Needs to Know: What's Normal, What's Not, and When to Seek Help*. New York: HarperCollins, 1998.

Richardson, Justin, M.D., and Mark A. Schuster, M.D., Ph.D. *Everything You Never Wanted Your Kids to Know about Sex (But Were Afraid They'd Ask)*. New York: Three Rivers Press, 2003.

Roffman, Deborah M. *But How'd I Get in There in the First Place? Talking to Your Young Child About Sex*. Cambridge, MA: Perseus Publishing, 2002.

Rutledge, Rebecca, Ph.D. *The Everything® Parent's Guide to Children with Depression*. Avon, MA: Adams Media, 2007.

Sember, Brette McWhorter. *How to Parent with Your Ex*. Naperville, IL: Sphinx Publishing, 2005.

Shimberg, Elaine Fantle. *Blending Families*. New York: Berkley Books, 1999.

Smith, Bert Kruger. *Grandparenting in Today's World*. Austin, TX: Hogg Foundation for Mental Health, University of Texas, 1989.

Sommers-Flanagan, Rita, Chelsea Elander, and John Sommers-Flanagan. *Don't Divorce Us!: Kids' Advice to Divorcing Parents*. Alexandria, VA: American Counseling Association, 2000.

Stephens, Yvonne. *Amazing 7-Minute Meals*. Austin, TX: Synergy Books, 2006.

Teyber, Edward. *Helping Children Cope with Divorce*. San Francisco: Jossey-Bass, 2001.

Witkin, Georgia, Ph.D. *KidStress*. New York: Penguin Group, 1999.

Wild, Russell, and Susan Ellis Wild. *The Unofficial Guide to Getting a Divorce*. Hoboken, NJ: Wiley, 2005.

Zonnebelt-Smeenge, Susan J. R.N., Ed.D., and, Robert C. DeVries, D.Min., Ph.D. *Getting to the Other Side of Grief : Overcoming the Loss of a Spouse*. Grand Rapids, MI: Baker Books, 2005.

# Appendix C

# Resources

# ORGANIZATIONS

## American Coalition for Fathers and Children

*www.acfc.org*
1-800-978-3237
Promotes equal rights for all parents affected by divorce.

## Center for Effective Parenting

*www.parenting-ed.org*
This Web site offers suggestions on how to handle specific issues as they arise.

## Father's Resource Center

*www.fathersworld.com*
This Web site offers tips on balancing work and family as well as good health and fitness.

## Kids Growth

*www.kidsgrowth.com*
This Web site is written by physicians, psychologists, and parenting experts and contains a variety of useful information, answers questions from viewers, and book reviews for children's books.

## Kid Source

*www.kidsource.com*
This Web site has information on children's health, education, and recreation, as well as parenting tips

## National Association for the Education of Young Children

*www.naeyc.org* (for general information)
*www.naeyc.org/accreditation* (to locate accredited centers on line)
This organization offers accreditation to preschools, kindergartens, and child-care centers. However, accreditation alone should not be your only criteria in selecting a program for your child.

## National Dissemination Center for Children with Disabilities (NICHCY)

P.O. Box 1492
Washington, D.C. 20013
1-800-695-0285
Fax: 202-884-8441
*nicjcy@aed.org*
*www.nichcy.org*
This Web site has a tremendous amount of information for parents about their child's disability.

## National Congress for Fathers and Children (NCFC)

760-758-0268
Helps single fathers remain active in their children's lives. Offers a newsletter.

## National Fatherhood Initiative

301-948-0599
*www.fatherhood.org*
Provides national advocacy for fathers to remain active in their children's lives. Also offers a newsletter and resource catalog.

## The National Fathers' Resource Center

*www.fathers4kids.org*
This Web site helps divorced dads with issues of child support, custody, and time sharing.

## Parents without Partners

1-800-637-7974
*www.parentswithoutpartners.org*
Although this is a national advocacy organization, its local chapters provide social and educational activities for single parents. Their newsletter is online.

# A SAMPLING OF CENTERS TREATING EATING DISORDERS

Penn State's Eating Disorder Program
Penn State Milton H. Hershey Medical
Center
500 University Drive
Hershey, PA 17033-0850
717-531-7146
1-800-243-1455

University of Iowa Hospital & Clinics
Eating and Weight Disorders Program
200 Hawkins Drive
Iowa City, Iowa 52242
319-356-1188
319-353-6314
1-877-384-8999
*www.uihealthcare.com/depts/uibehavioral*
*health/patients/directory_e.html#eating*

Stanford University Eating Disorders
Program
Palo Alto, CA
650-498-9111

Presbyterian Hospital of Dallas Eating
Disorders Program
8200 Walnut Hill Lane
Dallas, TX 75231
1-800-411-7081

Remuda Ranch in Arizona (residential treatment program for people with
anorexia)
One E. Apache Street
Wickenburg, AZ 85390
1-800-445-1900
928-684-4501
*www.remudaranch.com*

British Columbia Children's Hospital
Eating Disorder Program
4480 Oak Street, Room #D4
Vancouver, BC V6H 3V4
Canada
604-875-2200

Hotel Dieu Hospital
Eating Disorders Program
72 Barrie Street
Kingston, Ontario K7L 3J7
Canada
613-548-6121

Douglas Hospital
Eating Disorder Unit
6875 La Salle Blvd.
Montreal, Quebec H4H 1R3
Canada
514-761-6131, ext. 22895

# Index